THE ORIGINS AND EVOLUTION OF THE PROGRESS ESTATE

THE ORIGINS AND EVOLUTION OF THE PROGRESS ESTATE

By Keith Billinghurst

Copyright © Keith Billinghurst 2017

The right of Keith Billinghurst to be identified
as the author of this work has been asserted in accordance with
the Copyright, Designs & Patents Act 1988.

All rights reserved. No part of this book may be reproduced,
stored in a retrieval system, or transmitted in any form
or by any means, electronic, electrostatic, magnetic tape,
mechanical, photocopying, recording or otherwise,
without the written permission of the copyright holder.

Published under licence
by Brown Dog Books and The Self-Publishing Partnership,
7 Green Park Station, Bath BA1 1JB

www.selfpublishingpartnership.co.uk

ISBN printed book: 978-1-78545-178-2

Cover design by Kevin Rylands
Internal design by Tim Jollands

Printed and bound by CPI Group (UK) Ltd, Croydon CR0 4YY

Contents

Foreword	7
List of Tables and Illustrations	9
Acknowledgements	11

WHY THE ESTATE WAS BUILT
The Outbreak of the First World War	13
The Demand for Labour at the Royal Arsenal in Woolwich	16
The Housing Crisis in Woolwich	21

HOW GARDEN SUBURBS CAME TO BE
The Growth of Cities and Suburbs	25
70 years of Legislation	32
From Charity to Political Reform	44
Ruskin, Architecture and the Arts and Crafts Movement	51
A Chocolatier's Vision Becomes a Reality	61
Ebenezer Howard and the Garden City Movement	68
Barry Parker and Raymond Unwin	72
Joseph and Seebohm Rowntree and the Garden City Conference, 1901	79
Letchworth Garden City	87
Henrietta Barnett and Hampstead Garden Suburb	95
Town Planning Reaches the Statute Book: The Housing, Town-Planning, & C. Act, 1909	107
Raymond Unwin Heads for Whitehall	112
Charles Robert Ashbee and Frank Baines	122
The Housing Act, 1914	130

THE EVOLUTION OF THE ESTATE
Cecil Henry Polhill and the Site for the Estate	133
His Majesty's Office Goes to Work	147
How to Build 1,298 Homes Fast – Frank Baines-Style	160
The Estate's Road Names	176

1915-1924: The Estate's Early Years	205
1925-1938: The Early Co-op Years	210
1939-1944: Second World War Aerial Attacks	218
1945-1947: Post-War Rebuilding	228
1948-1966: Modernisation and Renewal	236
1967-2015: The Growth of Freehold Home Ownership	241
Afterword	245
Appendices	
A: Conversion of Pre-Decimal to Decimal Currency	247
B: Metric Equivalents of Imperial Weights and Measures	248
C: Inflation 1850-2017	249
Bibliography	250
Index	255

Foreword

The Progress Estate was built in 1915 to house some of the men employed at the Royal Arsenal munitions factories in Woolwich. The Progress Residents Association began to plan the estate's centenary celebrations in mid-2014 and, during 2015, held roughly one event each month in a varied programme intended to appeal to both residents and others living nearby.

During this planning stage, the Association also decided to publish a book about the Estate. Although a number of articles have been written about the Estate over the years and reference is made to it in many books, there does not appear to be a concise explanation of its roots in the history of the country's housing, how the site was acquired and the houses built, or the events that have shaped its appearance over the first 100 years of its existence. I undertook the task on the committee's behalf and am wholly responsible for any errors or omissions that might be found in its pages. Anyone who would like to comment on the text or offer corrections to any errors is invited to write to progressestatecomments@gmail.com. We are considering creating an addendum to this book to record verifiable new or revised information as it comes to light which the Association will publish on its website, www.progressestate.co.uk.

In the interests of brevity, 'the Estate' describes what at various times has been called 'the Woolwich Housing Scheme', 'the Government Housing Scheme at Well Hall', 'the Well Hall Estate' and 'the Progress Estate'.

'Site layout plans' describes H.M. Office of Works drawings for the layout of the east and west sides of the Estate, and 'detailed drawings' their architects' drawings for individual blocks of houses. 'Published plans' refers to the site plans for the east and west portions of the Estate that also show the four classes of accommodation as printed in *The Architects' and Builders' Journal*, 27 December 1916, vol. XLIV no. 1147 (Supplement). They are reproduced on pages 152 and 153.

The evolution of the Estate is described chronologically because this provides a clearer description of its development than would have been achieved by a thematic approach. Thus, some of the chapter titles include the years covered. As these divisions are somewhat arbitrary, there is occasionally some overlap between one group of years and the next; issues dealt with towards the end of one period sometimes continue into the following chapter.

Publications listed in the bibliography are cited in footnotes as (author's surname), (page no.). Where an author has more than one book or article listed, their surname is followed by the year of publication. If the year of publication is not known, it is followed by the first part of the title of the book or the name of the article, as the case may be. Square brackets enclose words or phrases added to quotations whose meanings might otherwise lack clarity.

I am very grateful to the Association for the free hand they have given me in the writing of this book, despite time delays caused partly by information coming to light that had not been envisaged at the outset. It is common for authors to thank their spouses for the tolerance they have shown whilst books were being researched and written. The experience of producing this book has taught me that such acknowledgements are by no means trite; my wife now numbers amongst those people without whose forbearance much history might not have been documented.

Finally, the Association would like to record its thanks to The Hyde Group and the Royal Borough of Greenwich for their grants under, respectively, the Pitch2Enrich initiative and the Ward Budget scheme. Our book would not have been published without their financial assistance.

Keith Billinghurst
Eltham
London SE9

February 2017

List of Tables and Illustrations

No.	Title	Page no.
1	From assassination to world war in 138 days	14
2	Average numbers of workers employed in the Manufacturing Departments at the Royal Arsenal, Woolwich	17
3	British municipal towns with 1851 populations greater than 100,000	26
4	Cellar dwellings, Manchester, 1840s	27
5	Changing structure of the British workforce 1851-1891	27
6	Liverpool back-to-backs, 1843	28
7	Annual passenger journeys by rail	36
8	Growth of three London suburbs 1851-1891	36
9	Late 19th-century by-law housing	41
10	York's best type of working-class house, 1900	41
11	By-law housing at Longford, Coventry, 1911	42
12	Charles Booth's map of St Giles, London 1898-99	47
13	John Ruskin	51
14	St Mark's, Venice, north-west portico, angled view (daguerreotype, Ruskin & Hill)	52
15	The architectural line from Ruskin to the end of the 19th century	54
16	Garth House, Edgbaston	59
17	William Alexander Harvey	62
18	Bournville's population, 1901	65
19	Houses in Sycamore Road, Bournville	66
20	Bournville, 1915	67
21	Garden City	69
22	Ward and Centre of Garden City	70
23	Parker and Unwin	72
24	Preliminary sketch for a hall near Derby	76
25	Early plan for New Earswick by Parker and Unwin (1902)	84
26	Poplar Grove in 1904	85
27	Parker and Unwin's layout for Letchworth (1902)	89

28	Parker and Unwin's layout for Bird's Hill, Letchworth	93
29	Cottages around the green in Ridge Road, Bird's Hill, Letchworth	94
30	Unwin's conceptual layout for the Central Square, Letchworth	103
31	Hampstead Garden Suburb street plan	105
32	Block of houses on Hogarth Hill	105
33	An imaginary irregular town from *Town Planning in Practice*	113
34	*Nothing Gained by Overcrowding!* Diagram I	117
35	72-75 Cheyne Walk, Chelsea	123
36	Investiture group in City Levée dress civil uniform at the Investiture of the Prince of Wales at Caernarfon Castle in 1911. Frank Baines is second from the left.	125
37	Plan of the Estate incorporated in the Indenture of 9th November 1915	141
38	Well Hall Road looking north, circa 1905	144
39	Elm trees growing in Dickson Road, looking east	144
40	West side of the Estate	152
41	East side of the Estate	153
42	Raised pavement in Ross Way	155
43	John Mowlem's weekly wage bill	157
44	Classes of accommodation	158
45	Moira Road flats	159
46	House construction showing narrow-gauge railway	161
47	Part of Ordnance Survey London Sheet P (revised 1914)	168
48	Estimated number of male residents aged 18 and over	208
49	Ross Way	216
50	WWII bomb damage	226

Front cover
H.M. Office of Works detailed drawing no. 34 for houses in Prince Rupert Road
Rear cover
The Estate under construction in 1915

Acknowledgements

The author is grateful to the staff of the following institutions whose patient assistance enabled him to carry out the necessary research:

- Borthwick Institute, York University, holders of the Joseph Rowntree Village Trust Archive
- British Architectural Library at the Royal Institute of British Architects, London
- British Library's London map room and its licensing and imaging departments
- Garden City Collection, Letchworth
- Greenwich Heritage Centre, Woolwich
- Joseph Rowntree Foundation, York
- Library of Birmingham, holders of the Bournville Village Trust Archive
- London Metropolitan Archive
- National Co-operative Archive, Manchester

Thanks are due to the following for permission to reproduce photographic illustrations:

- Bournville Village Trust (9, 17, 20)
- British Library (28, 39, 40, 41, 45, 46, 47, 49, rear cover)
- Courtauld Institute of Art, ref: Kersting H885 (35)
- Garden City Collection (21, 22, 23, 24)
- Hampstead Garden Suburb Trust (31)
- Historic England Archive (36)
- Joseph Rowntree Foundation (26)
- Land Registry (37)
- London School of Economics (lse.ac.uk) (12)
- Ruskin Foundation (13, 14)
- Greenwich Heritage Centre (front cover, 38)

Other photographic illustrations (excluding the author's own – nos. 19, 29, 30, 32, 42) are from:

- John Burnett, *A Social History of Housing* 1815-1985, Routledge, 1986 (4, 6, 11)
- en.wikipedia.org/wiki/History_of_rail_transport_in_Great_Britain (7)
- Jimmy Guano, en.wikipedia.org/wiki/File:Garth_House,_Edgbaston,_Birmingham_-_William_Bidlake.jpg (16)
- Frank Jackson, *Sir Raymond Unwin: Architect, Planner and Visionary*, A. Zwemmer Ltd., London, 1985 (25)
- Mervyn Miller, *Letchworth, the First Garden City*, Phillimore, 2002 (27)
- B. Seebohm Rowntree, *Poverty and Progress: A second social survey of York*, Longmans, Green and Co., London, 1941 (10)
- Raymond Unwin, *Town Planning in Practice*, T. Fisher Unwin, London, 1909 (33)
- Raymond Unwin, *Nothing Gained by Overcrowding!*, P. S. King & Son, London, for the Garden Cities & Town Planning Association, republished by the Town and Country Planning Association, 2012 (34)

The author would like to thank John Usher for providing information about Cecil Henry Polhill and Lynne Dixon for drawing his attention to the Estate plans which came to light at the Greenwich Heritage Centre during 2016. He would also like to record his gratitude to Gill Holmans and Avril Martin for saving Bill Venn's papers from destruction. A lifelong bachelor, Mr Venn became a tenant of Progress Estates Ltd. on 18 March 1946. He lived in the same house until he died in 2012 and throughout this time retained many if not all of the letters and circulars he received from his landlords. His only surviving relative was a niece who outlived him for just a few months. These papers have served as an archive for the period since The Hyde Group acquired the Estate's rented housing from the Royal Arsenal Co-operative Society in 1980. It is hoped that the Greenwich Heritage Centre will, in due course, accept them; their chief value is likely to be to students of the Rent Acts.

WHY THE ESTATE WAS BUILT

The Outbreak of the First World War

If it had not been for the First World War, the Estate would not have been built. Here, briefly, is the background to that conflict.

The Balkans had been chaotic for several years. The Balkan League, created from a series of bilateral treaties in 1912 between Greece, Bulgaria, Serbia and Montenegro was opposed to the Ottoman Empire.[1] The League won the First Balkan War (October 1912 to May 1913) and partitioned nearly all the Ottoman territories in Europe. However, Bulgaria's dissatisfaction with the division of Macedonia resulted in its starting the Second Balkan War in which it attacked its former allies, Serbia and Greece. This conflict ran from the end of June to the middle of August 1913. It backfired on its perpetrator; Bulgaria was forced to concede portions of its gains from the First War to Serbia and Greece, as well as to Romania. The latter was an enemy from previous conflicts and, as its troops approached Sofia, Bulgaria asked for an armistice.[2]

The Balkan League could not reconstruct itself. The heir presumptive to the Austro-Hungarian throne, Archduke Franz Ferdinand, wished to see Serbia crushed,[3] and the small states making up the Balkans were at the mercy of the surrounding empires. This powder keg was ignited on 28 June 1914 when a young Serb nationalist, Gavrilo Princip, assassinated the Archduke in Sarajevo.[4]

Thirty eight days days later, Great Britain declared war on Germany and, one hundred days after that, most of Europe, Asia Minor, Russia and Japan were at war:

---

[1] en.wikipedia.org/wiki/Balkan_League, accessed 26 May 2014.

[2] en.wikipedia.org/wiki/Second_Balkan_War, accessed 12 March 2015.

[3] Hogg, p. 947.

[4] Lee, p. 88.

FROM ASSASSINATION TO WORLD WAR IN 138 DAYS

28 June   Archduke Franz Ferdinand of Austria-Hungary assassinated in Sarajevo.

23 July   Franz Joseph, Emperor of Austria, and with the strong support of Germany, gave Serbia a 48-hour ultimatum to accept conditions that would have menaced her existence as an independent estate.
Austria partially mobilised against Serbia.

26 July   Russia put itself into a 'state of preparation for war'.

28 July   Austria-Hungary declared war on Serbia.

30 July   Russia mobilised.

31 July   Austria-Hungary mobilised.

1 August   France and Germany mobilised.
Germany declared war on Russia.

2 August   Germany sent a note to Belgium at 7 p.m., alleging that Germany must violate her soil in order to 'anticipate' a French attack in Belgium. The note demanded that Belgium should remain passive and required an answer in twelve hours.

3 August   Germany declared war on France.

4 August   Great Britain, bound to protect Belgium's independence under the Treaty of London, 1839 protested against Germany's invasion of Belgium, declared war on Germany, and mobilised.

5 August   Montenegro declared war on Austria.

6 August   Austria declared war on Russia.

12 August   Great Britain and France declared war on Austria.

23 August   Japan declared war on Germany.

5 November   Great Britain declared war on Turkey.

12 November   Turkey declared war on France, Great Britain and Russia.

Source: Hogg, pp.947-8.

WHY THE ESTATE WAS BUILT

In Britain, the Defence of the Realm Bill had its first and second readings, committee stage and third reading in the House of Commons on 7 August. The House of Lords passed it without amendment on the 8th, and it received Royal Assent on the 10th.[5] Its single paragraph gave 'His Majesty in Council power, during the continuance of the present war, to issue regulations as to the powers and duties of the Admiralty and Army Council, and of the members of His Majesty's forces, and other persons acting on His behalf, for securing the public safety and the defence of the realm'.

Britain was at war like never before. By the end of the first battle of Ypres in November 1914 her regular army would have lost more than half its 160,000 men in just three months.[6]

---

[5] hansard.millbanksystems.com/commons/1914/aug/07/defence-of-the-realm-bill and hansard.millbanksystems.com/lords/1914/aug/08/defence-of-the-realm-bill, accessed 29 August 2014.

[6] Tony Barber, 'Ripples across the century', *Financial Times,* London, 4 August 2014, p. 7.

The Demand for Labour at the Royal Arsenal in Woolwich

The purpose of this chapter is to provide an overview of the expansion of activity at the Royal Arsenal in Woolwich in the months following the outbreak of First World War, because this caused the Estate to be built.[7]

The levels of employment at Woolwich Arsenal had always been positively correlated to war: see table opposite.

In August 1914, the country's Ordnance Factories, of which the Royal Arsenal at Woolwich was pre-eminent, were controlled by the War Office. In parallel with the expansion of the Office's activities over the course of the war (staff grew from less than 2,000 in 1914 to over 22,000 by 1918), the government would establish three new ministries. The first of these was the Ministry of Munitions.[8] On 26 May 1915, the day after the coalition war government was formed, Prime Minister Herbert Asquith announced that 'Mr. Lloyd George has undertaken the formation and temporary direction of this department and during his tenure of office as Minister of Munitions will vacate the office of Chancellor of the Exchequer'.[9]

Whilst the Act of Parliament creating the new ministry was passed in June 1915, the handover of Woolwich Arsenal was a slow process, and one might assume many of the people involved with it as War Office personnel were in due course transferred to the new ministry. In introducing the second reading of the bill, Sir John Simon, Secretary of State for the Home Department, had explained its purpose was to 'supply munitions for the present War'. Although many of its activities were likely to be in co-operation with other, existing ministries (not least of which would be the War Office and the Admiralty), 'a start is to be made with the most urgent matters, and these obviously are the

---

[7] Hogg, pp. 949-991, 1000-1001 and 1288-1291.

[8] The other two were the Ministry of Pensions and the Air Ministry. The Ministry of National Service added to its existing duties by taking over from the Adjutant-General's Department in the autumn of 1917 the very important task of obtaining men for the Army. www.1914-1918.net/waroffice.html, accessed 23 July 2014.

[9] www.airfieldinformationexchange.org/community/showthread.php?11695-FIRST-WORLD-WAR-Ministry-of-Munitions-and-Munitions-Factories, accessed 24 July 2014.

AVERAGE NUMBER OF WORKERS EMPLOYED IN THE MANUFACTURING DEPARTMENTS AT THE ROYAL ARSENAL, WOOLWICH

Conflict/peacetime	Date	Average numbers
Crimean War and Indian Mutiny	1858	5,456
	1859	6,218
	1860	10,373
	1861	10,238
Interwar minimum	1872	4,627
South African (Boer) War	1899	17,013
	1900	20,015
	1901	20,005
First World War	August 1914	10,866
	January 1915	22,631
	December 1915	45,898
	May 1916	59,833
	December 1917	72,700
	May 1918	64,977
	August 1918	65,462
	November 1918	63,827
Immediate aftermath	January 1919	38,203
	April 1919	24,628
Interwar minimum	1933	6,746
Rearmament and the Second World War	1936	11,050
	1937	15,725
	1938	19,050
	September 1940	32,500
	November 1940	19,000
	February 1943	23,000
	August 1945	15,500
Post-war	1947	8,300
Ordnance Factory closed	1967	

Sources: Hogg, pp 1289-90 and, for year of closure, en.wikipedia.org/wiki/Royal_Arsenal, accessed 2 July 2014.

supply of shells, rifles and guns, including machine guns, explosives and the like'. The new Ministry would cease to exist when the war ended.[10]

Until 1914, no one had envisaged a conflict that would engulf the majority of the world's nations and the Royal Arsenal had grown piecemeal without any central planning. Much of the machinery was out of date and many of the badly lit and ill-ventilated workshops were not suitable for modern plant. Planning for replacements had been haphazard, and favourable conditions of employment already promised to staff militated against economical production. Whilst in due course larger projects such as the new small arms ammunition factory were moved to more open ground, making it possible to improve layouts, the initial expansion was to the existing Royal Gun and Carriage Factory, shell factories and the inspection buildings.

The first expansion in the Royal Gun and Carriage Factory was on the outbreak of war. The Front's immediate requirement was for the breech-loading 60-pounder 5-inch heavy field gun. This had been designed in 1903-05 and was moved by either horse-drawn or mechanical traction.[11] The Ordnance QF 4½-inch howitzer was also required. It had entered service in 1910 and would be an important weapon throughout the war, in due course replacing a quarter of the 5-inch guns.[12] Ordnance QF 18-pounder guns, which became the backbone of the Royal Field Artillery, were also in demand[13] as were carriages and vehicles of all descriptions.

The second expansion in 1915 was caused by calls from the Army for 8-inch Mark VI howitzers (a Vickers design approved in August 1915)[14] and increased demand for the aforementioned 60-pounders and 4½-inch howitzers. Orders for carriages were met by private manufacturers because the carriage department had no room to expand. At the same time, the Royal Gun and Carriage Factory had to supply the Royal Laboratory fuse factory, another of the factories in the

---

[10] House of Commons Debate, *Hansard*, vol. 72 cc88-152, 7 June 1915.

[11] en.wikipedia.org/wiki/BL_60-pounder_gun, accessed 23 July 2014.

[12] en.wikipedia.org/wiki/QF_4.5-inch_howitzer, accessed 23 July 2014.

[13] en.wikipedia.org/wiki/Ordnance_QF_18-pounder, accessed 23 July 2014.

[14] en.wikipedia.org/wiki/BL_8 inch_howitzer_Mk_VI_%E2%80%93_VIII#Mark_VI, accessed 23 July 2014.

complex where all kinds of ammunition were made and filled, with a large amount of additional stamping plant.[15]

Between the outbreak of war and spring 1915, shell filling was concentrated in the Royal Arsenal and large extensions were made to the Royal Laboratory.[16] Its area was increased by 1,520,572 square feet – the equivalent of about 20 Premiership football pitches. Prior to 1914, output had typically been 10,000 lb of explosives a week and had never exceeded 30,000 lb. Within a week of war being declared it rose to 100,000 lb by the adoption of night shifts and overtime working.

A weekly increase of at least 5,000,000 rounds of small ammunition was required in September 1914, resulting in the construction of a new factory and the acquisition of the requisite plant and machinery for increasing the output of fuses and cartridge cases.

War turned the Royal Arsenal into an enormous construction site. Erection of the first new factory began in September 1915. Other than during November 1915, additions and new works were carried out every month until March 1918. The final new building was in October 1918 when new premises were built for the cleaning of cartridge cases. A gross 3,433,609 square feet were built during the war – 45 Premiership football pitches.

The Royal Arsenal had always favoured building by direct labour. New premises generally had to be erected at short notice to satisfy the demands of war. Had contractors been used, the drawing-up of detailed contracts (particularly for work connected with danger buildings) would have resulted in unacceptable delays. By using direct labour, details could be worked out as building was underway. The scarcity of men was to some extent overcome by employing military labour and navvies from Ireland.

Economical production was never a prime consideration in Woolwich. Although armaments were manufactured by the private sector, contracts were only let once all preliminary testing had been

---

[15] Stamping plant marked fuse heads with lot numbers and the dates of filling.

[16] Woolwich could not provide anything like enough facilities for all the shell filling that was required, and so in July 1915 the first National Filling Factories were started at Aintree and Coventry. A Principal Architect to H.M. Office of Works, Frank Baines, became responsible for all new NFF building designs. By the end of the war, eighteen were in operation. (www.airfieldinformationexchange.org/community/showthread.php?11695-FIRST-WORLD-WAR-Ministry-of-Munitions-and-Munitions-Factories, accessed 24 July 2014).

completed in order to minimise disruptive alterations once production was underway. The Royal Arsenal's prime function was to provide the nation's Army and Navy, at short notice, with the tools to win wars. This necessary mindset on the part of those responsible for its role in the war effort made the construction of the Estate on a cost-plus basis the obvious way to proceed; tendering was simply too time-consuming.[17]

---

[17] Cooper, p. 48. During the war, the Government let contracts on the basis of paying the costs, plus an agree percentage for overheads and profit.

The Housing Crisis in Woolwich

Dr. Sidney Davies, Medical Officer of Health for Woolwich, was interred in Germany at the beginning of August 1914. He was released at the end of October on the grounds of age and was none the worse for the experience, save for being weary[18]. He had been elected President of the Metropolitan branch of the Incorporated Society of Medical Officers of Health in 1908.[19]

His concern with public health matters dated from at least 1903 when, as Medical Officer for the Borough, he delivered his address 'Consumption: Its Causes and Prevention'. *The Woolwich Labour Journal* described it as 'one of the simplest, clearest, and wisest statements on the subject that we have yet seen. It is full of practical information, especially for working people, and its advice if acted upon would greatly lessen the suffering and pitiable loss of life among the poor. Dr. Davies dwells chiefly upon the preventative and curative effects of fresh air, light, and keeping the house thoroughly clean (not by *dusting*, but by *washing with water*). We hope the lecture will be printed in pamphlet form – its wide circulation would do unbounded good'.[20]

Dr. Davies spoke at the Proceedings of the National Conference on the Prevention of Destitution held at Caxton Hall, Westminster, on 12 June 1912. He supported the notion of a National Health Service whilst reminding the audience that the excellent advice received by many local authorities (including his own) 'did not receive any attention'. The Army had appreciated it could not be successful in war unless it were a healthy army, yet had not succeeded in convincing public bodies or the public themselves that it would pay to increase people's health. The public looked upon public health as a nice but expensive fad and he was afraid that until they were convinced it meant saving and making

---

[18] *Woolwich Pioneer*, 30 October 1914, In: www.worldwar1schoolarchives.org/manchester-grammar-school, ULULA, February 1915, p. 5, accessed 20 August 2014.

[19] www.publichealthjrnl.com/article/S0033-3506%2808%2980041-8/abstract?cc=y?cc=y, accessed 19 August 2014. The Society's successor organisation is the Association of Directors of Public Health (www.adph.org.uk/about-adph/history, accessed 27 August 2014).

[20] ILP News, March 1903, In: dds.crl.edu/loadStream.asp?iid=7385, accessed 19 August 2014.

money the desired progress would not be made.[21] To build up data for his assertions, his annual reports as Medical Officer of Health for Woolwich began, from the same year, to include notes on the habits of persons suffering and dying from cancer in the borough.[22]

Dr. Davies had reported on the borough's supply of houses to the Borough Council in October 1913, and on the great demand for working-class houses.[23] Just over a year later, on 2 December 1914, he noted that whilst 227 had been built, a large number had been demolished and the supply was diminishing. The increase in demand caused by additional workers at the Arsenal had been exacerbated by the number of Army recruits quartered in the borough and the removal of families from married quarters. The Council resolved to bring the matter to the attention of Will Crooks, the town's Member of Parliament.[24] Crooks duly arranged for a deputation appointed by the Borough Council to meet the President of the Local Government Board on 30 December. The representatives took a prepared a statement:

> The difficulty has arisen, as it did in 1901, out of the war, and the consequent increase in the number of men employed in the Royal Arsenal and Dockyard. The census population of the Borough in 1901 was 117,178, it is now estimated to be 140,000. The number of houses in 1901 was 18,086, now it is 22,051. In 1901 the unoccupied houses numbered 234. In consequence of the

---

[21] www.mocavo.co.uk/Report-of-the-Proceedings-of-the-National-Conference-on-the-Prevention-of-Destitution-Held-at-the-Caxton-Hall-Westminster-on-June-11th-12th-13th-and-14th-1912/290741/91, accessed 19 August 2014.

[22] scans.library.utoronto.ca/pdf/5/22/.../canadalancetprac52torouoft_bw.pdf, accessed 19 August 2014.

[23] Hills (unpublished thesis) and Jones (unpublished project).

[24] Will Crooks, born 6 April 1852 in Poplar, the third son of a ship's stoker who lost his arm in an accident three years after his son's birth. Despite his mother's endeavours to support the family by working as a seamstress, all five of her children were temporarily forced into the Poplar workhouse in 1861 which profoundly informed Crooks' views of poverty. Began making political speeches early in his adult life and was one of the earliest Labour members of the London County Council in 1889. Labour MP for Woolwich (and only the fourth Labour MP in the Commons) in 1902. Apparently did not raise the matter of housing in Woolwich in the House. en.wikipedia.org/wiki/Will_Crooks and hansard.millbanksystems.com/people/mr-william-crooks, accessed 18 August 2014. Road named after him in Eltham – Will Crooks Gardens, SE9 6HZ.

large reduction in the Arsenal in the years following the South African War, in 1911 there were as many as 1,296 unoccupied houses. Since then these houses have been filling up, until in April this year there were only 305, and at the present time only 128, these 128 almost entirely representing business premises and houses let at quarterly rents exceeding £30 p.a. and therefore unsuitable for working-class occupation.[25]

The council had made enquiries of eight estate agents. They did not have a single house vacant, and the Secretary of the Royal Arsenal Co-operative Society said he could fill 200 in a week.

The Local Government Board accepted the case put forward by the Council, and accordingly the Town Clerk reported to the Council on 10 February 1915 'that the Principal Architect of H.M. Office of Works has received instructions to erect about 1,000 dwellings on land at Well Hall, Eltham'. The Council report was, however, behind the game. This was wartime and there was a desperate need for munitions; the sedate routine of local government meetings was, at least temporarily, a thing of the past. The initial site surveys and the very earliest of the house designs had been completed by 25 January[26] and on the 29th, *The Pioneer*[27] reported on its front page:

> It will be good news to Arsenal men to learn that, following the recent deputation from the Borough Council to the Local Government Board, the Government has decided to proceed at once with a large housing scheme for Government workmen. The site chosen is at Eltham on the Well Hall road ... Ninety acres of land have been purchased and the Estate will be laid out as a Garden City ...

The front-page headline for their 5 February edition was: 'The Housing Scheme for Government Workmen – where to apply for houses'. The same columnist (writing under the pseudonym 'Free Lance') reported:

---

[25] £30 per annum equates to 11/6d. per week. Come 1915, a two-bedroomed flat on the Well Hall Estate would be rentable for between 7/- and 7/6d. per week.

[26] Analysis of drawings held in the Greenwich Heritage Centre.

[27] *The Pioneer and Labour Journal*, a weekly newspaper published in Woolwich that was supportive of the Labour Party.

> The notice (exclusively reported in the Pioneer last Week) of the intention of the Government to proceed at once with a large housing scheme at Eltham, has brought a large crop of inquiries from Arsenal men where application is to be made for houses. At the moment details of lettings have not been decided and applications should be made to Mr F. Baines, Principal Architect, H.M. Office of Works, Storey's Gate, S.W. [London]. I have had the opportunity of seeing the plans of the Estate and houses and if the scheme materialises as laid out in the plans, and there is every reason to believe it will, Woolwich will have a Garden City of which it will be justly proud. The plans provide for four classes of houses so that all pockets will be catered for.

One can only imagine the joy with which Frank Baines would have learned that his Office was supposed to add unpaid letting agent duties to those of being the Estate's architect. He and his colleagues would be working seven days a week for more or less the whole of 1915 just to build it.

If *The Pioneer*'s 5 February report was accurate, the decision to build the Estate as a Garden City either was taken during January 1915 or had been a matter of government policy for state-funded housing before the end of 1914. Therefore, in order for the Estate's place in the evolution of urban housing to be understood, it is time to consider how housing had evolved from the mid-1800s, when the emerging Industrial Revolution required ever-increasing numbers of people to live within short distances of the factories in which they worked.

HOW GARDEN SUBURBS CAME TO BE

The Growth of Cities and Suburbs

As the 19th century proceeded, the manufacturing economy overtook agriculture as the main source of employment. Factories' labour forces needed to be able to travel to and from work reasonably quickly, so more and more people began to live closer to one another as time passed. In addition, raw materials and finished products needed to be transported as economically as possible. In broad terms, that meant siting factories near canals in the first half of the 19th century and railways in the second.[28] These, generally, were in existing towns whose populations expanded accordingly.

The English and Welsh population doubled from 8.9ml to 17.9ml between 1801 and 1851, which equated to a growth rate of 1.4% per annum. However, the proportion living in towns and cities rose from a third to well over a half, thereby increasing urban populations by a multiple of three to four and delivering an overall growth rate of 2¼-2½% per annum.[29] For comparison, the UK population increased by 7.6% in the ten years to 2013 – only ¾% per annum.[30] As has always been the case, resettlers tended to move to those towns and cities that offered employment. The population living in the London area (broadly, the area that now has London postcodes) grew from 1.0ml in 1801 to 2.3ml in 1851,[31] representing, respectively, 11.0% and 12.8% of the population of England and Wales. Mid-century, it was continuing to grow at 20% per decade. About 60% of the new arrivals were coming from the home and southern counties or East Anglia. The Irish, Scots and people from overseas made up a significant portion of the remainder.[32]

---

[28] en.wikipedia.org/wiki/Canals_of_the_United_Kingdom, accessed 6 January 2016.

[29] Burnett, pp. 4-10.

[30] 'Big Read', *Financial Times*, 2 June 2015.

[31] en.wikipedia.org/wiki/Demography_of_London, accessed 6 January 2016.

[32] Burnett, p. 57.

Despite the huge increase in London's population, the fastest rates of growth were seen in the largest industrial cities:

BRITISH MUNICIPAL TOWNS WITH 1851
POPULATIONS GREATER THAN 100,000 (000s)

Town	1801	1851	Change p.a.
Birmingham	71	233	2.4%
Bradford	13	104	4.2%
Glasgow	77	345	3.0%
Leeds	53	172	2.4%
Liverpool	82	376	3.1%
Manchester	75	303	2.8%
Sheffield	46	135	2.2%
Totals	417	1,668	2.8%

Source: Hopkins, p 18.

The chief cause of worsening housing conditions in the first half of the 19th century was the subdivision of large, previously gentrified houses into rooms for letting. As new arrivals who could afford nothing better (or possibly simply needed to live in a certain area) moved in, those with the wherewithal left town. Thus, in 1842, Charles Darwin moved his family to Down House in Kent 'to escape an increasingly overcrowded and dirty London'.[33] In the worst instances, cellars, never built for human habitation, were also let. These often had no drainage, sanitation or ventilation, and sometimes only soil floors. Continuous flooding was not uncommon because some were below river level and had to be bailed out by buckets carried up to street level every day. They became breeding grounds for typhus and other infectious diseases. In 1883, Dr. Peter Gaskell thought that 'upwards of 20,000 individuals

---

[33] Chris Packham, 'Following in Darwin's Footsteps', *English Heritage Members' Magazine*, October 2014, p. 24.

live in cellars in Manchester alone'[34] – some 5% of the population. If the Mancunian suburbs were included, the total had been at least twice this some 40 years earlier.[35] Dr. Duncan, a medical officer in Liverpool, estimated 40,000 people in his city lived in cellars in the late-1830s – perhaps 10% of the population.

Cellar dwellings, Manchester, 1840s.

This table shows the change in the make-up of the British workforce between 1851 and 1891.

CHANGING STRUCTURE OF THE BRITISH WORKFORCE 1851–1891

	1851		*1891*	
	Number (ml)	*%*	*Number (ml)*	*%*
Agriculture, forestry and fishing	2.1	21.9	1.6	11.2
Manufacturing, mining and building	4.1	42.7	6.5	45.4
Trade and transport	1.5	15.6	3.4	23.8
Domestic and personal	1.3	13.5	2.0	14.0
Other	0.6	6.3	0.8	5.6
Totals	9.6	100.0	14.3	100.0

Source: P. Deane and W.A. Cole, *British Economic Growth 1688-1959: Trends and Structure*, Cambridge University Press 1969, pp.142-3. In: Benson, p 10.

[34] Dr Peter Gaskell, *The manufacturing population of England, 1883*. In: Burnett, p. 55.

[35] Friedrich Engels, *The Condition of the Working Class in England in 1844*. In: Burnett, p. 56.

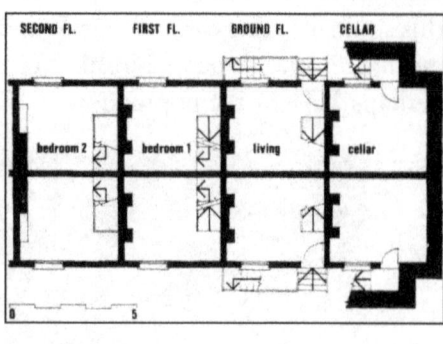

Liverpool back-to-backs, 1843.

Over these 40 years the combined numbers employed in manufacturing, mining, building, trade and transport increased by 4.3ml – from 5.6ml to 9.9ml. This represented 91% of the 4.7ml increase in the working population as a whole (from 9.6ml to 14.3ml).

The first houses to be constructed specifically for the urban working classes were back-to-backs. The illustration above shows plans for those built in 1843 near Liverpool's docks in Dukes Terrace. Each house cost a little over £100 to build and would rent for around 3/- per week. The cellar, if constructed, was not normally inhabited. All the activities of daytime living took place in the ground-floor living room. It was usual for the husband and wife to sleep in the first-floor bedroom and the children on the second floor where the ceiling was lower, as it followed the line of the roof. Couples without children (or whose children had left home) might let the top room to a lodger. Every room measured 12½ x 10¾ feet.

Back-to-backs were built in their thousands, principally in the main manufacturing cities of Birmingham and northwards, from the 1840s. Relative to its population, Leeds had more than any other city. By 1886, 49,000, representing 71% of the city's entire housing stock, had been built at a density of 70 or 80 to the acre.[36]

The sanitary problems caused by these housing developments soon came to light. In 1842 Edwin Chadwick, a barrister and Secretary to the

---

[36] Burnett, pp. 70-77.

Board of the Poor Law Commissioners, wrote his *Report on the Sanitary Condition of the Labouring Population of Great Britain*.[37] Describing back-to-backs, he said:

> An immense number of small houses occupied by the poorer classes in the suburbs of Manchester are of the most superficial character; they are built by the members of building clubs, and other individuals, and new cottages are erected with a rapidity that astonishes persons who are unacquainted with their flimsy structure. They have certainly avoided the objectionable mode of forming underground dwellings but have run into the opposite extreme, having neither cellar nor foundation. The walls are only half a brick thick, or what the bricklayers call 'brick noggin', and the whole of the materials are slight and unfit for the purpose… They are built back to back; without ventilation or drainage; and, like a honeycomb, every particle of space is occupied. Double rows of these houses form courts, with, perhaps, a pump at one end and a privy at the other, common to the occupants of about twenty houses.[38]

The work of the Committee on the Health of Towns led to the Metropolitan Buildings Act, 1844. Its purpose, as explained by William Alexander Mackinnon,[39] one of the Committee members during the bill's committee stage on 16 July 1844, vividly describes the insanitary state of much inner-city housing at the time:[40]

> As far as buildings in Towns were concerned, the attention of the Committee on Public Health was particularly directed to three points which required to be amended by the Legislature. The first was the necessity of allowing a free ventilation of air by not permitting blind alleys or streets not open at both ends to be erected in future, and I trust this measure will be adopted in the

---

[37] Printed by William Clowes and Sons, Stamford Street, for Her Majesty's Stationery Office.

[38] Lords Sessional Papers (1842), vol XXVII, p. 240. In: John Burnett, *ibid.*, pp. 70.

[39] William Alexander Mackinnon (1784-1870), Member of Parliament for Lymington, 1835-52. Liberal Conservative and free-trader. H. C. G. Matthew, 'Mackinnon, William Alexander, of Mackinnon (1784–1870)', *Oxford Dictionary of National Biography*, Oxford University Press, 2004 [www.oxforddnb.com/view/article/17619, accessed 25 Jan 2016}.

[40] hansard.millbanksystems.com/commons/1844/jul/16/metropolitan-buildings#S3V0076P0_18440716_HOC_12, accessed 25 January 2016.

present Bill. Every street or alley to be erected in future ought to have a way through, not to be choked up at one end, to be what the French call a 'cul de sac.' It appeared before the Committee that great unhealthiness prevailed amongst the poor in those districts in the metropolis, and in all large towns where such blind alleys or streets were occupied by any class of persons. The next point was, that houses should be ventilated by not being so constructed as to stand back to back; that is, if the front of the house was towards the street or the entrance, the back part should be open towards a yard or some open space, so as to allow a free current of air to pass from the front to the rear of the house, which could not be the case if a house had no open space behind, but in place of it there was another house built up behind, so that by no possible means could any ventilation take place, as no current of air could go through the house. I beg leave to call the attention of the House and of the noble Lord[41] to this mode of building, that it may in this Bill be corrected. The next point that was deemed of the utmost importance was the drainage of houses and streets, that no house should be constructed without a direct communication under ground, either with the main sewer or branch drain leading to such sewer, so that a drain should be formed for every dwelling. That no cess pool or dead well should be under any house or dwelling, or within a certain distance from it, so that no miasma[42] or noisome evaporation or gas should arise from such dead well or cess pool injurious to the health of the inhabitants, which noisome gas has been deemed by medical men (after that arising from churchyards) the most injurious to public health. In stating this, I do not mean to say that this metropolis is not well drained, it is by far the best drained town in Europe, but although much has been done, yet much remains to be done to improve the present drainage of London.

The Bill received Royal Assent on 9 August 1844 and, in broad terms, applied to new buildings in the whole of London within what are now the North and South Circular Roads.[43] It imposed minimum widths for new streets, alleys and mews. Houses were to have an open rear

---

[41] The Earl of Lincoln, First Commissioner of Woods and Forests and, at this time, Chairman of the Metropolitan Improvements Commission. www.oxforddnb.com/view/article/5686?docPos=4, accessed 28 January 2016.

[42] Noxious vapours.

[43] Section III, archive.org/stream/metropolitanbui00britgoog#page/n22/mode/2up, accessed 25 January 2016.

space of at least 100 square feet, thus calling a halt to the construction of new back-to-backs in the metropolis.

The second half of the 19th century and the first two decades of the twentieth would see housing become the chief cause of new legislation, spurred on by social reformers inside and outside Parliament.

70 Years of Legislation

The years 1847 to 1919 saw fifty-six Acts of Parliament that impacted directly on housing. Their sheet number probably reflects the incremental steps that, perforce, must be taken when vested interests are ranged against substantial change. The aim of them all was to improve what could be broadly described as the housing of the working classes. Some of these were borne of the eight reports by Royal Commissions. Twelve Select Committee reports dwelt upon the impact of some of this legislation. Countless Bills were brought forward by Members of both the Commons and the Lords. Many of these were designed to promote parliamentary debate and, whilst often failing to obtain even a second reading, gave their promoters an insight into what legislation might be possible.[44]

The difference wrought by most of these individual pieces of legislation was a lot less than that for which their promoters had hoped. The principal reason for these recurring disappointments was because it was not until 1919 that central government finally obtained powers to compel recalcitrant local authorities to take the action national governments considered essential. Legislation until then had been permissive; it allowed local authorities to do (or, as the case may be, not do) certain things if they so chose. This reflected a general belief of the time that authority had no right to interfere with private property or control its development. Writing in *The Nineteenth Century*, C. L. Lewis said 'Liberty to do what you like with your own is the inalienable privilege of every Briton; but there is always the proviso *subauditum* that in doing what you like you shall not hurt others'.[45] The Latin word describes something that is not stated but implied or inferred. The intellectual change in the last third of the 19th century was therefore an increasing realisation on the part of lawmakers that in the interests of the population as a whole legislation had to become more specific in order for the majority of people not to be disadvantaged by private property owners whose interpretation of the law had been far too literal.

The Metropolis was usually at the forefront of the adoption of new

---

[44] Gauldie, pp. 13 and 311.

[45] 'How to ensure breathing spaces', vol. xxi (May 1887), p. 679. In: Tarn, p. 125.

powers and, indeed, had its own legislation as far back as 1774.[46] Its public servants were well aware that building controls were necessary to ensure decent (healthy) standards of housebuilding. George Godwin, an architect and district surveyor, wrote in the 1860s that 'we are much disposed to think that the legislature should interfere, and that some properly constituted officer should certify that every new house is built in such a manner as to be fit to live in'.[47] There were a few enlightened local authorities who were also often early adopters. This group was led by Sheffield, Bradford, Liverpool and Manchester, all of whom had histories of artisan strength. For the rest, there were two problems. Firstly, people living a distance from the Metropolis were fiercely proud of their independence and resented what they saw as interference from London. Secondly, local government was too often prone to corruption by those with a financial interest in property as either builders or owners.

This chapter will look briefly at the most significant of these Acts. Garden suburbs were not the direct result of legislation and never provided housing for the poorest labouring classes. They were, however, developed by those who saw the uncontrolled growth of cities as a social disaster and so, to that extent, their creators informed the work of lawmakers as the right to vote spread to include increasingly wider sections of the population.

All cities with large, transitory populations saw vast increases in the numbers of their inhabitants living in lodging houses. This was an especial problem in London, Manchester and Liverpool and quickly became the focus of social reformers. Lord Ashley (soon to become the 7th Earl of Shaftesbury when his father died on 2 June 1851)[48] introduced a debate on lodging houses on 8 April 1851 with some statistics that, these days, are almost impossible to believe. A return of house-to-house visitations in St. George's, Hanover Square, was made in 1842 and reported to the Statistical Society. It stated that 1,465 families of the labouring classes were found to reside in only 2,174 rooms. Of these, 929 had but one room for the whole family, 408 had two, 94 three, 17 four, 8 five, 4 six,

---

[46] London Building Act 1774, intended to prevent dangerous structures and reduce fire risk (Burnett, *op. cit.*, p. 114).

[47] Burnett, pp. 87-88.

[48] en.wikipedia.org/wiki/Cropley_Ashley-Cooper,_6th_Earl_of_Shaftesbury, accessed 17 January 2017.

1 seven, and 1 eight. The remaining three families were returned 'not ascertained'. If this was so in one of the best parishes in London, what must be the condition of the overpopulous and more needy parishes in the east [end]? This return said nothing of the condition of a great many of the residences of the working people, in which there was not one family in a room, but two, three, four, and, as he had himself seen, five: four occupying the corners, and the fifth in the middle of the room. To look first at the moral aspect of the subject: in these rooms there were grown-up persons, male and female, of different families, or the same family, all living together; in these rooms every function of nature was performed. How could decency be preserved? Education was impossible: pernicious example was ever before the child. Who could wonder that in these receptacles nine-tenths of the great crimes, the burglaries, murders and violence that desolated society, were conceived and hatched? Or if the physical state of these people was considered, what must be the condition of dwellings with 8, 10, 20 or 25 persons, or even more, living in a single room? Nothing produced so evil an effect upon the sanitary condition of the population as overcrowding within limited spaces. If people were in a low sanitary condition, it was absolutely impossible to raise them to a just moral elevation. Their general state of health and capacity for work reduced, they must be brought upon the parish, and the general charity of the community.[49]

Although the Public Health Act of 1848 had empowered local Boards of Health to make by-laws regulating the occupation of common lodging houses,[50] the Lodging Houses Act, 1851 was the first piece of national legislation aimed at controlling the use of the nation's stock of housing. It obliged local authorities to determine the maximum number of people who could occupy each room in a lodging house. However, those administering the Act found it difficult to differentiate, by way of written definition, between the filthy, overcrowded conditions Lord Ashley had described and the comfortable boarding houses for artisans, commercial travellers, clerks and students, thereby making control of the former problematic.

---

[49] House of Commons debate, 8th April 1851, Hansard, vol 115, cc 1258-76. hansard.millbanksystems.com/commons/1851/apr/08/lodging-houses#S3V0115P0_18510408_HOC_46, accessed 12 January 2016.

[50] www.parliament.uk/about/living-heritage/transformingsociety/towncountry/towns/tyne-and-wear-case-study/about-the-group/housing/lodging-houses, accessed 16 January 2016.

Further Acts in 1855 and 1878 attempted to regulate buildings' foundations, ceiling heights and the quality of materials[51].

In 1875, Benjamin Disraeli's second Conservative government placed the Artisans' and Labourers' Dwellings Improvement Act on the statute book. As permissive legislation it allowed, but did not enforce, local authorities to compel slum owners to sell their properties to councils. The councils would then take advantage of reduced interest rates offered by the government to demolish the slum housing before allowing it to be redeveloped by commercial builders. The take-up was lower than expected and for reasons at both ends of the economic spectrum. At one, the Act's lack of compulsion mirrored the laissez-faire attitude of the ruling political party of the day. Some owners of capital would have viewed the Act as an attack on landlords. The less spent on repairs and maintenance, the higher the return on money invested in their properties. At the other, there was a concern that the working classes would be driven into lodgings. Many would not pay more than the 3/- to 4/- weekly rent for which a back-to-back was obtainable. Whilst they could afford to do so in good times, they would certainly not be able to when economic life deteriorated. For many, it was 'when' and not 'if'. Even skilled workers could be laid off at only a few hours' notice.[52]

The more enlightened local authorities made use of the permissive legislation that was passed to seek private Acts of Parliament for the creation of their own by-laws. Thus, for example, some began to obtain Acts to control new back-to-back housing. Leeds was empowered by its eponymous Improvement Act of 1842 to insist upon proper privies in newly built developments. An Act obtained by Manchester in 1844 enabled them to ban outright their further construction, and Bradford, in 1860, obtained legislation limiting the size of new builds to a maximum of two pairs per block.

Even as legislation to rein in poor back-to-back development was reaching the statute book, a new problem was in the making as the development of railways made commuting an economic reality.

The graph on the following page shows the huge increase in the number of passenger journeys each year between 1830 and the outbreak

[51] Burnett, p. 157.

[52] Burnett, pp. 76-77.

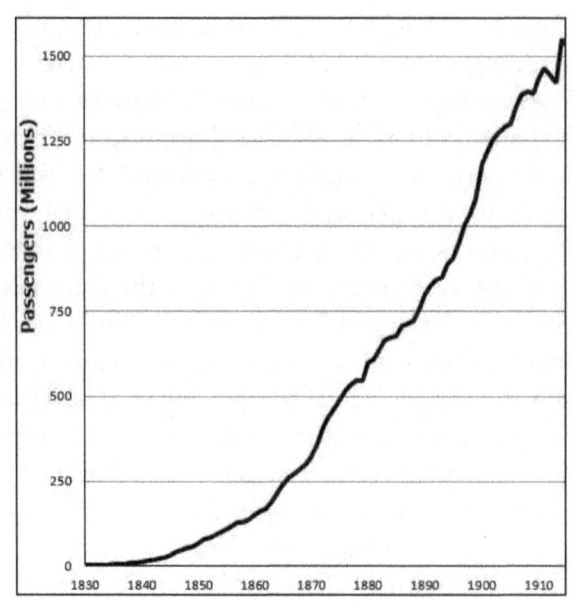

Annual passenger journeys by rail.

of the First World War. They rose from about 80ml per annum in 1850 to 500ml in 1875, 1bn by 1897 and 1½ bn by 1915.

Suburban growth was greatest in London. This table shows, by way of examples, the increase in the population of three suburbs between 1851 and 1891.

GROWTH OF THREE LONDON SUBURBS 1851-1891

Town	Area of Greater London	Distance from Central London	Population 000s 1851	Population 000s 1891	Population growth rate % p.a.
Willesden	North-west	6.8 ml	3	114	9.5%
West Ham	East	9.2 ml	19	267	6.8%
Leyton	North-east	10.8 ml	5	98	7.7%

Primary source:: Burnett, p 164

Commuting was boosted by the Cheap Trains Act, 1883 (effective from 1 October of that year) which exempted the railway companies from duty on fares not exceeding 1d. per mile 'where the Board of

Trade are satisfied that any two or more railway stations are within an area which has a continuous urban as distinguished from a rural or suburban character, and contains a population of not less than one hundred thousand inhabitants'.[53]

Absent London, where the Metropolitan Buildings Act, 1844 set minima for road widths and open rear spaces,[54] only those few towns that had obtained private Acts of Parliament had any control over the building industry. The growth of the railways therefore presented developers with the ability to build suburbs around the manufacturing conurbations in a more or less uncontrolled manner. There was a hope in certain quarters that those living in poor quality, inner-city housing would move to these new developments, freeing up rentable accommodation for those living in inner-city lodgings and thus, at the bottom of the chain, causing the worst forms of housing to become unlettable. However, this optimism was not fulfilled. Populations continued to rise, as did the value of undeveloped land. Furthermore, public health concerns led to legislation that increased building costs. Whilst it would be wrong to describe all construction businesses as jerry-builders, bad practices were not uncommon. The business model was to build houses for renting, not owner-occupation; even by 1914, ninety per cent of houses in England and Wales would be rented from private landlords.[55] Thus the economic equation was expected rents expressed as a percentage of the cost of the houses. Rents were fixed by what the population as a whole would pay, so minimising costs improved builders' outcomes if and when they sold the completed properties to landlords. Housebuilding was a highly fragmented trade in the second half of the 19th century. For example, in Camberwell, South London, 416 different firms or individuals constructed 5,670 houses between 1878 and 1880, of which over half built six houses or less in this three-year period.[56] For these smaller businesses, housebuilding was often a way of keeping a (small) labour force intact when repair and maintenance work fell away.

[53] Section 2. www.railwaysarchive.co.uk/documents/HMG_ActCheap1883.pdf, accessed 26 January 2016.

[54] Burnett, pp. 157.

[55] Parker, J. and Mirrlees, C, 1972. Housing. *In:* Halsey, p. 377.

[56] Burnett, p. 24.

As had been the case with legislation concerning back-to-back housing, the problem of jerry-built housing came to be addressed as a public health concern. An article in the medical journal *The Lancet* on 21 November 1874 opined:

> It is difficult to understand the argument of those who contend that the labouring-classes ought to live in the suburbs – i.e. in unhealthy, cheap, undrained districts, often beyond the pale of sanitary legislation, and in adulterated houses whose foundations were rotten, whose walls were scarcely weatherproof, and whose owners but too often belong to the most unscrupulously dishonest class to be found among us.[57]

Much of the improvement in standards of new housing began with the Local Government Act, 1858. Its Form of By-laws permitted local authorities to adopt regulations that would deal with the width and construction of new streets, the structure of walls, the adequacy of airspace around new houses, their drainage and sewerage, room height, the area of windows, and the construction of flues. The Form allowed them to modify the recommendations in the light of local customs and building practice. Although the Act lacked compulsion, it set a precedent for national involvement in housing matters.

The Local Government Board was created by its eponymous Act of 1871 which consolidated responsibility for public health and local government that had previously been divided between the Home Secretary and the Privy Council. It also took on all the functions of the Poor Law Board, which was abolished. Although not a housing issue in itself, the Board was to be made the agency through which future governments of the day would operate and police housing and public health legislation.

The Sanitary Law Amendment Act, 1874 allowed local authorities to regulate paving, the drainage of premises and the ventilation of rooms. The Public Health Act, 1875 continued to allow local authorities to regulate all those matters the 1858 Act's Form of By-laws had enabled them to control and, in addition, permitted them to prohibit the habitation of buildings (or parts of buildings) they deemed to be unfit

---

[57] Burnett, p. 157.

for human habitation.⁵⁸ In 1877 the Local Government Board issued a new set of model by-laws for the guidance of local authorities, clarifying and considerably extending those in the Form under the 1858 Act. Streets over 100 feet in length were to be at least 36 feet wide. The minimum space at the rear of a house was increased from 100 to 150 square feet. Windows were to be at least equal to one-tenth of the floor space and a minimum of half were to be openable.

The Artisans' and Labourers' Dwellings Improvement Act, 1875 reached the statute book very shortly before the aforementioned Public Health Act. Its main intention was to encourage local authorities to undertake large-scale slum clearance. This satisfied a public demand for these buildings to be removed, but there was almost no support (locally or within Parliament) for authorities to rebuild houses for those made homeless as a consequence.⁵⁹ Whilst the authorities were to carry out the redevelopment of the streets and sewers, any houses they built were to be sold to private owners within ten years. The Act was an early, tentative step on the road that would lead to council housing as we know it when *Homes fit for Heroes* became, towards the end of hostilities in 1918, the slogan under which Lloyd George's Coalition Government proposed to house ½ml returning troops and their families, the costs of which in excess of a penny on local rates rate would be borne by the State.⁶⁰

As implied by an earlier reference to the London Building Act of 1774 London was, until the 1890s, generally excluded from national (permissive) legislation concerning building controls and, instead, obtained its own legislation. Since 1844, the Metropolis had included Paddington, Hampstead, Tottenham and Hackney to the north and Greenwich, Lambeth and Streatham to the south.⁶¹ In 1878 the Metropolis Management and Building Acts Amendment Act, attempting to control the worst forms of jerry-building, gave the Metropolitan Board of Works powers to regulate the construction of foundations and to control the materials used in housebuilding.⁶²

---

⁵⁸ Section 157.

⁵⁹ Gauldie, p. 276.

⁶⁰ Burnett, p. 226.

⁶¹ Tarn, p. 124. The Metropolitan Building Act 1844 further provided for its provisions to be operative within the whole of a radius of twelve miles of Charing Cross.

⁶² Tarn, p. 125.

Come the late-1880s, the unresolved problems were threefold:

1. Whilst local authorities were tending to become more responsible,[63] they did not have to adopt the model by-laws and many stood out for a long time despite the Local Government Board's efforts to persuade them to the contrary.
2. Towns that had previously obtained local Acts could continue to operate under them, even though their requirements became increasingly less stringent than the model by-laws.
3. The regulations only applied to new building, leaving aside the problems inherited from the past.

The Public Health Acts Amendment Act, 1890 granted local authorities permission to control the structure of floors, hearths and staircases, and the height of rooms. They could forbid the building of houses over privies or cesspools and the erection of houses on ground filled with offensive matter. The Housing Act of the same year (and various re-enactments up to 1903) allowed local authorities, with the approval of the Local Government Board, to demolish insanitary buildings and develop plans to improve unhealthy areas in urban districts. They could also acquire land on which to build and manage working-class lodgings, houses and cottages. Whilst the compensation and enquiry procedures proved to be over-laborious, thus discouraging local authorities from making use of the powers, the Act's provisions made local authorities reasonably successful in controlling the slums. They did little, however, to promote new layouts that would stop the expansion of uniform blocks of terraced housing.[64]

The thrust of these legislative changes led to the spread of by-law housing over London and provincial towns in the 19th century. It comprised terraces of identical rows of houses built on grids of roads. Whilst monotonous, it offered many of the working classes affordable minimum environmental and sanitation standards for the first time.[65] By the end of the century, improvements in sewerage and water supply

---

[63] Tarn, p. 124.

[64] Jackson, p. 100.

[65] Burnett, p. 161.

Late 19th-century by-law housing.

allowed closets to be incorporated within the structure of houses instead of as external privies.

It would be wrong for this chapter to end by giving the impression that all by-law housing was bad – it was not. Seebohm Rowntree, whose social investigations in York will be described in due course, considered these late-Victorian by-law terraced houses to be the best type of working-class houses in that city in 1900; similar buildings continue to provide accommodation in many an English town today.

York's best type of working-class house, 1900.

Three years before the outbreak of the First World War, by-law terraced housing of the style shown in these plans was being built at Longford in Coventry.

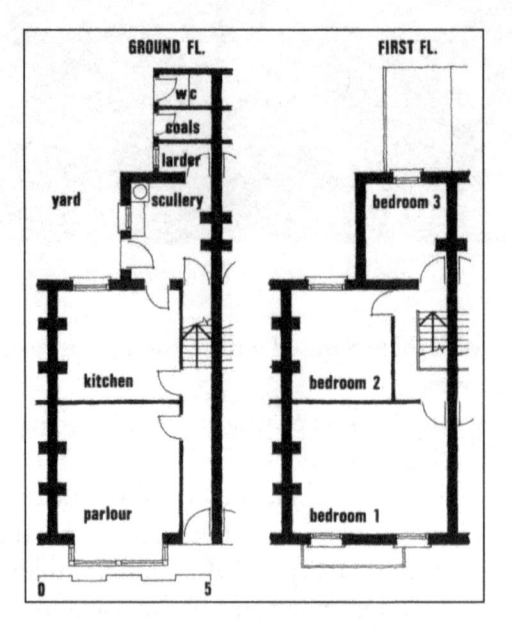

By-law housing at Longford, Coventry, 1911.

These three-bedroomed houses, complete with front parlour, represented the final development of this type of housing. Although reasonably spacious (and financially beyond the reach of the unskilled) they still exhibited some of the features for which the style of housing as a whole was criticised:

- They formed monotonous, repetitive terraces in treeless streets.
- They were often built down to the lowest permitted standards.
- Some towns believed they forced up building costs and thus increased rents to the disadvantage of lower-paid workers.
- Aesthetic standards were sacrificed to pay for better construction and sanitation.
- Front doors often opened directly onto the street.

It would also be wrong to criticise Parliament for not resolving the nation's housing problems with greater speed. Victorian towns were often fiercely independent and, apart from Londoners, the population felt remote from national government. People were used to their local authority making the by-laws that framed their daily lives and viewed any encroachment on their activities from Whitehall with suspicion. At the same time, patronage played a significant part in local politics. Land and property owners were used to having a far greater influence on local affairs than would be tolerated today.

From Charity to Political Reform

A history of 19th-century housing in Great Britain would be incomplete without a mention of charity, because in a pre-welfare state that was all that stood between the poorer members of society and abject poverty. Submission to the Poor Law was an ever-present fear amongst the working classes. It could be caused by accident, age, or the failure of one's chosen friendly society.[66] The first purpose of this chapter is, therefore, to give a very brief outline of how charity impacted directly on housing. The reader whose interest is awakened in this fascinating branch of British social history should look further into the sources mentioned in the footnotes and the bibliography at the end of this book. The second is to explain how the widening of the electoral franchise and concerns about the health of the nation increased Parliament's determination to legislate for social issues, one of which was housing.

The initial mid-18th century response to the social problems borne of poor housing was to seek a cure through the private sector. In 1844 Lord Ashley, the 33-year-old scion of the Shaftesbury dynasty who seven years later would see the Bill that became the Lodging Houses Act, 1851 through its Parliamentary stages, founded and became chair of the Society for Improving the Condition of the Labouring Classes.[67] It enjoyed the patronage of Queen Victoria and its president was her husband, Prince Albert. The Society, along with the Metropolitan Association for Improving the Dwellings of the Industrious Classes (long, descriptive names were not uncommon in Victorian times) became the first two Model Dwellings Companies. They built new homes for the working classes whilst seeking a competitive rate of return on their capital.[68] 'A competitive rate' meant 5% per annum at a time when the average

---

[66] The threat continued to exist until well into the 20th century, for example Progress Estates Ltd, 15 July 1936, minute no. 7: 'Read letter dated 7th instant, from Mr. Winn, Estate Manager, asking what course to be pursued in the matter of arrears [of rent] amounting to £10. 10. 7d. owing by Holverstone, 53 Ross Way. It was reported that the man and his family were in the Lewisham workhouse. Resolved – that the arrears be written off'. Ross Way is a road on the Progress Estate.

[67] The Society's name was changed in 1959 to the 1830 Housing Society prior to its being taken over by the Peabody Trust in 1965 (en.wikipedia.org/wiki/Labourer%27s_Friend_Society, accessed 24 September 2014).

[68] en.wikipedia.org/wiki/Model_dwellings_company, accessed 12 January 2016.

yield on Government debt, in the shape of Consuls, was 3.11%,[69] and thus was born the generic description 'five per cent philanthropy'. With similar ambitions, the Peabody Trust was constituted in 1862 to manage the enormous donation of £150,000 from the American banker George Peabody. In total, about eight large and maybe fifteen smaller companies were created. The final quarter of the 19th century probably marked their zenith; they were included in the 1875 Artisans' and Labourers' Dwellings Improvement Act's definition of 'commercial builders'. Whilst only ten out of eighty-seven eligible towns in England and Wales used the permitted powers created by the Act,[70] these included the Metropolis (London), Glasgow and Liverpool.[71]

The Society for Improving the Condition of the Labouring Classes built model lodging houses of one to three rooms in London's Clerkenwell in 1845. The project was widely acclaimed, and they went on to construct a five-storey model lodging block for one hundred and four people in St Giles, the heart of London's most notorious slum area near where Centre Point now stands. The work of the Model Dwellings Companies as a whole increased the public's attention to the problem of bad housing.

Through the whole of the second half of the 19th century, the delivery of 'charity' was seen as a social duty to be carried out by the middle and upper classes as penance for their financial well-being. It was a matter of duty and its scale was huge. It has been calculated that in the early 1860s the annual expenditure of charities in London alone was very nearly equivalent to the combined expenditure of all the Poor Law authorities throughout England and Wales.[72] Whilst there is no doubt that the individual recipients benefited, the size of the problem was beyond the ability of hundreds of individual and small charitable organisations to resolve. There was also a concern on the part

---

[69] *Three centuries of data – version 1.0, Money, interest and prices*, www.bankofengland.co.uk/Pages/Search.aspx?q=money%20interest%20and%20prices, accessed 12 January 2016.

[70] en.wikipedia.org/wiki/Artisans'_and_Labourers'_Dwellings_Improvement_Act_1875, accessed 12 January 2016.

[71] hansard.millbanksystems.com/lords/1879/jul/24/artizans-and-labourers-dwellings-act, accessed 3 February 2016.

[72] H. Hunt, *British Labour History 1815-1914*, Weidenfeld & Nicolson, 1981, pp. 126-134. In: Benson, p. 49.

of the Fabian Society[73] and other like-minded groups that these bodies' actions were serving to institutionalise poverty because they were not tackling its root causes.

The Charity Organisation Society was set up in 1869 to put London's charities on a sensible footing, although over the following fifteen years progress was increasingly hampered by a growing belief amongst its leaders that the theories of Self-Help, epitomised by Samuel Smiles,[74] were the way forward. The alcoholic, the chronic idler and the totally depraved were rejected as hopeless cases whilst a widow could be given a mangle so she could take in washing because she was worthy of help. Poverty was seen as, mostly, the result of personal failing. The underlying causes of charity should be addressed by the promotion of moral improvement.[75] Canon Samuel Barnett, husband of Henrietta Barnett whose central role in the development of Hampstead Garden Suburb will be explained in due course, was one of the Organisation's founders but resigned from the national body as he, unlike its leaders, began to understand that the state had an irreplaceable role in the diminution of poverty.

The Poverty Line

The philanthropist and social researcher Charles Booth had been born to a middle-class family of shippers in Liverpool in 1840.[76] He was a cousin of the Fabian Beatrice Webb, with whom he worked closely in his researches into poverty[77]. His interest in elective politics began to wane after he canvassed, unsuccessfully, as a Liberal candidate in the 1865 general election, and diminished further after Conservative victories in municipal elections the following year. He decided that his time was better spent in educating the electorate, rather than directly

---

[73] Fabian Society, formed 1844, rejected violent upheaval as a method of change, preferring to use the power of local government and trade unionism. Prominent early members included George Bernard Shaw and Sidney and Beatrice Webb. www.fabians.org.uk/about/the-fabian-story, accessed 3 February 2016.

[74] Samuel Smiles (1812-1904), *Self-Help*, Routledge, 1859.

[75] Fraser, pp. 124-145.

[76] Gilbert, pp. 53-56.

[77] en.wikipedia.org/wiki/Charles_Booth_%28philanthropist%29, accessed 7 October 2014. Beatrice Webb was the wife of Sidney Webb – see fn 73.

representing them, and so he rejected Prime Minister Gladstone's subsequent offer of a peerage and thus a seat in the House of Lords. He was President of the Royal Statistical Society from 1892 to 1894, during which time he brought the disciplines of the Society to bear upon the issue of poverty by building up a statistical picture of various communities, as opposed to the then more usual method of relying upon anecdotal stories of distress.

Booth is credited with the invention of the phrase 'the poverty line'. He defined it as being the 21/- per week he calculated a family of five needed to maintain themselves. His surveys, published between 1889 and 1903 under the title *The Life and Labour of the People in London*, came to the general conclusion that thirty per cent of London's population were living in poverty.

The map illustrated below includes St Giles. The darker the shading, the worse the housing. The buildings in black were occupied by 'a vicious, semi-criminal class'. Slightly lighter are properties held by 'very poor, casual labourers whose families live in chronic want', and those a touch lighter still by 'the poor, living on 18/- to 21/- per week'. The originals are meticulously coloured and the reader interested in greater detail should visit the Charles Booth Online Archive created by the Library of the London School of Economics and Political Science and the Senate House Library. His four further classifications categorised houses whose occupants ranged from 'mixed – some comfortable, others poor' to 'upper-middle and upper classes: wealthy'.

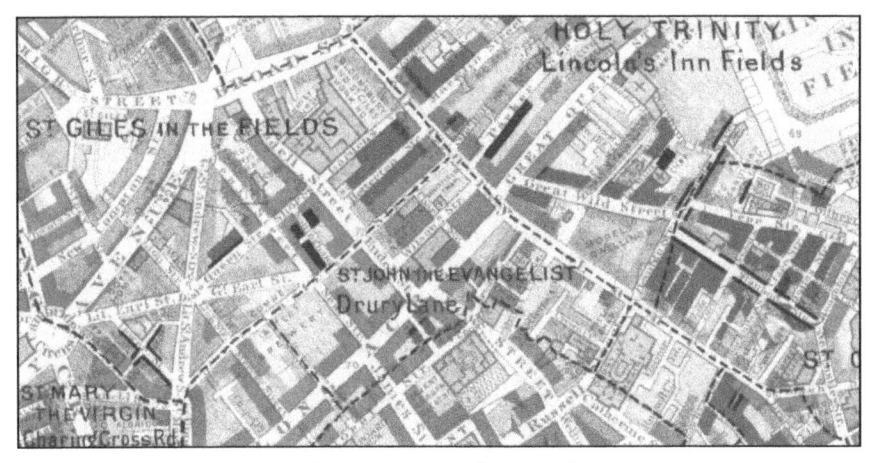

Charles Booth's map of St Giles, London 1898-99.

There was some backlash when Booth's findings were first published, based upon arguments as to whether or not he had drawn his poverty line in the right place. However, the importance of his work was to bring home that the relief of distress, simply by reason of the sheer numbers involved, could not be resolved by individuals giving arms or the efforts of private charitable agencies. His message was to be practical, not sentimental, about poverty.

The Condition of the People

Social workers and political reformers had been concerned with 'the condition of the people' since the 1880s[78]. The force of public opinion had increased following the passing of Gladstone's Representation of the People Act, 1884 and the Redistribution of Seats Act, 1885.[79] As Sidney Webb[80] told the Royal Commission on Labour in 1892:

> It appears to me that if you allow the tramway conductor to vote he will not forever be satisfied with exercising that vote over such matters as the appointment of the Ambassador to Paris, or even the position of the franchise. He will realise that the forces that keep him at work for sixteen hours a day for three shillings a day are not the forces of hostile kings, or nobles, or priests; but whatever forces they are he will, it seems to me, seek so far as possible to control them by his vote. That is to say, he will seek to convert his political democracy into what one may roughly term an industrial democracy, so that he may obtain some kind of control as a voter over the conditions under which he lives.

---

[78] Gilbert, chapters 1-2.

[79] The 1884 Act established one-member parliamentary constituencies as the norm, and extended the franchise to all men paying rent of £10 per annum or holding land to the value of £10. This gave the vote to 60% of males over the age of 21. The 1885 Act redistributed the constituencies, granting greater representation to London and other urban areas.

[80] Sidney James Webb, 1st Baron Passfield (13 July 1859-13 October 1947), British Socialist, economist, reformer and a co-founder of the London School of Economics. One of the early members of the Fabian Society in 1884 who, along with George Bernard Shaw (they joined three months after its inception) helped to turn it into the pre-eminent political-intellectual society of England in the Edwardian era and beyond. He wrote the original Clause IV for the British Labour Party.

Legislation between 1884 and 1897 included an Act improving employees' ability to claim compensation for industrial accidents, another permitting citizens to receive medical treatment under the Poor Law without incurring the disenfranchisement of pauperism, and a third authorising Poor Law Guardians to disregard sums up to 5/- per week received by the applicant from a friendly society. They were evidence of Sidney Webb's predictions; by 1900, 58% of males over the age of 21 were on the electoral roll.[81]

The outbreak of the Boer War in October 1899 interrupted this progress. The government pleaded it had no money to spend on improving welfare, and the immense rise in imperialism accompanying the conflict turned the working man's mind away from the society in which he lived. Mafeking was a town about the size of Watford and 6,000 miles away, yet its relief brought tens of thousands of people onto the streets between Mansion House and Piccadilly at 9:30 p.m., and a performance at the Lyceum was interrupted by the manager who read a dispatch before leading the audience in a rendition of the national anthem.

It was only after reports began to emerge in the spring of 1900 about the widespread weakness and physical disabilities exhibited by the working classes who were volunteering for active service that the reformers had a chance to regain the initiative. Of 12,000 volunteers examined at the Manchester Depot in 1899, 8,000 had been rejected as virtual invalids and, of the 4,000 accepted, only 1,200 were found after Army service to be physically fit in all respects. Were contemporary notions of the inevitable superiority of the British race and its social system correct? If so, why had it taken three years and £250ml to defeat a handful of unorganised farmers?[82]

Social reform was thus given the status of a respectable political question – it linked imperialism and 'the condition of the people', because only an efficient nation could maintain a vigorous and expanding empire. Improvements in housing were one of the themes

---

[81] en.wikipedia.org/wiki/Reform_Act_1867, accessed 27 August 2014 and David Butler, Electors and the Elected, In: Hasley, p. 297.

[82] In retrospect, part of the answer was that, for the first time, the cavalry-based British Army had faced guerrilla tactics. See en.wikipedia.org/wiki/Second_Boer_War#Final_overview, accessed 1 October 2014.

that emerged from this awareness, and the emergence of town planning was chief amongst them. Come August 1914, the First World War would slow progress, although the standards for new housing (along with the beginnings of public sector housing) would by then have improved them considerably.

Ruskin, Architecture and the Arts and Crafts Movement

Charles Dickens was at the height of his powers in the middle of the 19th century, publishing *Great Expectations* in 1861. Whilst it would take a further 32 years for the first MPs to be elected for what became, in 1893, the Independent Labour Party,[83] the social conditions that led to their success in the polls can be traced back to this time.

The purpose of this chapter is to explain how a few people – principally architects[84] – who were linked by pupillage or employment formed a chain of knowledge during the second half of the 19th century. It began with Ruskin making a connection between the workmanship that was inherent in Gothic architecture and the manner in which he believed society should develop, continued through prominent architects whose practices were substantially in commissions for churches, and finally spread out to secular building design as the century drew to a close.

John Ruskin (1819-1900)

Ruskin was a leading Victorian patron of the arts, art critic and something of a polymath. He was a draughtsman, a watercolourist, a prominent social thinker, and (following the inheritance of his wealthy father's estate after the latter's death on 3 March 1864) a philanthropist. For a period, he concentrated on architectural research. He visited Venice in 1846 and, in 1848, Salisbury Cathedral in July and the churches of Normandy from August to October. This led to his publishing *The Seven Lamps of Architecture* in May 1849.[85]

---

[83] Gilbert, p. 57.

[84] The Institute of British Architects had been founded in 1834 and was awarded its Royal Charter in 1837. Its Examination in Architecture was established in 1863 and became compulsory for admission as a member in 1882. www.architecture.com/RIBA, accessed 22 February 2016.

[85] Robert Hewison, 'Ruskin, John (1819-1900)', *Oxford Dictionary of National Biography*, Oxford University Press, 2004; online edn, January 2016 [http://www.oxforddnb.com/view/article/24291, accessed 21 February 2016].

St Mark's, Venice.

Ruskin wished to protect what survived and referred to the depredations of 'the Restorer, or Revolutionist'. He drew certain principles from his investigations which would influence the direction of the Gothic Revival in architecture. These were the 'lamps' in the title of his book – sacrifice, truth, power, beauty, life, memory, and obedience. Whilst abstract notions, to Ruskin they manifested themselves in the Gothic buildings of Italy and Northern France. The principles he drew from their design and structure would influence the direction of the Gothic Revival, notably towards its use in secular buildings. He went on to publish *The Stones of Venice* in three volumes between 1851 and 1853 following further long visits to that city in November 1849 and June 1852. The volumes reflected his view of contemporary England and acted as a warning about the moral and spiritual health of society. Venice had slowly deteriorated in his view. Its cultural achievements had been compromised, and its society corrupted, by the decline of true Christian faith. Instead of revering the divine, Renaissance artists honoured themselves, arrogantly celebrating human sensuousness. His reasons for pursuing social reform were expressed in the second volume:

> We want one man to be always thinking, and another to be always working, and we call one a gentleman and the other an operative; whereas the workman ought often to be thinking, and the thinker often to be working, and both should be gentlemen, in the best sense. As it is, we make both ungentle, the

one envying, the other despising, his brother; and the mass of society is made up of morbid thinkers and miserable workers. Now it is only by labour that thought can be made healthy, and only by thought that labour can be made happy, and the two cannot be separated with impunity.[86]

For Ruskin, the Gothic buildings he had visited represented a manifestation of his social thinking. Their intricate workmanship, especially on the part of the stone-carvers whose work is illustrated on the opposite page, would indeed lead to a fulfilling life for their creators.[87] Whilst Ruskin did not invent the Gothic Revival of English architecture, it was this aspect of his thinking that influenced the architects of what became known as the Arts and Crafts movement.

Sir George Gilbert Scott (1811-1878)

George Scott, knighted in 1872, lived in the same era as Ruskin. He was the son of a clergyman and many members of his large, extended family were also men of the cloth.[88] It was these connections that led to many ecclesiastical commissions. His achievements were summed up in an obituary in *Building News* on 19 April 1878:

> [His architecture had] the merit of being a thoroughly national revival of the Gothic style. In sentiment and in detail it neither offended by its violence nor sacrificed English[ness] to modern sympathies. If not remarkable for its originality, or its energy, it was always pleasing, moderate, and sensible. Indeed it had, in common with its author, a geniality that was eminently impressed upon everything he did.

Scott's importance to this book is that he was the first link in the architectural chain from Ruskin, through the Arts and Crafts movement, to the end of the 1800s, as shown in the text box on the following page.

---

[86] en.wikipedia.org/wiki/The_Stones_of_Venice_(book), accessed 22 February 2016.

[87] en.wikipedia.org/wiki/Gothic_Revival_architecture, accessed 1 March 2016.

[88] Gavin Stamp, 'Scott, Sir George Gilbert (1811-1878)', *Oxford Dictionary of National Biography*, Oxford University Press, 2004 [http://www.oxforddnb.com/view/article/24869, accessed 1 March 2016].

THE ARCHITECTURAL LINE
FROM RUSKIN TO THE END OF THE 19th CENTURY

	GG Scott 1811-1878	GE Street 1824-1881	GF Bodley 1827-1907	PS Webb 1831-1915	Wm Morris 1834-1896	WH Bidlake 1861-1938	W Alexander Harvey 1874-1951
1844	Employed Street (1844-49) and Bodley (1846-52)						
1845							
1846		Employee of Scott					
1847							
1848			Pupil, then employee, of Scott				
1849							
1850							
1851							
1852							
1854		Employed Webb		Employee of Street			
1856		Pupiled Morris			Pupiled to Street		
1857							
1858-1865			Commissions for Morris		Commissions from Bodley		
1885			Employed Bidlake			Employee of Bodley	
1886							
1892-1901						Devised Birmingham School of Art's architectural courses	Studied under Bidlake (see next chapter)

George Edmund Street (1824-1881)

Like Scott, George Street was an adherent of the High Anglican tradition and the majority of his work was for ecclesiastical purposes. He became an employee at Scott's Oxford-based practice in 1844. Along with George Frederick Bodley who joined it in 1846 (see below) he was destined to become one of the leading architects of his generation. He was a brilliant draughtsman with a flair for producing fluid pen-and-ink perspectives. He set up his own practice in 1849 and, come 1852, operated it from Oxford where he had been appointed Diocesan Architect in 1850.

Street's travels through France, Germany, the Low Countries and Italy during the 1850s informed his many lectures and publications. The latter included his 1855 book on northern Italian Gothic, *Brick and Marble Architecture in the Middle Ages; notes on tours in the north of Italy* which widened the appreciation of Ruskin's views.[89] Today, he is best known for designing the Royal Courts of Justice in London. He won the architectural competition for its design in 1867 and was appointed sole architect in June 1868, although the building was incomplete when he died in December 1881.

George Frederick Bodley (1827-1907)

Bodley's sister Georgina was married to Samuel Scott, brother of the aforementioned George Gilbert Scott. He, Bodley, having discovered an interest in architecture, became a pupil and then employee of Scott's from 1846 to 1852 before setting up practice on his own. Along with his fellow ex-Scott employee, George Edmund Street, he developed an architectural style which was based on both Continental and English Gothic and became known as High Victorian.

His commissions for All Saints Church at Selsey, Gloucestershire (1859-62), St Michael's, Brighton (designed in 1858), St Martin's, Scarborough (1860-61) and St Stephen's, Guernsey (1861-65) all included stained glass by Morris, Marshall, Faulkner & Co., the firm set up by William Morris (see below) in 1861. Bodley, who had met the firm's partners when Morris was a pupil in Street's office, is said to have

---

[89] David B. Brownlee, 'Street, George Edmund (1824-1881)', *Oxford Dictionary of National Biography*, Oxford University Press, 2004; online edn, January 2008 [http://www.oxforddnb.com/view/article/26659, accessed 1 March 2016].

designed two of its early wallpapers. The stained glass commissions were sufficiently important in the firm's early days for its partners to suggest that Bodley might become a partner. However, his methods were the antithesis of the Arts and Crafts movement's approach. He believed in subsuming the identity of the craftsman into the architect's controlling vision and strove to ensure that nothing would disturb the integrated harmony of his buildings. Thus, in the early 1870s, he abandoned Morris in favour of craftsmen he could control more tightly.

Bodley's biographer[90] regards him as 'the most influential architect at work in the Anglican Church during the last third of the nineteenth century'.

Philip Speakman Webb (1831-1915)

Philip Webb was only seventeen when his father died in 1849. He decided upon a career in architecture because it offered greater financial security than his earlier choice of painting. He became articled to John Billing, who had a varied practice in Berkshire's county town of Reading. Billing trained Webb in the Gothic and classical styles, and provided ample practical experience in and around the then unspoilt old market town. After his apprenticeship was completed, Webb worked as Billing's assistant for two years until 17 March 1854, when he joined the practice of Bidlake and Lovatt in Wolverhampton.[91] Here he encountered the appalling effects on the area of heavy industries, which influenced his subsequent thinking about architecture. He returned to Oxford only two months later on 15 May 1854 to work at half the salary for the previously-mentioned diocesan architect, George Edmund Street, who soon appointed him chief assistant.[92] He left Street to set up his own

---

[90] Michael Hall, 'Bodley, George Frederick (1827-1907)', *Oxford Dictionary of National Biography*, Oxford University Press, 2004; online edn, January 2016 [http://www.oxforddnb.com/view/article/31944, accessed 1 March 2016].

[91] George Bidlake (1830-1892) was the father of William Henry Bidlake, discussed later in this chapter. See Trevor Mitchell, 'Bidlake, William Henry (1861-1938)', *Oxford Dictionary of National Biography*, Oxford University Press, October 2013; online edn, May 2014 [http://www.oxforddnb.com/view/article/61673, accessed 2 March 2016].

[92] Sheila Kirk, 'Webb, Philip Speakman (1831-1915)', *Oxford Dictionary of National Biography*, Oxford University Press, 2004 [http://www.oxforddnb.com/view/article/36801, accessed 3 February 2016].

practice in 1858.

Webb's biographer has stated that, although the office of Richard Norman Shaw (1831-1912) provided the leading architectural practitioners and campaigners in the Arts and Crafts movement, it was Philip Webb's buildings that were more influential, and Philip Webb himself who provided the movement's morality and theory. Architecture to Webb was first of all a common tradition of honest building. The great architectures of the past had been noble, customary ways of building, naturally developed by the craftsmen engaged in the actual works. He believed building was a folk art; all art meant folk expression embodied and expanding in the several mediums of different materials. Architecture is naturally found out in doing; it is the very opposite to the 'whim' designs the profession was so excited about exhibiting. In a word, architecture is building traditionally.[93]

William Morris (1834-1896)

William Morris was born into a wealthy middle-class family in Walthamstow. Whilst studying Classics at the University of Oxford he adopted Ruskin's philosophy, rejecting the tawdry industrial manufacture of decorative arts and architecture in favour of a return to hand craftsmanship that he expected would raise artisans to the status of artists and so create affordable and handmade art.[94] He envisioned a Socialist society centred upon useful work as opposed to useless toil. He believed all work should be artistic, in the sense that the worker should find it a pleasurable outlet for creativity.[95]

Having obtained his Bachelor of Arts degree, Morris became articled to the previously-discussed architect George Edmund Street at the latter's Oxford-based practice in January 1856 where he was trained by Street's principal assistant, the aforementioned Philip Webb. All three had a common interest in Ruskin's work and Street was putting Gothic Revival into practice.[96] Morris moved to London with the practice the

[93] W. R. Lethaby, *Philip Webb and his work*, 1935, pp. 119-120. In: Richardson, pp. 14-15.

[94] en.wikipedia.org/wiki/William_Morris, accessed 1 October 2014. For a fuller biography, see www.oxforddnb.com/view/article/19322?docPos=3, accessed 3 February 2016.

[95] en.wikipedia.org/wiki/Utopian_socialism, accessed 22 October 2014.

[96] en.wikipedia.org/wiki/John_Ruskin#Architecture, accessed 24 November 2014.

following August, yet his interests were already shifting to painting as he became influenced by Dante Gabriel Rossetti. Morris seems to have been temperamentally indisposed to dealing with the day-to-day nuts and bolts of being an architect. He saw architecture as a union of the arts and the crafts, rather than a profession that stood apart from them.[97]

By 1857, Morris had moved on from his architectural career although he maintained a lifelong friendship with Philip Webb. Webb designed Morris's home, The Red House in Bexleyheath, Kent, in 1859 and together they founded the Society for the Protection of Ancient Buildings in 1877. Morris was particularly concerned about the practice, which he described as 'forgery', of attempting to return buildings to an idealised state from the distant past because it often involved the removal of elements added in their later development. He saw these as contributing to their interest as documents of the past. The Society still exists today and must be notified of all applications in England and Wales to demolish in whole or in part any listed building.[98] Its manifesto is a key document in the history of building conservation.[99]

The contribution of Morris to housing design was philosophical. He wanted artisans to be free to make a positive contribution to a building's appearance and sought to restore pleasurable work and the pursuit of handicrafts and leisure activities for all. Was he a dreamer? Yes, he probably was. His legacy, at least insofar as this book is concerned, was to inspire future planners and architects to develop economically viable housing for the working classes that would allow the latter to improve their lives, both physically and emotionally. A hint of his thinking about house design is contained in his Utopian novel *News From Nowhere*, published in book form following its serialisation in the British Socialist newspaper *The Commonweal* that commenced in January 1890:[100]

> ... the little hill of Hinksley, with two or three very pretty stone houses new-grown on it (I use the word advisedly, for they seemed to belong to it) ...

---

[97] Miele, pp. 1-26.

[98] www.spab.org.uk/what-is-spab-/history-of-the-spab, accessed 3 February 2016.

[99] en.wikipedia.org/wiki/Philip_Webb, accessed 24 November 2014.

[100] en.wikipedia.org/wiki/News_from_Nowhere, accessed 3 March 2016, and Morris, p. 160.

A defining similarity between architects who took the Arts and Crafts movement's principles to heart was respect for the site; no longer should land be something to be ploughed up by man and machine in order to build some predetermined style of housing.

William Henry Bidlake (1861-1938)

William Bidlake's architectural training began in 1882 in London at the office of R. W. Edis. In 1883, he entered the Royal Academy Architecture School and joined the Architectural Association. He became an employee at the office of George Bodley (discussed earlier in this chapter and, at this time, in partnership with another former pupil of George Scott's, Thomas Garner) in 1885. He joined the Birmingham Architectural Association in 1887 and began to teach in 1888. In 1890, he supported the foundation of the Birmingham Guild of Handicraft. He was instrumental in introducing the architectural course at the Birmingham School of Art in 1892 and was responsible for its design from then until 1901.[101] Famously ambidextrous, his party trick was to sketch with both hands simultaneously.[102]

Between 1895 and 1901 Bidlake won more than 30 commissions that included ten houses, two churches and a school of art. The commission for Garth House, Edgbaston (1900) helped establish his reputation.

Garth House, Edgbaston.

[101] Trevor Mitchell, 'Bidlake, William Henry (1861-1938)', *Oxford Dictionary of National Biography*, Oxford University Press, October 2013; online edn, May 2014 [http://www.oxforddnb.com/view/article/61673, accessed 2 March 2016].

[102] en.wikipedia.org/wiki/William_Bidlake, accessed 17 November 2015.

Philip Webb had designed high-pitched roofs and prominent chimney breasts into his house for William Morris near Bexleyheath, Kent (The Red House, 1859-70) and at Standen House, Sussex (1892-94). Bidlake incorporated these features into his more modest (albeit still large) house. The style would continue to influence those designing garden suburbs in the early years of the 20th century.

This chapter has shown how over a 50-year period Ruskin's social ideas began to inform an approach to the country's secular architecture. Earlier chapters discussed the contribution made by legislation and political reform in the provision of dwellings for the working classes, albeit the improvement of the existing housing stock was something of an intractable problem. Now it is time to look at the part played by two industrial philanthropists who sought to provide a new style of housing for those needing to live near the factories in which they worked.

A Chocolatier's Vision Becomes a Reality

Like so many other towns and cities in the final quarter of the 19th century, Birmingham was more or less devoid of planning regulations and controls. This chapter will look at how the Cadbury brothers created houses for the working classes adjacent to their new factory at Selly Oak, some four miles south-west of the city centre. Their vision was borne of their business acumen and moral instincts. The architectural ideas that emerged led to the birth of Garden City movement as the 19th century drew to a close.

Between 1866 and 1870, George and Richard Cadbury turned a struggling business into a chocolate empire[103] with a payroll that had expanded from 'only eleven girls' to a workforce of two hundred.[104] There was no room to enlarge their factory in Birmingham's slums and, furthermore, they questioned the contrast between the image of the pure products the firm was producing and the factory in the densely-packed and smoke-laden area from which they operated. Ruskin's political and economic thinking also chimed with their all-embracing Quaker sensibilities; the idea of material success for its own sake was abhorrent and they were determined to use their growing business in a way that 'enlarged the riches of human experience'. The brothers began to nurture the idea that they could create a 'factory in a garden' to replace their premises in Birmingham's slums. It would be a model factory, a New Jerusalem in England's green and pleasant land. They bought a fifteen-acre plot on which to erect it at auction in June 1878. Then known as Bournbrook, it was adjacent to the Birmingham West Suburban Railway (thereby offering transport to and from the factory for employees living in Birmingham city) and the Worcester and Birmingham Canal (a route for supplies to the factory and for the dispatch of finished products). The River Bourn offered a supply of clean, fresh water. At the time, the finest food products were considered to be French, so the Cadburys' sales people changed the name to Bournville because they thought it had French overtones.

The new factory opened in September 1879. Initially one detached house and sixteen semis were built for the company's key workers (in

[103] Cadbury, p. 104.

[104] Harrison, p. 23.

Laburnum Road, immediately to its north);[105] the idea of developing a housing estate emulating village life developed subsequently.

George Cadbury began to discreetly buy land surrounding the factory in 1893, using his personal resources, so as to reduce the risk of speculators and suburban slum builders thwarting his housing plans.[106] His voluntary work for the Adult School movement in Birmingham's inner city had convinced him that if slum dwellers were provided with homes that gave them a sense of dignity they would thrive and their health would improve. By providing each home with a garden in which food could be grown, diet would improve. In 1895, he purchased Bournbrook Hall itself which, along with its 118-acre estate, shared a common boundary with Bournville to the west. Further acquisitions were made between 1898 and 1911.

In 1895, George appointed William Alexander Harvey, a young local architect to help him build the first 142 homes, and so began to turn the garden factory into a garden city.

William Alexander Harvey (1874-1951)

William Alexander Harvey was only twenty years old when George Cadbury appointed him Estate Architect at Bournville in 1895. He had been a pupil of William Bidlake's at the Birmingham School of Art where he won prizes for his sketches of local medieval and vernacular buildings.[107] That he developed the ideas of the Arts and Crafts movement in the realm of domestic architecture is clear from his 1906 book in which he recalls the principles of his work at Bournville.[108] If artisans were to be attracted away from villas in long, stereotyped rows, the two movements of housing reform and the revival of domestic architecture needed to advance hand in hand. For Bournville's smaller

[105] Harrison, p. 34.

[106] Cadbury, pp. 146-149.

[107] Harrison, p. 41.

[108] Harvey, p. 6.

cottages, a pleasing appearance had been aimed at by controlling the cost of materials. This had been achieved not by purchasing cheap materials, but by avoiding waste. For example, a 12-foot 6-inch wide room required 13-foot 2-inch joists, obtained by purchasing stock 14-foot timbers and cutting 10 inches off each. A reduction in the room width of only 2 inches to 12 feet 4 inches meant stock 13-foot timbers could be utilised, with no waste or labour costs for cutting. Similarly, it was traditional to use 9x3inch timbers for joints. Harvey found that these were no stronger than 11x2inch timbers. The saving in buying wood of 5 inch less cube was greater than the cost of building the walls a few inches higher.[109]

At first, Cadbury provided building plots on long leases to anyone who wished to build houses. Later he built houses to rent.[110] Nearly all were cottage-style, giving a great variety of size and design. Each had a garden of 'not less than one sixth of an acre'. Certain provisos were stipulated for the purchasers of plots:

- No house was to occupy more than a quarter of the plot.
- No one could purchase more than two plots (this to prevent speculation).
- Each property was to have a minimum of six fruit trees planted to provide fresh fruit for the household.

Alexander Harvey drew up the plans for all these houses, creating an ordered informality by designing them in different styles.[111] When work commenced in 1896 the houses were advertised as being on the Bournville Building Estate.[112] By 1915, Harvey's ability to combine economic building methods with variation in design resulted in his being regarded as 'one of the greatest experts in the cheap cottage problem'.[113]

In order to prevent speculative builders from moving in, yet allow the village to expand later on without becoming overdeveloped, George

---

[109] Harvey, pp. 21-22.

[110] BVT, MS1536, Box 59, *The Story of Bournville*, Bournville Village Trust, 1983, p. 2.

[111] BVT, MS1536.

[112] BVT, MS1536, Box 5, correspondence of George Cadbury.

[113] L. Weaver, *The 'Country Life' Book of Cottages* (1919 edition), p. 20. In: Harrison, p. 42.

Cadbury set up the Bournville Village Trust by Deed of Foundation on 14 December 1900. Its purpose was to administer and develop the village for the benefit of the residents as a whole and to prevent any exploitation of the area by builders and property developers – something which was by then happening all round the village. Its major object was '… the amelioration of the condition of the working class and labouring population in and around Birmingham and elsewhere in Great Britain by the provision of improved dwellings with gardens and open spaces to be enjoyed therewith …'[114]

Houses were to be individually designed and would nestle around a green that incorporated the estate's established trees. Winding walkways set out at curves and angles would follow the contours of the land. The earlier housing schemes of Titus Salt in Yorkshire's woollen industry town of Saltaire (1852) and William Lever's Port Sunlight (1888) had been constructed to benefit their own workers. George's plan was to construct housing for a broad mix of people drawn from all walks of life so that 'all classes may live in kindly neighbourliness'.[115] It would, he hoped, provide a template for raising the standards of the poor elsewhere in the country.[116]

40 years' experience of employing men in Birmingham city centre had convinced George Cadbury that the greatest drawback to their moral and physical progress was the lack of any healthful occupation for their leisure. Working men could not be healthy and have healthy families when the only pursuits available outside factory hours were the institute, the club-room or the public house. Providing men with a garden – and he would find they took to its cultivation very readily – replaced their spending their money in such places and enabled them and their families to consume fresh garden produce. A 1901 survey of Bournville found the economic value of these crops, after associated outgoings, was 1/11d per week, compensation for the amount by which Bournville's rents exceeded the rent for similarly-sized city-centre houses.

[114] BVT, MS1536, Box 5, correspondence of George Cadbury.

[115] Quotation from the Trust's documentation.

[116] George Cadbury secured the services of 'a clever young lawyer' to take up for him 'the question of the Bournville Trust'. When ascertaining how Sir Titus's property was secured, it was discovered that 'no arrangements had been made for its future and it was in the hands of the debenture holders'. BVT, MS1536, Box 5, correspondence of George Cadbury, copy of a letter to John Burns, MP, 20 November 1899.

All this fulfilled Cadbury's intentions expressed in the Trust's Deed of Foundation:

> The Founder is desirous of alleviating the evils which arise from the insanitary and insufficient housing accommodation supplied to large numbers of the working classes, and of securing to workers in factories some of the advantages of outdoor village life, with opportunities for the natural and helpful occupation of cultivating the soil.[117]

Creating the Model Village some sixteen years after the factory had out-grown its Birmingham city centre site was as much a social as an architectural experiment. The Trust was achieving its ambition of attracting workers other than its own employees, as was demonstrated by the 1901 Census when 315 houses, some for long leases of 999 years and others for weekly rent, had been built:[118]

BOURNVILLE'S POPULATION, 1901

Householders' places of work		Householders' occupations	
Bournville	41.2%	Indoor factory work	50.7%
Villages within a mile of Bournville	18.6%	Clerks/travellers	13.3%
Birmingham	40.2%	Mechanics, carpenters, bricklayers & others	36.0%

Source:: Harvey, p 11.

Harvey's designs were an early – possibly the earliest – attempt to build houses available to anyone at a standard above speculative builders' terraces, certainly aesthetically and often structurally, albeit the rents were beyond the means of the poorest of the working classes. He left the service of the Trust in 1904 whereupon he became employed by

---

[117] Harrison, p. 34.

[118] BVT, MS1536 Box 5, correspondence of George Cadbury.

Cadbury directly to superintend the erection of the village's public buildings, all of which he designed.[119] His place as Trust architect was taken over by Henry Bedford Tyler[120] who adopted his predecessor's ideals in a town planning sense and, along with other architects of subsequent garden cities and suburbs, created houses at lower costs and rents. Whilst the initial houses were semi-detached, by 1915 blocks of four, and occasionally more, were being built in the western, northern and north-east parts of the site.

Houses in Sycamore Road, Bournville.

---

[119] BVT, MS1536, Box 26: *A Ten Years Record, The Bournville Village Trust December 1900 to December 1910*, ms signed by John H. Barlow, Secretary.

[120] Harrison, p. 53.

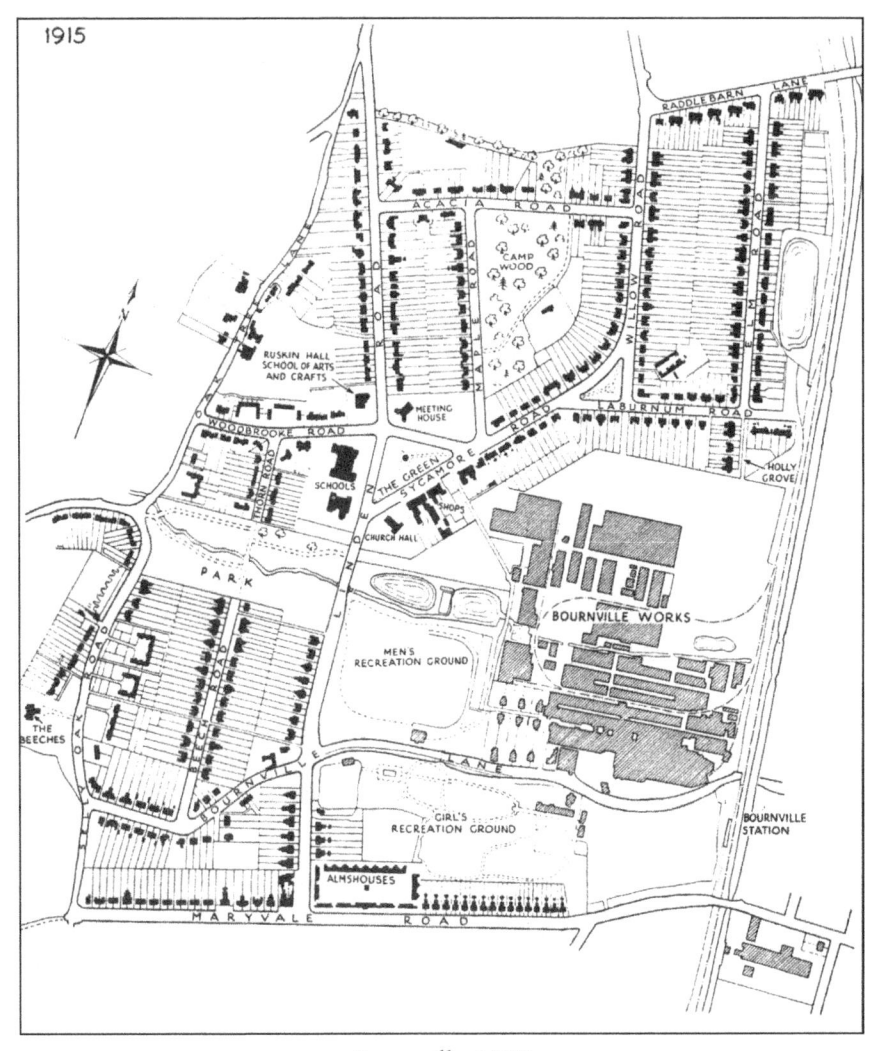

Bournville, 1915.

Ebenezer Howard
and the Garden City Movement

A couple of years after Alexander Harvey was beginning to design his first houses at Bournville in 1896, Ebenezer Howard (1850-1928) was publishing his book that led to the Garden City movement.

A Londoner, Howard taught himself shorthand after leaving school at the age of fifteen.[121] In 1871, he went to America with two friends to start a farm in Nebraska. Discovering that agriculture was not for him, he moved some 600 miles east to Chicago and gained employment with the official stenographers at the city's law courts. Chicago was being rebuilt after a serious fire (also in 1871). The new western suburbs included large, public parks and 'garden city' was the term used to describe this new environment. Here, he became acquainted with a number of American intellectuals concerned with humanism and individualism[122] although he continued to worship at the Congregational Church; he had been employed as private secretary to the influential Congregational preacher Dr. Joseph Parker before moving to the States.

Howard returned to England in 1876 and started to work for Gurney & Sons, whose verbatim reports of parliamentary proceedings form the basis for Hansard's daily parliamentary reports. He would have listened to parliamentary debates dealing with the social issues of the day. In the final quarter of the 19th century, he would have seen both Conservative and Liberal governments – the Conservative premiership of Benjamin Disraeli, followed by the alternating governments of Gladstone (Liberal) and the Marquess of Salisbury (Conservative). Proceedings were no doubt enlivened by the arrival of the first Independent Labour Party MPs – Keir Hardie and two others in 1892, for example, whose views were supported by a number of radical Liberals.

Howard's only book was published in 1898. Its original title, *To-morrow: A Peaceful Path to Real Reform*, was changed for the 1902 reprint to *Garden Cities of To-morrow*, the name by which it became

---

[121] Mervyn Miller, 'Howard, Sir Ebenezer (1850-1928)', *Oxford Dictionary of National Biography*, Oxford University Press, 2004 [http://www.oxforddnb.com/view/article/34016, accessed 9 March 2016].

[122] en.wikipedia.org/wiki/Ebenezer_Howard, accessed 9 March 2016.

HOW GARDEN SUBURBS CAME TO BE

widely known. He founded the Garden Cities Association in 1899 which was in due course renamed the Town and Country Planning Association. It remains an active body to this day, its aim being 'to make the planning system more responsive to people's needs and aspirations and to promote sustainable development'.

Howard's book starts with a quotation from Ruskin:

> ... and then the building of more [houses], strongly, beautifully, and in groups of limited extent, kept in proportion to their streams and walled around, so that there may be no festering or wretched suburb anywhere, ... so that from any part of the city perfectly fresh air and grass and sight of far horizon might be reachable in a few minutes' walk.[123]

Such thoughts underpin the ideas that Howard went on to describe. His book describes a theoretical city, named Garden City.

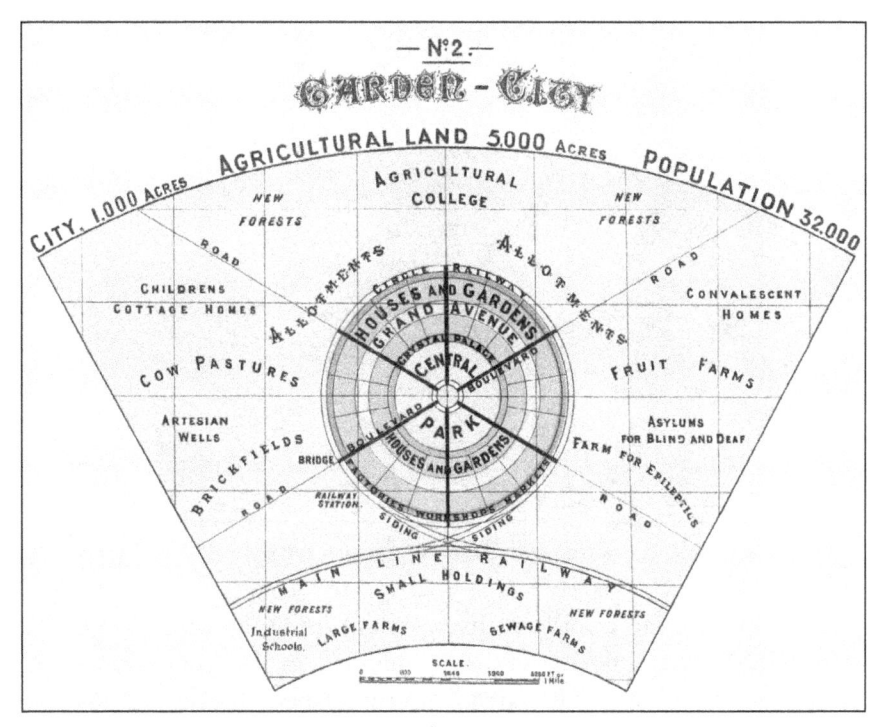

Garden City.

---
[123] John Ruskin, *Sesame and Lilies*, 1865. In: Howard, p. 1.

The built-up circle has as its hub a central park surrounded by public buildings. Houses and factories form an outer ring. Outside this built-up circle are spaces for allotments, cows, an artesian water supply, brickfields, and homes for the elderly and disabled. To the south, the railway line that transports goods to and from Garden City also runs around it to take people to and from work in the factories and workshops on its south side. A diagram of a segment of the city shows the central public park with public buildings around its very centre.

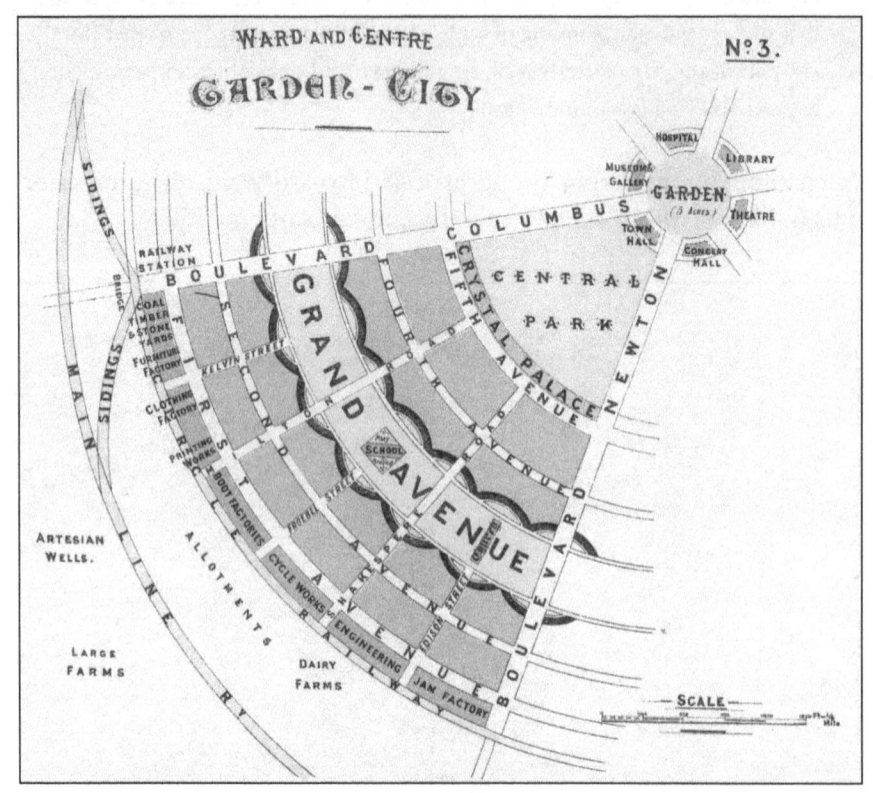

Ward and Centre of Garden City.

Grand Avenue, the middle of five avenues going all around the city, was envisioned as a 420-foot-wide boulevard. It was almost a second, circular park and only 240 yards from the furthest house. Schools and their playgrounds and gardens would front onto it as would churches of various denominations. Howard envisaged a population of 30,000 living in 5,500 homes in the inner circle – an average of 5½ per home

– with minimum and average plot sizes of 20x100 feet and 20x130 feet respectively. Based on his diagram *Ward and Centre*, roads would take up about 30% of the land allocated for housing. He therefore envisaged a housing density in these zones of about twelve per acre. At the time, Bournville's houses were being built at seven per acre. The Progress Estate would be built at fourteen per acre.

Four out of the twelve chapters in Howard's book are given over to the economics of Garden City's revenue and expenditure and most of the rest of it is devoted to Garden City's organisation. It is a treatise about how such a city might be built and run, not a description of what its buildings might look like. It was nevertheless a key publication, because it led to the Garden City Conference at Bournville in 1901. This was to be a significant conference in the development of working-class housing, as will be explained once some background has been given to two of the architects whose work would come to define the movement's achievements.

Barry Parker and Raymond Unwin

Parker and Unwin, to the right and left, respectively, of this family group photograph taken in 1898.

Barry Parker (1867-1947) and Raymond Unwin (1863-1940) formed an architectural partnership that lasted from 1896 until its amicable dissolution in 1915. They were half cousins, Barry's mother, Frances being a half-sister of Unwin's father, William.[124] Their influence on the design of garden suburbs and the emergence of town planning is hard to overstate. Before discussing how their talents exhibited themselves, we need to look briefly at their early lives in order to understand the influences that would make them the people they became.

Parker was the junior of the two by four years and sixteen days; they were November children, his birthday being the 18th and Unwin's the 2nd. He was born in Chesterfield, Derbyshire, the son of a bank manager, Robert Parker. The family's move to Buxton in the 1880s, 25 miles west and in the Peak District, may have been caused by his father's ill health. Barry studied at T. C. Simmonds Atelier of Art in Derby between 1886 and 1889. An atelier is the private workshop or studio of a

---

[124] 'Staveley was the home town of a brother-in-law of [Unwin's] father, Robert Parker'. In: Andrew Saint, 'Unwin, Sir Raymond (1863-1940)', *Oxford Dictionary of National Biography*, Oxford University Press, 2004; online edn, January 2008 [http://www.oxforddnb.com/view/article/36613, accessed 18 January 2017].

professional artist in the fine or decorative arts, where a principal master and a number of assistants, students and apprentices work together producing pieces of fine or visual art which are then released under the master's name or supervision. Parker sat the external examinations of the South Kensington Schools, London, whilst a pupil of Simmonds.[125] The Schools were the forerunner of the Royal College of Art and Parker may well have met Edwin Lutyens (1869-1944) there in 1886 or 1887.[126]

In 1889, Parker took up articles under George Faulkner Armitage of Altrincham, 27 miles north-west of Buxton and nowadays a commuter town ten miles south-west of Manchester city centre. G. Faulker Armitage (as he chose to be known) was the son of a prosperous Manchester cotton merchant, one of the founders of Armitage and Rigby who had mills in Manchester and Warrington. The Armitage family (he was one of thirteen children) were active Congregationalists and were linked to the Rigby's by a number of marriages as well as by commerce.[127] Faulker Armitage's Altrincham premises show his debt to both Ruskin and Morris[128] and his studio embraced furniture and textile workshops as well as architecture. Parker was Clerk of Works on several of the buildings Armitage designed.[129]

Raymond Unwin's influence was far-reaching and led to his being appointed President of the Royal Institute of British Architects in 1931. He was granted a knighthood for his services to planning in 1932 and awarded the RIBA's Royal Gold Medal in 1937.[130] Born near Rotherham, seven miles north-east of Sheffield, he was devoted to his father, Edward, a graduate of Balliol College, Oxford. When

---

[125] Mervyn Miller, 'Parker, (Richard) Barry (1867-1947)', *Oxford Dictionary of National Biography*, Oxford University Press, 2004; online edn, January 2011 [http://www.oxforddnb.com/view/article/61684, accessed 14 March 2016].

[126] Richardson, p. 127.

[127] Fitzpatrick, Gill. 'Portrait of a Studio: George Faulkner Armitage and His Apprentices', *The Journal of the Decorative Arts Society 1850 – the Present 31* (2007), www.jstor.org/stable/41809380?seq=1#page_scan_tab_contents, accessed 14 March 2016.

[128] Rosamund Allwood, 'George Faulkner Armitage 1849—1937'. *Furniture History*, vol. 23 (1987), pp. 67-87, Furniture History Society. www.jstor.org/stable/23406699, accessed 14 March 2016.

[129] Miller (2002), p. 39.

[130] Jackson, p. 178.

the family textile business collapsed in the late-1860s they moved to Oxford[131] and Unwin senior took up a Fellowship at the University. However, the conflict between the literal Biblical description of man's origins and the work of Charles Darwin became, to his mind, irreconcilable.[132] At this time, holding Holy Orders was a prerequisite for maintaining a Fellowship. Unwin concluded that Darwin's theories were correct (or at least that Biblical literalism was not), resigned Holy Orders and thus had to discontinue his Fellowship. Thereafter the family survived on his meagre earnings as an extra-collegiate tutor and he began to move in progressive circles, becoming acquainted with the Revd. Samuel Barnett. Barnett's work with the Charity Organisation Society has already been mentioned and he will reappear in the chapter about Hampstead Garden Suburb.

Raymond Unwin was educated at the grant-aided Magdalen College Choir School, Oxford, a secondary school that guaranteed a quarter of its places to free scholarships for pupils from public elementary schools. In his history of the School, Robert Spenser Stanier stated:

> To allow the School to develop into another rich man's Public School would have been to betray a heritage and a tradition. Magdalen School had never been a school of rich men's sons, and genuine democracy had flourished in it …[133]

Ruskin was by this time the first Slade Professor at Oxford. He believed art should 're-enter life' and become the reflection of a healthy society because 'all most lovely forms and thoughts are directly taken from natural objects'.[134] Both Unwin and Barry Parker avidly read Ruskin's

---

[131] Jackson, p. 11. Andrew Saint, 'Unwin, Sir Raymond (1863-1940)', *Oxford Dictionary of National Biography*, Oxford University Press, 2004; online edn, January 2008 [http://www.oxforddnb.com/view/article/36613, accessed 14 March 2016] states that Edward Unwin's business was a tannery he had inherited from his father, whose management he gave up to move to Oxford. This difference does not detract from both authors' views of his personality.

[132] *On the Origin of Species* had been published on 24 November 1859 (en.wikipedia.org/wiki/On_the_Origin_of_Species, accessed 17 March 2016).

[133] Robert Spenser Stanier, *Magdalen School*, Oxford Historical Society, 1958 edition. In: freepages.genealogy.rootsweb.ancestry.com/~stanier/archive/whoswho.html, accessed 17 March 2016.

[134] John Ruskin, *The Seven Lamps of Architecture*, 1849, quotations from 'The Lamp of Beauty' and 'The Lamp of Life'. In: Jackson, p. 13.

works. Unwin later recalled attending lectures by Ruskin and becoming familiar with Morris's work: 'One who was privileged to hear the beautiful voice of John Ruskin declaiming against the degradation of *laissez faire* theories of life, to know William Morris and his works ... could hardly fail to follow the ideals of a more ordered society, and a better planned environment for it, than that which he saw around him in the [eighteen] seventies and eighties'.[135] One must assume Unwin saw the village architecture of the Cotswolds, spreading out to the north-west of Oxford, as a manifestation of these men's opinions.

Unwin became an apprentice engineer at the Staveley Coal and Iron Company near Chesterfield in 1883 and then, in 1886, an engineering draughtsman at a cotton mill in Manchester. There he joined the Manchester Socialist Society and became the first Secretary to the newly-formed Manchester branch of William Morris's Socialist League.[136] In 1887, aged 24, he returned to the Staveley Coal and Iron Company as chief draughtsman and joined Edward Carpenter's Sheffield Socialist Society. Carpenter was a writer and poet whose poem 'Towards Democracy' introduced Walt Whitman's ideals to this country; Whitman was one of the American intellectuals who had influenced Ebenezer Howard whilst he was living in Chicago. Unwin described the poem thus:

> [Its two or three main conceptions] begin with a new understanding, relation and unity to be realised between the spirit of man and his body, the animal man no longer a beast to be ridden, but an equal friend to be loved, cherished, and inspired. ... There then emerges a new sense of equality and freedom in all human intercourse and relationships. Content, in happy unity with its body, the soul of man, thus accepting equality of spiritual status, and enjoying free communication with its fellows, discovers a new relation to the universe, to nature, and to the Great Spirit which pervades it; a new faith, not of belief in this or that, but of trust.[137]

---

[135] The Royal Gold Medal – presentation to Sir Raymond Unwin, *Journal of the Royal Institute of British Architects*, s33. 144 (12), 24 April 1937, p. 582. In: Mervyn Miller, *Letchworth: The First Garden City*, second edition, Phillimore & Co., 2002, p. 40.

[136] Jackson, p. 13.

[137] Edward Carpenter and *Towards Democracy*, p. 234-6. In: Swenarton (1989).

Preliminary sketch for a hall near Derby.

Carpenter's ideas informed Unwin's unfolding realisation that architecture and, as time passed, planning, had social as well as design implications.[138] He began to think about houses from the point of view of their occupants rather than of those who built them (as had been at least partially proposed by the artisanship of the Ruskin/Morris tradition) and came to the realisation that the state, involvement with which was intentionally avoided by Morris, could be used to further Socialist reform.[139] Unwin acknowledged his intellectual debt to all three in his acceptance speech for the RIBA Gold Medal.[140] Ruskin and Morris may have influenced how Parker's and Unwin's houses looked, but Carpenter informed how he, Unwin, thought about them. Thus he and his partner Barry Parker would write to the introduction of their book *The Art of Building a Home*: 'It is too often evident that people, instead of being assisted, and their lives added to, by the houses they occupy, are but living as well as may be in spite of them. The house planned to meet supposed wants which never occur, and sacrificed to

---

[138] Jackson, p. 16.

[139] Swenarton (1989), p. 127.

[140] Swenarton (1981), p. 126.

convention and custom, neither satisfies the real needs of its occupants nor expresses in any way their individuality'.[141]

Attendance at the Sheffield Socialist Society also resulted in Unwin forming a lifelong friendship with Keir Hardie, the Miners' Union official in the late-1870s and the first Independent Labour Party MP (1892) and his meeting Charles Robert Ashbee[142] who would in due course tutor Frank Baines. Baines rose to become a Principal Architect at H.M. Office of Works, the architect for the Estate in 1915. In the early 1890s Unwin joined the Labour Church, a denomination that attracted those who could not align themselves with the conservative established Church. Keir Hardie was one of its speakers.[143]

Although Unwin had been re-employed by the Staveley Coal and Iron Company to design cranes, steam engines and air compressors he had, by the early 1890s, begun to plan their mining townships. In 1893 he and Ethel Parker, Barry Parker's sister, finally married. They had known each other since childhood yet did not become formally engaged until 1891, the year her father died.[144] He had apparently prohibited correspondence between them which caused Raymond to keep a diary comprising entries addressed to her that substituted for what would otherwise have been his letters.[145] By then, Ethel was 26 and he 28. It was also the case that Barry did not agree with the Socialist ideals espoused by Raymond and his friends[146] and finally, of course, the familial relationship of Ethel and Raymond as half-cousins would merely have added to concerns as to their marriage.

Despite Parker's rejection of Unwin's Socialist beliefs, he was influenced by his architectural ideas and they formed their partnership

---

[141] Parker and Unwin, p. i.

[142] Discussed more fully in the chapter *Charles Robert Ashbee and Frank Baines*.

[143] Jackson, p. 18.

[144] Mervyn Miller, 'Parker, (Richard) Barry (1867-1947)', *Oxford Dictionary of National Biography*, Oxford University Press, 2004; online edn, Jan 2011 [http://www.oxforddnb.com/view/article/61684, accessed 15 July 2016].

[145] University of Manchester Department of Architecture and Planning, Unwin Papers, 1887 Diary. In: Swenarton (1989), p. 134.

[146] Andrew Saint, 'Unwin, Sir Raymond (1863-1940)', *Oxford Dictionary of National Biography*, Oxford University Press, 2004; online edn, Jan 2008 [http://www.oxforddnb.com/view/article/36613, accessed 17 March 2016 and Miller (2002), p. 39.

in 1896. Parker's wife saw them as a combination of social and aesthetic zeal: 'Each has a deep affection for the other's gifts – so profoundly different yet complementary'.[147] Unwin would concentrate on strategy, layout and costings, and Parker on aesthetic detail. The partnership, which by all accounts ran very affably, always concentrated on housing. Their initial focus was on individual arts and crafts homes, often for progressive businessmen, complete with ample living rooms and inglenooks.[148] The illustration on page 76 is an example of these designs.

Their work would move from small groups of houses to complete suburban and civic layouts as Unwin's mastery of all aspects of 'the housing question' grew.

---

[147] Barry Parker Collection, Letchworth. In: Jackson, p. 24.

[148] John Simkin, spartacus-educational.com/Barry_Parker.htm, accessed 17 March 2016.

Joseph and Seebohm Rowntree and the Garden City Conference, 1901

Like his fellow chocolatier and contemporary George Cadbury, Joseph Rowntree (1836-1925) was a Quaker. Prosperity came to him and his family in the 1890s as a result of the successful development of pastilles after years of experimentation and the construction of a purpose-built factory.[149] Commercially, the two first collaborated in 1895 when, along with Fry's, they worked together to defend their businesses from European competition.[150]

Benjamin Seebohm Rowntree (1871-1954) was the second of four sons from Joseph's marriage to Antoinette Seebohm in 1867, the cousin of his first wife Julia who had died in 1863. Antoinette also bore him two daughters.[151]

Inspired by Charles Booth's statistical analysis of poverty in London, Seebohm (as the second son was always known) investigated York's working-class homes, publishing his findings in *Poverty: A Study of Town Life in 1901*.[152] He found that 12% were back-to-backs and two-thirds of the rest 'uninspiring', having thin walls of damp-absorbent bricks, inferior mortar, green wood that caused floors, window frames and doors to shrink in under a year, and no gardens. He described them as 'the slums of a not-very-distant future'.[153] His findings implied that only one-fifth of York's houses were, at a minimum, adequate and well built. His father decided to conduct an experiment in working-class housing and so he acquired 123 acres of agricultural land in the countryside just outside the village of Earswick, three miles north of the city of York, in 1901, for £72 per acre.[154] To use today's parlance, he

---

[149] Cadbury, pp. 137-141.

[150] Cadbury, p. 156.

[151] Robert Fitzgerald, 'Rowntree, Joseph (1836-1925)', *Oxford Dictionary of National Biography*, Oxford University Press, 2004 [http://www.oxforddnb.com/view/article/35857, accessed 21 March 2016].

[152] Macmillan & Co, London.

[153] Anne Vernon, *A Quaker Businessman: The Life of Joseph Rowntree*, William Sessions, York, 1987, p. 146. Copy of text provided by Joseph Rowntree Foundation & Joseph Rowntree Housing Trust, 12 June 2015.

[154] Waddilove, p. 31.

appointed Seebohm, then 30 years old and the Labour Director of the family chocolate business,[155] as the CEO of what has since come to be known as New Earswick whilst he, then aged 65, became Chair.

In 1903, at the age of 67 and with his threescore years and ten not far off, Joseph contemplated 'how [my wealth] can be so applied in the future as to secure results equal to those which might have been secured had I had the administration of it over a lengthened period'.[156] Thus it was that, with the assent of his wife and children, he created his Village Trust, the Charitable Trust and the Social Service Trust.[157] The three collectively became the recipients of the larger part of his fortune and the New Earswick enterprise was transferred to the Joseph Rowntree Village Trust in December 1904,[158] by which time about 26 cottages had been constructed. The assets (which included shares in Rowntree and Company Limited) were valued at the time at £62,165/5/2½d.[159] Joseph had been advised by the same Counsel as had prepared the deed for Cadbury's Bournville Village Trust in December 1900.[160]

Local authorities had been empowered to acquire land and erect houses since the passing of the Housing of the Working Classes Act, 1890[161] and could, with the consent of the Local Government Board, apply for loans for the purpose from the Public Works Loan Commissioners.[162] Joseph's hope was to demonstrate to local government that decent working-class housing was a financially viable public enterprise, affordable by men earning about 25/- per week.[163]

There was never any intention to subsidise the cost of the village's homes. A conference about New Earswick's financing held on 16

---

[155] Brian Harrison, 'Rowntree, (Benjamin) Seebohm (1871-1954)', *Oxford Dictionary of National Biography*, Oxford University Press, 2004; online edn, January 2008 [http://www.oxforddnb.com/view/article/35856, accessed 28 March 2016].

[156] Waddilove, p. 4.

[157] Cadbury, p. 307.

[158] Waddilove, p. 7.

[159] Miller (2002), p. 43.

[160] Harrison, p. 44.

[161] Burnett, p. 138.

[162] Thompson, p. 7.

[163] Waddilove, pp. 7-8.

March 1906 concluded: 'We ought to earn a minimum of at least 3% on the village building scheme if it is to be considered anything but a philanthropic enterprise'.[164] Later, Joseph reinforced this during a speech he made when the village hall – the Folk Hall – was opened in 1907:

> I spoke just now of the interest with which experiments such as we are carrying out at Earswick are watched by many throughout the country. In connection with that there is one point I want to bring before you. We want at Earswick to do something towards the Housing Problem, and the value of our experiment will very much depend upon whether we are able to make it pay. If we can say to Manufacturers or to Town or County Councils that a Village such as ours can pay something like 3 per cent upon the money expended, it is probable that we shall have many imitators, but if, on the other hand, the experiment is commercially a failure, the number of imitators will be few. It is, however, only by the utmost vigilance and economy that as much as 3 per cent interest upon our expenditure can be made, and you will therefore understand why, in connection with the houses, we find it necessary to decline many requests that are made to us.[165]

He went on to say: 'The Hall will be a free gift to the Village, and, consequently, the finance of the Village will not be burdened with any interest payments upon the cost of the Folk Hall'. This reflected the March conference's decision that the cost associated with what, in a town, would be services that already existed or would be provided by a local authority out of general public funds ought not to drive up the rents of the houses in order to meet the associated financing costs. Thus, a modern dairy on a local farm to produce milk to a high standard, the aforementioned village hall, a children's playground and the schools would be kept out of account. On the other hand, the expenditure on shops, site development, a sewage disposal works, street lighting and other services specific to the community's needs were to be included in the village's capital requirement.[166]

---

[164] Waddilove, p. 31.

[165] JRVT NE 21/2(b), Joseph Rowntree's speech at the opening of the Folk Hall, 5 October 1907.

[166] Waddilove, pp. 32-33.

Unlike George Cadbury, Joseph Rowntree was not building an estate with employment on its doorstep; his own factory was on the edge of York. Seebohm Rowntree was concerned the village might fail to draw tenants to its homes. Living in New Earswick would, for many, entail travelling three or four miles to work and back again along a low-quality road with poor transport links.[167] Even if rents were compatible, people would only move to the village if their perception of the quality of life it offered more than outweighed this inconvenience. York had few industries and often a thousand reasonably good yet empty homes. The cheaper ones – Seebohm's slums of the future – never lacked tenants and he thought the return on capital might be below their target of 3% per annum, the rate they considered the Public Works Loan Commissioners would be likely to charge local authorities for housing schemes.

Ebenezer Howard had formed the Garden City Association in 1899 to promote his ideas. They attracted widespread interest; his biographer, Dugald Macfadyen, states that 'three months after its formation Mr. Howard was able to declare: 'The Association numbers among its members manufacturers, co-operators, architects, artists, medical men, financial experts, lawyers, merchants, ministers of religion, members of the London County Council [Moderate and Progressive] Socialists and Individualists, Radicals and Conservatives'.[168] Barry Parker and Raymond Unwin were both early members and had participated in its meetings and discussions. Howard's concepts were more widely debated at the inaugural Garden City Conference, hosted by George Cadbury at Bournville in 1901.[169] Unwin presented his paper 'On the Building of Houses in the Garden City' at the conference. The layout was to be:

> arranged in conformity with the land ... Wide avenues or roads must be planned to lead off [from the sites of civic buildings] in all directions, so that glimpses of the country beyond shall be obtained from all parts ... and vistas leading up to the finest buildings shall greet the visitor from every direction ... In the arrangement of the space devoted to dwellings ... a complete acceptance of natural conditions must be combined with some definite design. No weak

[167] Waddilove, p. 14.

[168] Macfadyen, chapter VI: 1899.

[169] Burnett, p. 292.

compound of town and country, composed of meandering suburban roads, lined with semi-detached villas, set each in a scrap of garden, will ever deserve the name of 'Garden City'.

His eight-page paper laid down the framework for modern town planning. There was to be a broad overall plan and detailed design standards. Aesthetic control was to be exercised by committees.[170] This was in complete contrast to the permissive Victorian approach described earlier in this book. He declared: 'It is not in the row or semi-detached villa that we must look for the solution to the housing problem in towns, but to the quiet quadrangle with its wide expanse of grass, or the square with its spacious garden'.[171]

Seebohm Rowntree also attended the conference and, on his advice, Joseph Rowntree appointed Parker and Unwin as New Earswick's architects.[172] Because the rate at which people would move to the village was unknown, development was at an intentionally slow pace. Seebohm Rowntree's concerns were to some extent borne out. Construction of the first thirty-four cottages began in 1902. Come 1908, there were around fifty families present and a provisional decision was taken by the Village Trust to limit the number of houses to one hundred.[173]

For the purposes of this book, the interest in New Earswick lies as much in Parker and Unwin's site plan as the architecture of the early houses. It was to be built on virgin land. The initial design challenge was to organise the site in such a way as would cope with further, but undefined, expansion. Their principle of 'respect for the site'[174] is reflected in the way the roads acknowledge the line of the River Foss. Most trees on the site were preserved. The earliest part to be developed

---

[170] Garden City Association (1901), p. 69. In: Miller, pp. 41-42.

[171] Garden City Association, *Garden City Conference at Bournville: Report of Proceedings (1901)*, p. 71. In: Harrison, p. 52.

[172] Jackson, p. 51. Waddilove, pp. 13 & 17 states that Unwin was commissioned as architect in 1901 and Parker in 1919 when Unwin was appointed Chief Architect to the newly created Ministry of Health. This may well be correct at a formal level.

[173] The village comprised 247 houses by 1919, 506 by 1939 (government subsidies for housing having been available from 1919), and 584 by 1954 (Waddilove, p. 142). Transport links have also improved over the years.

[174] Jackson, pp. 64-65.

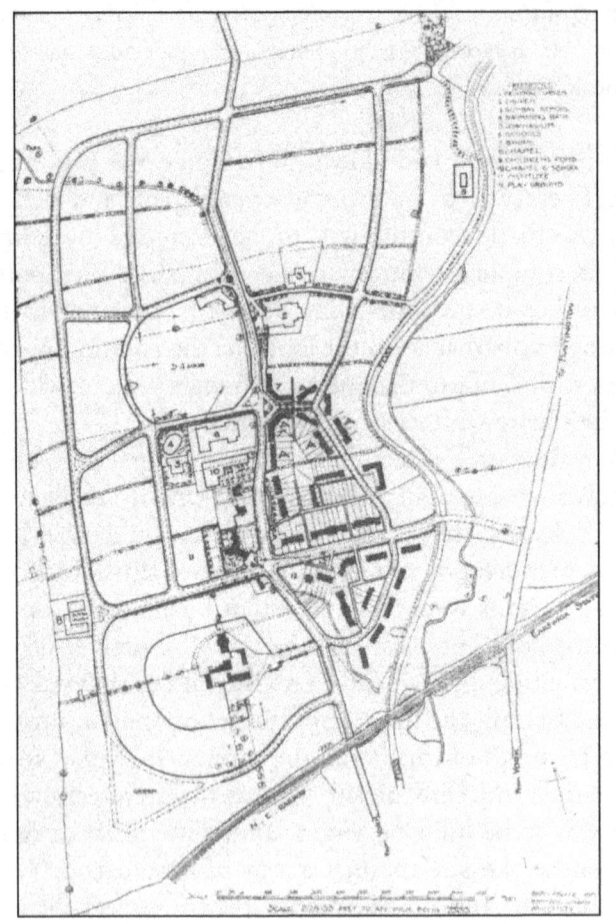

THE ORIGINS AND EVOLUTION OF THE PROGRESS ESTATE

Early plan for New Earswick by Parker and Unwin (1902).

was the lower south-east portion; Poplar Grove is the road immediately west of the Foss.

It proved to be a real struggle to build cottages that were affordable for the lower working classes. Although the first to be built had been let at between 4/9d and 5/3d per week, a 1907 conference on the village's financings concluded that the costs had proved to be such that rents needed to be increased to an average of 6/1d per week if the target rate of return was to remain intact, and that was before adding a contribution to a sinking fund for the repayment of capital. The only way out of the dilemma was to reduce the standard of accommodation available at the lowest rents. This involved increasing the density to a minimum of

Poplar Grove in 1904.

fourteen dwellings to the acre[175] and excluding both a bath and a hot water supply. The rents for these would be 4/- per week. However, four other types would be constructed. The first, with a bath in the kitchen and hot water, might be let for 4/6d. The next group would have a reduced density of twelve per acre, somewhat increasing the room sizes and rent for 5/3d. The third type would still have a bath in the kitchen but would also offer a parlour, renting for 6/2d. The largest, offering a parlour and a separate bathroom, would rent for 7/-.[176]

Notwithstanding the Rowntrees' interest in Ebenezer Howard's Garden City movement, New Earswick had only ever been planned as a garden village. Joseph's idea had been to show that it was possible to build decent working-class homes without subsidy, and the Village Trust had just about managed to do so. The primary duty of the Village Trust was the creation of village communities where the tenants would pay rents that gave a commercial return on the capital invested.[177] Possibly reflecting an acceptance of Seebohm's concerns, Joseph subsequently wrote: 'it is doubtful if there will be a great and continuous demand for houses at Earswick and I think it is just possible that before very long the income of the Trust may be applied elsewhere, and possibly

---

[175] The original density had been planned at twelve to the acre. Joseph Rowntree Village Trust Archive, Borthwick Institute for Archives, University of York, *The Report of a Conference on the Finance of the Earswick Village* (16 November 1906).

[176] Waddilove, pp. 34-35.

[177] Waddilove, p. 4.

it may be the most useful thing to make a number of small model village communities – say a hundred houses – rather than anything approaching a garden city'.[178]

The Rowntrees' sponsorship of the architectural competition for Letchworth Garden City, announced in the early autumn of 1903, was the next instalment of this ongoing social experiment.[179]

For Parker & Unwin, their experiences at New Earswick stood them in good stead at Letchworth and later – for Unwin – Hampstead Garden Suburb. It confirmed for Unwin that the planner's role lay in guiding and controlling the activities of a growing community by bringing order and a conscious overall sense of design to a complex social operation.[180]

---

[178] Waddilove, pp. 6-7.

[179] Jackson, p. 67.

[180] Jackson, p. 60.

Letchworth Garden City

The second half of the 19th century had seen towns enlarged by the construction of suburbs because ever-increasing numbers of people were needed to work in their rising numbers of factories and workshops. The growth of cities' railway networks was a major factor because it made commuting a viable economic option for many of the working population. Town planning as we now know it did not exist. Instead, legislation had gradually increased minimum building standards in the interests of public health. These suburbs were therefore filled with by-law housing that met these standards, yet created what progressive thinkers regarded as soulless living environments. Additionally, much inner-city squalor continued to exist in the tenement and back-to-back housing that preceded the suburbs.

In his book *Garden Cities of To-morrow*, Ebenezer Howard had theorised that this state of affairs could be cured by the creation of garden cities. The 1901 Garden City Conference led him to believe there was practical and financial support for his ideas. The Garden City Pioneer Company ('the Pioneer Company') was formed by Howard's Garden City Association on 16 July 1902 'to promote and further the distribution of the industrial population upon the lines suggested in Mr. Ebenezer Howard's book ... and to form a garden city, that is to say, a town or settlement for agricultural, industrial, commercial and residential purposes, or any of them, in accordance with Mr. Howard's scheme or any modification thereof'. George Cadbury was one of its directors, and he and his family were significant investors in the enterprise.[181]

After some astute negotiations, begun in April 1903 by Herbert Warren, the Pioneer Company's solicitor whose practice in Baldock in Hertfordshire was some five miles from Hitchin and on the north-east edge of what is now Letchworth, and his clerk James Brown (also the Baldock Postmaster) a 3,818-acre ring-fenced site was assembled from fifteen separate owners at a cost of £155,587 – an average of £40/15/- per acre.[182] Although only about two-thirds of the size Howard had envisaged in his book, the price was in line with his expected £40 per

---

[181] Miller (2002), p. 20.

[182] Miller (2002), pp. 22-23.

acre, the average price of agricultural land in 1898.[183]

The Pioneer Company was replaced by First Garden City Co. Ltd. on 1 September 1903.[184] Its intentions were: 'Firstly, the provision of hygienic conditions of life for a considerable working population. Secondly, the stimulation of agriculture by bringing a market to the farmer's door. Thirdly, the relief of the tedium of agricultural life by accessibility to a large town. Fourthly, that the inhabitants will have the satisfaction of knowing that the increment of value of the land created by themselves will be devoted to their own benefit.'[185] These mirrored precisely the aims Howard had stated in his book.[186]

Presumably due to their close association with the Garden City Association, Parker and Unwin were told, in confidence, the whereabouts of the site before completion of the legal formalities. By August 1903, Unwin had visited the site twice and reported on it to the Pioneer Company's Engineering Committee. In late-October 1903 Parker and Unwin along with two other firms were invited to submit master plans for the development,[187] whereupon they devoted considerable resources to the project. Unwin and Robert Bennett, one of six assistants who, together with a secretary, were dedicated to it took up lodgings in Letchworth and immersed themselves in developing a deep understanding of the site's attributes. Parker was a frequent visitor and the plans were completed in Buxton one or two months later in December 1903.[188] The Pioneer Company's board resolved to adopt Parker & Unwin's plan on 11 February 1904 and it was duly published as the Company's Plan in April 1904.

---

[183] Howard, p. 2. The author does not state the source of his estimate. Edward Cadbury (eldest son of George Cadbury and Chair of Letchworth's Building Committee) wrote to Ebebezer Howard after the site assembly was announced saying 'he had supposed land would have been bought at £20/acre in one of the neglected areas of England' (Miller (2002), pp. 23 & 48).

[184] Jackson, p. 65.

[185] C. B. Purdom, *The Building of Satellite Towns*, 1925, pp. 57-58 & 60. In: Tarn, pp. 164-165.

[186] Howard, p. 2.

[187] Miller (2002), p. 39.

[188] Miller (2002), p. 44.

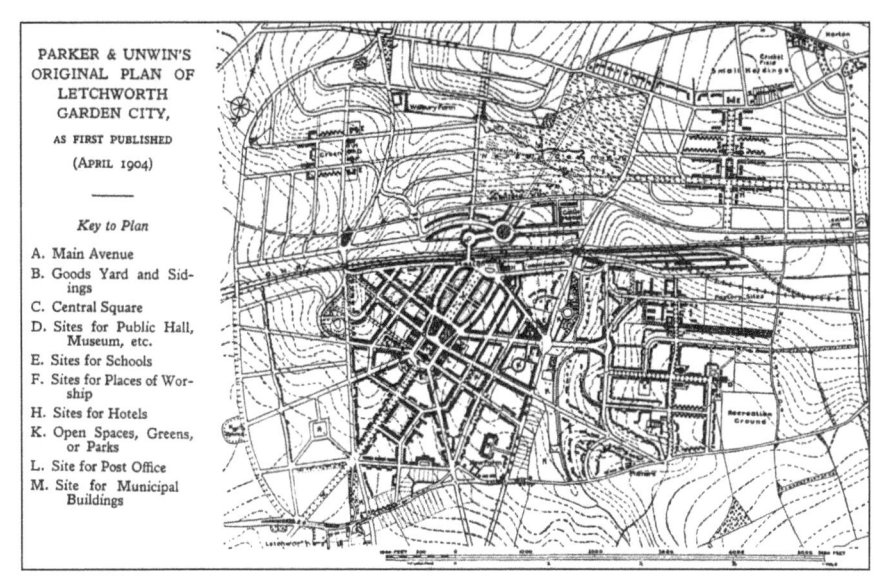

PARKER & UNWIN'S
ORIGINAL PLAN OF
LETCHWORTH
GARDEN CITY,
AS FIRST PUBLISHED
(APRIL 1904)

Key to Plan

A. Main Avenue
B. Goods Yard and Sidings
C. Central Square
D. Sites for Public Hall, Museum, etc.
E. Sites for Schools
F. Sites for Places of Worship
H. Sites for Hotels
K. Open Spaces, Greens, or Parks
L. Site for Post Office
M. Site for Municipal Buildings

Parker and Unwin's layout for Letchworth (1902).

The layout itself was very much the work of Unwin. His contribution to the partnership had always been to do with organisation and planning, whereas Parker's talents lay in the design of houses; the firm was rarely commissioned for anything else. He (Unwin) had written to Ethel Parker in 1891, during their long engagement, saying 'Barry seems to think we might join up someday and set up as architects, he [Parker] doing the artistic part and me the practical'.[189] Unwin's contribution, doubtless driven by his Socialist beliefs, was to design localities that would allow people from all walks of life to live together and enjoy pleasant and fulfilling lives. To achieve this, it was necessary to provide a layout that could grow organically over time, yet simultaneously to oversee the design and construction of buildings in order to ensure high standards were maintained. Parker's contribution was to design houses – in groups as much as individually – that ordinary people could afford without sacrificing the aesthetic principles of the Arts and Crafts movement.

Parker and Unwin were appointed Consulting Architects to First Garden City Ltd. on 23 March 1904. They were to oversee its building

---

[189] Hitchcock Collection: correspondence between Raymond Unwin and Ethel Parker. In: Miller (2002), p. 40.

and exercise design control.[190] Come June, Unwin drafted building regulations 'regarding buildings other than factories' for adoption by Hitchin Rural District Council:

> The Directors of First Garden City Limited are convinced that the high standard of beauty, which they desire to attain in Garden City, can only result from simple, straightforward buildings and from the use of good and harmonious materials. They desire as far as possible to discourage useless ornamentation, and to secure that buildings shall be suitably designed for their purpose and position.

The Council issued regulations in 1905 that largely followed his draft. They included rules for the grouping and aspect of houses and for the use of hedges to form boundaries. The range of densities was relative to price. Houses costing over £500 could be built at four to the acre. At the other extreme, there could be twelve to the acre for those below £200, with the smallest having a living room of 144 square feet. On the whole, all concerned abided by them,[191] save for the designers of a smallish portion of the City immediately to the north of the railway line that was given over in 1905 to the Cheap Cottages Exhibition.

Thomas Adams (1871-1940) had been made Secretary to Howard's Garden City Association in April 1901. He was interested in rural regeneration and had acted as a Liberal Party agent.[192] When the Pioneer Company was considering the three plans submitted for Garden City, he had favoured the compact formality of a layout submitted by Lethaby and Ricardo.[193] Both, especially Lethaby, had close connections with the Arts and Crafts movement.[194] He appears to have viewed Parker and Unwin's appointment as Consulting Architects more narrowly than they wished. Matters came to a head when an early group of indifferently designed cottages erected by a local contractor caused Unwin to write to Howard, stressing the need for high standards. Adams, by now

---

[190] Miller (2002), p. 47.

[191] Miller (2002), pp. 47-48.

[192] Miller (2002), pp. 18.

[193] Miller (2002), pp. 46.

[194] Miller (2002), p. 38.

Letchworth's Estate Manager,[195] responded in July 1904 by advertising for an independent consultant at £200 a year. Unwin wrote to him on 11 July:

> People are expecting that the Garden City will be a more interesting and beautiful place than an ordinary new building suburb ... The general effect ... may be made or marred by the way in which the plan is carried out in detail ...[and] will depend not only on the detail of the roads, but on the planning of buildings, and their arrangement on the plots, and the treatment of corner sites ... it seems to me to be very important to make suggestions to builders.[196]

The Board, having shortlisted some of the 150 applicants for the role Adams had publicised, awarded the appointment to Parker and Unwin at the stated fee, plus expenses.

Parker and Unwin were firmly of the view that cottages should be 'healthy, comfortable and comely, in that order'.[197] By 1903 they had developed four-roomed cottages in blocks of four that could be built for £132 each and which, for not much more, could be improved enormously.[198] Yet the depressed level of agricultural wages in the early 1900s made it difficult for agricultural workers, nationally, to afford the accommodation on offer in their localities. Their cause was taken up by *The Country Gentleman* and *The Spectator* magazines. They decided to promote a competition to design cottages costing £150 or less.[199] In November,1904 Adams, one might assume motivated by his interest in rural regeneration, obtained Board approval to offer these promoters a site, at a peppercorn rent, for their venture. In agreeing to the competition, the Board warned Unwin against overzealous control, ruling that 'Architects [are] not to be interfered with as regards details or matters of taste by [the] Consulting Architect'.[200]

[195] Miller(2002), pp. 37.

[196] Miller (2002), pp. 48.

[197] The Cheap Cottage – What is really Needed, *The Garden City*, June 1905. In: Jackson, p. 77.

[198] R. Unwin, 'Cottage Building in Garden City', *The Garden City*, June 1906. In: Jackson, pp. 77-78.

[199] Jackson, p. 76.

[200] Miller (2002), pp. 55.

Parker and Unwin were shocked. To them, the competition created two unacceptable problems. Firstly, it undermined their belief that aesthetic standards should not be subordinated to costs, the exhibition encouraging its competitors to adopt unconventional building methods in the interest of price. Secondly, it reinforced the idea that Letchworth was an ideal location for Londoners to acquire an affordable weekend retreat, thus conflicting with their concept of creating a living, working community.[201] As to the first, Unwin subsequently wrote: 'Many a £150 cottage is an excessively dear cottage … it is one of the curses of our times that this idea of cheapness … acquires an artificial and altogether misleading meaning … [We] may be quite certain that we are on the wrong track … if we do not build [cottages] well'.[202] As to the second, C. B. Purdom, who had joined the Garden City Association as an assistant accountant in November 1902 and became a constant campaigner for the garden city ideal,[203] described the Cheap Cottages Exhibition as Letchworth's 'first considerable architectural blunder … due to the anxiety of the directors to assist in solving the cottage problem'.[204] His opinion had not changed when, in 1913, he wrote: 'there can be no question that the exhibition … did no little harm. It set a range of cheapness from which Garden City has hardly yet recovered, it gave the town the character of a village of tiny weekend cottages not very well built; its curiosities of planning, construction and material, which had nothing in common with the objects of the town, gave the place a name for cranky buildings.'[205]

Despite these problems, Parker and Unwin's influence on the subsequent planning and design of garden suburbs is prominent in Letchworth's layout and house design. The illustration opposite shows the partnership's plan for Bird's Hill. The site was developed as working-class housing adjacent to an industrial estate that was placed immediately to the north-east of the boundary trees and about ¼-½ml

---

[201] Jackson, pp. 76-77.

[202] UN 9/3, Unwin Papers, British Architectural Library, Royal Institute of British Architects, London. In: Miller (2002), p. 56.

[203] Miller (2002), pp. 21 and 213.

[204] C. B. Purdom, *The Garden City: A Study in the Development of a Modern Town*, Temple Press, 1908. In: Lees and Lees, pp. 65-66.

[205] C. B. Purdom, *The Garden City*, Dent, 1913, p. 50-51. In: Miller, p. 56.

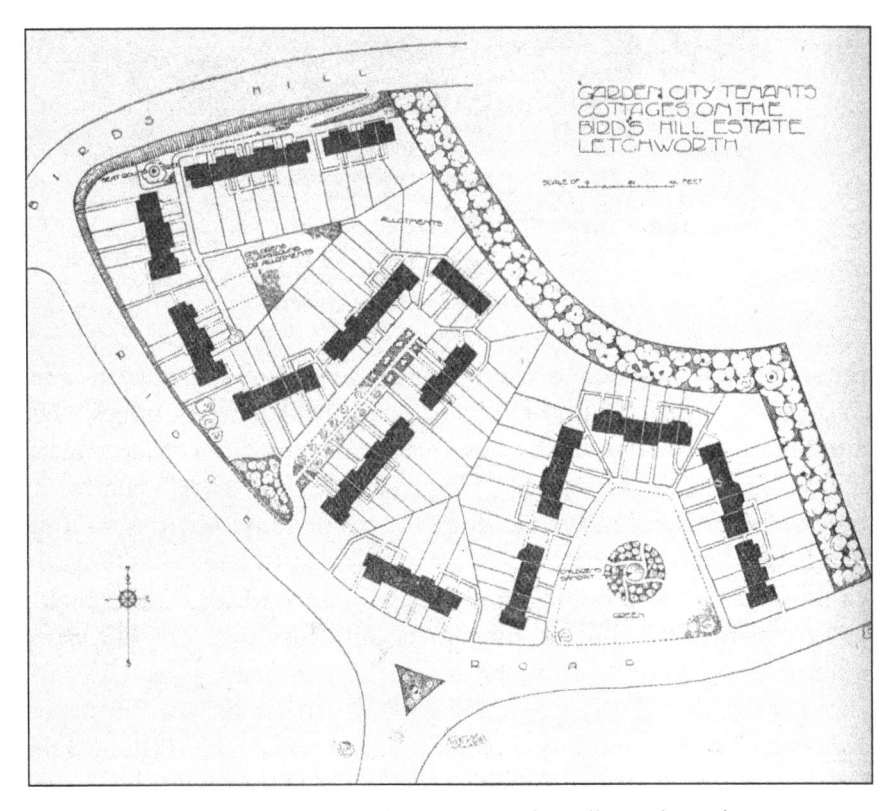

Parker and Unwin's layout for Bird's Hill, Letchworth.

east of Letchworth railway station. The lack of roads on a grid would become a leitmotif for subsequent garden suburb designs by both the partnership and others. The comparison between the design of the houses and their juxtaposition to the road bears obvious comparison with the Progress Estate and other garden suburbs.

Parker and Unwin were, respectively, 38 and 42 years of age when they designed Bird's Hill. They were mature enough to leave their indelible mark on Letchworth, yet young enough for their experiences at Garden City to inform their future careers. Parker's training had focussed relentlessly on design, and his Quaker background[206] fed into its application. G. Faulker Armitage, to whom he was articled after he completed the South Kensington Schools examinations, passed on the influence of William Morris. In 1895, he (Parker) told an audience that

[206] Jackson, p. 22.

*Cottages around the green in
Ridge Road, Bird's Hill, Letchworth.*

the architect should design a house down to its smallest details, in order to create the special quality of unity or what he called 'reposefulness'. His guiding aims in designing a home were to achieve qualities of 'restfulness, unity, comfort and tranquillity'. He rejected the average home for its over-decoration and mechanically-produced patterns. Morris's writings had taught him that simplicity of treatment and adherence to function could create a more ordered and nature-orientated life.[207] He moved to Letchworth in 1904 and lived there until his death in 1947, three years after he had retired from his consultancy at First Garden City Ltd. Between 1910 and 1912 he published 29 articles in *The Craftsman*, and American Arts and Crafts periodical, and was made a Fellow of the Royal Institute of British Architects in 1913. He redesigned the civic centre in Porto, Portugal over six months during 1915 and spent 1917 to 1919 working in São Paulo, Brazil on the Jardim America Garden suburb. He was continuously active during the inter-war years in UK housing design, including many council housing schemes, following which he held a planning consultancy for Wythenshawe, Manchester's garden satellite. Made President of the Town Planning Institute for 1929, he was awarded the Howard Medal for services to town planning by the Town and Country Planning Association (previously the Garden Cities Association) in 1941.[208]

Unwin became Parker's neighbour when they and their families moved to a pair of semi-detached houses the latter had designed in Letchworth Lane in 1904. Unwin's layout plans evolved into what

---

[207] Jackson, pp. 22-23.

[208] Mervyn Miller, 'Parker, (Richard) Barry (1867-1947)', *Oxford Dictionary of National Biography*, Oxford University Press, 2004; online edn, Jan 2011 [http://www.oxforddnb.com/view/article/61684, accessed 14 June 2016].

became town planning. His Socialist beliefs lead him to strive to design housing that fitted into, and was not foisted upon, the landscape with the intention of creating communities where people would live fulfilling lives. Although their partnership, and Unwin's involvement at Letchworth, would last until 1914, Unwin's career path took a new turn in 1906. Their future architectural contribution was to be in creating not Garden Cities, but Garden Suburbs.

Henrietta Barnett and Hampstead Garden Suburb

Henrietta Barnett (née Rowland) was born in Clapham, London on 4 May 1851. Her father was the wealthy businessman Alexander William Rowland whose fortune derived from the family business, the Macassar Oil Company. It manufactured hair oils widely used by the royal family and nobility of England as well as several sovereigns and courts in Europe. The queen's patronage was boldly proclaimed on the double-fronted Macassar Oil and Kalydor warehouse at 20 Hatton Garden.[209] Henrietta's mother, Henrietta Monica Margaretta Ditges, appears to have been born and brought up in Cologne.[210] She died at the age of 32, shortly after giving birth to Henrietta. Alexander continued to raise the family of eight children in comfort at the family home in Clapham and a country house in Kent.

In 1866, Alexander sent Henrietta to a boarding school in Devon run by the Haddon sisters. They were committed to social altruism – the taking of actions with the conscious intention of helping others.[211] Alexander died in 1869, whereupon Henrietta and two of her sisters moved to Bayswater in London's West End. It was here that she met Octavia Hill.

Octavia's father, James Hill, had married Caroline Southwood Smith, the lady who would become her mother, in 1835. He had six

---

[209] T. A. B. Corley, 'Rowland, Alexander (*bap.* 1783, *d.* 1854)', *Oxford Dictionary of National Biography*, Oxford University Press, 2004; online edn, Jan 2008 [http://www.oxforddnb.com/view/article/59286, accessed 12 November 2015].

[210] Seth Koven, 'Barnett , Dame Henrietta Octavia Weston (1851-1936)', *Oxford Dictionary of National Biography*, Oxford University Press, 2004; online edn, Sept 2013 [http://www.oxforddnb.com/view/article/30610, accessed 12 November 2015] and http://www.rowlandgenerations.org/family-trees/, accessed 12 November 2015.

[211] The sisters were the sisters-in-law of James Hinton, the leading and pioneering ear surgeon of his day. Became the first aural surgeon at Guy's in 1863. Was also a controversial philosopher who advocated that the moral centre of gravity should be shifted from self-regard to regard for others. This was perhaps a seductive argument for doing as one likes as long as one persuades oneself that the main object is to give pleasure to others. Unfortunately he took this to include providing sexual satisfaction for all sorts of women. Caroline Haddon, one of the two sisters, confirmed that he was in 'a disturbed sexual state' shortly before his death in 1875. Neil Weir, 'Hinton, James (1822-1875)', *Oxford Dictionary of National Biography*, Oxford University Press, 2004; online edn, May 2006 [http://www.oxforddnb.com/view/article/13354, accessed 12 November 2015].

children from his first two marriages (having been a widower twice) and would have three more by Caroline. Following his bankruptcy in 1840 and subsequent mental collapse, Caroline's father, Dr Thomas Southwood Smith, a pioneer of sanitary reform, provided the family with financial support. He and Caroline shared a desire to see both the use of children as mining labourers and the housing of the urban poor reformed. The latter inspired Octavia whose education was provided solely by her mother, at home.

In 1851, at the age of 13, Octavia joined a co-operative guild for 'distressed gentlewomen' and during the following year took charge of the workroom when the guild started to provide toy-making work for destitute children. In 1853, she became a spare-time copyist for John Ruskin at the Dulwich Picture Gallery and the National Gallery.[212]

A severe shortage of property meant that over the next decade Hill could not find accommodation for her workers so she decided she would have to become a landlord. Ruskin had inherited a substantial sum from his father in 1865 and was thus in a position to finance the purchase of eight dirty and neglected properties in Marylebone for Hill to manage on the understanding that she would achieve a yield of 5% per annum.[213] Any revenue in excess of a 5% yield would be reinvested in the properties for the benefit of the tenants. Thus it was that in the year of Ruskin's inheritance, at the age of 27, Hill began to build a housing business which, by the time she was 36 (in 1874), would encompass fifteen housing schemes with around 3,000 tenants. She was opposed to the municipal provision of housing, believing it to be bureaucratic and impersonal. Concerned with the availability of open spaces for poor people, she would go on to become one of the three founders of the National Trust.

Octavia may well have introduced Henrietta to the writings of John Ruskin and certainly did introduce her to many influential people who sought to improve the condition of London's poor. One of these was Canon Samuel Barnett.

Samuel Barnett had been born in Bristol in 1844 to wealthy parents. His father was a manufacturer of iron bedsteads and his mother came from a merchant family of overseas shippers. He obtained a second-

---

[212] https://en.wikipedia.org/wiki/Octavia_Hill, accessed 20 January 2015.

[213] Hill's obituary, *The Times*, 15 August 1912.

class degree in Law and Modern History from Wadham College, Oxford, in 1865. He became a curate at St. Mary's Bryanston Square in 1867 where he quickly demonstrated his ability as a worker on behalf of Marylebone's poor. His involvement with the Charity Organisation Society began in 1869 where he became influenced by Octavia Hill, one of the Society's founders. She introduced him to one of her 'fellow-workers'[214] – Henrietta Rowland. Samuel and Henrietta married on 28 January 1873.

Later in the same year, Bishop Jackson of London offered Samuel Barnett the parish of St Jude's in Whitechapel. It was, said the Bishop, 'the worst parish in my diocese, inhabited mainly by a criminal population and one which has, I fear, been much corrupted by the dole'.[215]

For about the next 20 years the Barnetts carried on their influential activities in and from Whitechapel. Disraeli's Home Secretary Sir Richard Cross was persuaded to enact an amendment to the Artisans' Dwellings Act after Canon Barnett took him on a tour of slum properties in the East End. They continuously protested to the local authorities about the lax enforcement of sanitary and police regulations.[216] They persuaded Charles Booth of the need for old-age pensions in 1883. In the following year, 1884, Canon Barnett was one of the founders of the East End Dwellings Company whose aim was to 'house the very poor while realising some profit'.[217] Georges Clemenceau[218] designated him one of the three greatest men he had met in England. Samuel and Henrietta Barnett were the kind of people whose numbers, had they been alive today, would have been stored in the iPhones of every Cabinet minister and Opposition front bench spokesperson.

With the passage of time, the Barnetts created a heterogeneous set of young men whose number included brilliant Oxford scholars and self-educated working-men. Settlement Work (as it became known) meant

---

[214] Volunteers who collected rents from tenants of Octavia Hill's properties. Gillian Darley, 'Hill, Octavia (1838–1912)', *Oxford Dictionary of National Biography*, Oxford University Press, 2004; online edn, May 2012. [www.oxforddnb.com/view/article/33873, accessed 2 May 2017].

[215] Gilbert, pp. 40-42.

[216] Gilbert, p. 41.

[217] en.wikipedia.org/wiki/East_End_Dwellings_Company, accessed 12 November 2015.

[218] Georges Clemenceau, Prime Minister of France, 1906-1909 and 1917-1920.

that those who would become influential leaders took their first-hand experience of poverty, and ways of dealing with it that worked, with them.

The Barnetts' lasting memorial was the creation of the Toynbee Hall. Canon Barnett proposed it as the first university settlement on 17 November 1883, at St John's College, Oxford. It would be a permanent institution to carry on their work among the poor and he concluded that reform could not be conducted from the outside; it was essential to 'live within sight of the poor'.

The building opened on Commercial Street in 1884. In Henrietta Barnett's own words,[219] it was:

> built to accommodate the many public-spirited men and women who gathered around us and became fellow-workers once Oxford and Cambridge began sending their young men to help us, our vicarage being too small a house to meet the needs for hospitality.
>
> Toynbee's big reception rooms became the meeting-place of thinkers and workers, of rich and poor, of young and old, of the learned and the ignorant, a veritable 'gathering place of souls' from which many deep friendships arose. To reach the Hall everyone had to travel, the West End eastwards and the East End westwards. They would however only come together if there was an occasion, a class, a lecture, a party, a meeting. Although it was laborious work to create the machinery necessary to effect these introductions, it was well worth while, because 'culture comes by contact'. The good that each class gains from knowledge of and friendship with another is beyond price, and is not yet valued adequately.

In 1888, one Charles Robert Ashbee, a then resident at Toynbee Hall, set up his Guild and School of Handicraft in Essex House on the East End's Mile End Road and, whilst at the People's Palace School in Mile End, a pupil by the name of Frank Baines had joined a boys' club formed by Ashbee and other teachers based at Toynbee Hall. On leaving school in 1892, Baines became apprenticed to Ashbee.[220] We will return to this connection later in this book.

---

[219] Barnett, p. 5.

[220] C. C. Pond, 'Baines, Sir Frank (1877-1933)', *Oxford Dictionary of National Biography*, Oxford University Press, October 2014; online edn, January 2015 [http://www.oxforddnb.com/view/article/60657, accessed 26 November 2014].

Mrs Barnett described the idea that was to become Hampstead Garden Suburb in the introduction to her book about its development:[221] 'If', I said one day to Canon Barnett, 'we could only buy a huge estate and build so that all classes could live in neighbourliness together, the friendships would come about quite naturally, and the artificial efforts to build bridges need not be made'. She and Canon Barnett 'found it absolutely essential for health' to have somewhere to go away from the noise and dirt (of Whitechapel) and towards the end of the 19th century bought a cottage overlooking Hampstead Heath, to which they would later add a convalescent home. Like Octavia Hill, both she and her husband mistrusted local authority housing, believing it was 'too easy and too cheap a remedy'. A reaction to the deprivations of Whitechapel and similar areas of poverty, the Suburb would be home to a mix of classes and provide a range of amenities, thereby alleviating discontent and increasing prosperity.[222]

An extension to what is now London's Northern underground line was sanctioned by Act of Parliament in November 1902. One of its proposed new stations presented a threat to the country around their cottage. Not only would hundreds of people flood out of the station over the nearby Heath; it was also known that Eaton College wished to sell a large tract of land adjacent to the Heath. Were this to be bought by speculative builders, the prospect from the cottage's window would become a view over terraces of brick boxes with slate lids. Mrs Barnett's reaction was: 'There was nothing to do but to enlarge the Heath'.[223]

In September 1904 she read a pamphlet by Raymond Unwin whilst staying away from Whitechapel with a close friend who was seriously ill. This was, she decided, 'the man for my beautiful green golden scheme'.[224] A few weeks later, Lord Brassey[225] introduced them, whereupon Unwin

---

[221] Barnett, p. 5.

[222] Jackson, p. 83.

[223] Cobb and Saunders, p. 3.

[224] Barnett, p. 7.

[225] Thomas Brassey, 1st Earl Brassey, 11 February 1836 - 23 February 1918, educated at Rugby and University College, Oxford. Called to the Bar, Lincoln's Inn, 1864. Liberal MP for Devonport (1865) and subsequently Hastings (1868-86). Raised to the peerage as Baron Brassey in 1886 [en.wikipedia.org/wiki/Thomas_Brassey,_1st_Earl_Brassey, accessed 9 March 2015].

reminded her that he had been among her social service followers, visiting Toynbee Hall whilst at the University of Oxford. He had, at the time, discussed taking Holy Orders with Canon Barnett. When Barnett realised Unwin was more concerned about man's unhappiness than his wickedness, he advised against the idea.[226] 'Both my husband and I recalled him with pleasure'.[227]

In 1905 Henrietta Barnett appointed Parker and Unwin as architects. By March 1906 control of the land had been passed to the Hampstead Garden Suburb Trust and Unwin alone became its architect and surveyor.

Unwin's ethos as a planner (at the time, a descriptor yet to fully enter the architectural vocabulary) was predicated on the considered opinions of Ruskin, Morris, Howard *et al*; small community (village) life comprised a mosaic of social classes and its loss was society's loss. Villages created balanced communities which maintained social cohesion. The rise of industrial production, with its need for large workforces in close or commutable proximity to its factories, was destroying societies. It was the planner's job to rethink how mixed socio-economic communities could be re-created in an industrial age. As he wrote in 1909:[228]

> There is nothing whatsoever in the prejudices of people to justify the large covering of areas with houses of exactly the same size and type ... the growing up of suburbs occupied by any individual class is bad socially, economically and aesthetically. It is due to the wholesale and thoughtless character of town development and it is quite foreign to the traditions of our country; it results very often in bad municipal government and unfair distribution of the burdens of local taxation, misunderstanding and want of trust between different classes of people and in the development and exaggeration of differences of thought and habit; it leads, too, to a dreary monotony of effect which is almost as depressing as it is ugly.

The Trust appointed Edwin Lutyens as Consulting Architect in May 1906, probably on the recommendation of his patron, Alfred

---

[226] Miller (2002), p. 39 and Miller (2010), p. 24.

[227] Barnett, p. 7.

[228] Unwin (1909), p. 294.

Lyttelton,[229] who sat on its Board. Lutyens became a Fellow of the Royal Institute of British Architects in the same year. He appears to have been assiduous in cultivating wealthy clients and building grand houses for them. His greatest claims to fame would, in due course, be his appointment by the Indian Government as architect to design the Secretariat Buildings in Delhi (1913), for his unpaid advice to the Commonwealth War Graves Commission (starting in 1917) and his design of the Cenotaph in London's Whitehall (1919). He was knighted in the 1918 New Year honours list for the first two.[230]

Under the direction of Lutyens, Unwin's plan for a bustling area of shops and community buildings was replaced with a dignified and symmetrical religious and cultural centre with two large churches and a Quaker meeting house. Although Mrs. Barnett may not have been in favour of the change when it was proposed, Unwin felt his duties as site-planner were uppermost and averted her potential clash with Lutyens. In due course she had evidently changed her mind: 'To his sense of symmetry and unerring instinct for true proportion we owe the Central Square, the Church, Free Church, Institute, and surrounding houses, as well as those of both its approaches'.[231] Somewhat similarly, Unwin was to design buildings for Letchworth's Central Square in 1912 in obvious tribute to Sir Christopher Wren. They were never built and

---

[229] Alfred Lyttelton (7 February 1857-5 July 1913), British politician and sportsman. Excelled at cricket (1876-79), football (1876-78), athletics (hammer throwing; 1876), rackets (1877-79) and real tennis (1877-79), arguably the pre-eminent sportsman of his generation and the first man to represent England at both football and cricket. Twelfth and youngest child of George Lyttelton, 4th Baron Lyttelton, by his first wife Mary, daughter of Sir Stephen Glynne, 8th Baronet. Prime Minister Gladstone was an uncle by marriage. Great-uncle of jazz trumpeter Humphrey Lyttelton. After Cambridge, served as legal private secretary to the Attorney General, Sir Henry James. Entered the House of Commons at the 1895 general election as Liberal Unionist Member of Parliament for Warwick and Leamington. Appointed Queen's Counsel in January 1900 and later that year was sent by Colonial Secretary Joseph Chamberlain to South Africa as chairman of the committee planning reconstruction following the Boer War. Served as Secretary of State for the Colonies 1903-05. Supported women's suffrage. en.wikipedia.org/wiki/Alfred_Lyttelton, accessed 28 January 2015.

[230] Gavin Stamp, 'Lutyens, Sir Edwin Landseer (1869-1944)', *Oxford Dictionary of National Biography*, Oxford University Press, 2004; online edn, May 2012 [http://www.oxforddnb.com/view/article/34638, accessed 21 January 2015.

[231] Barnett, p. 7.

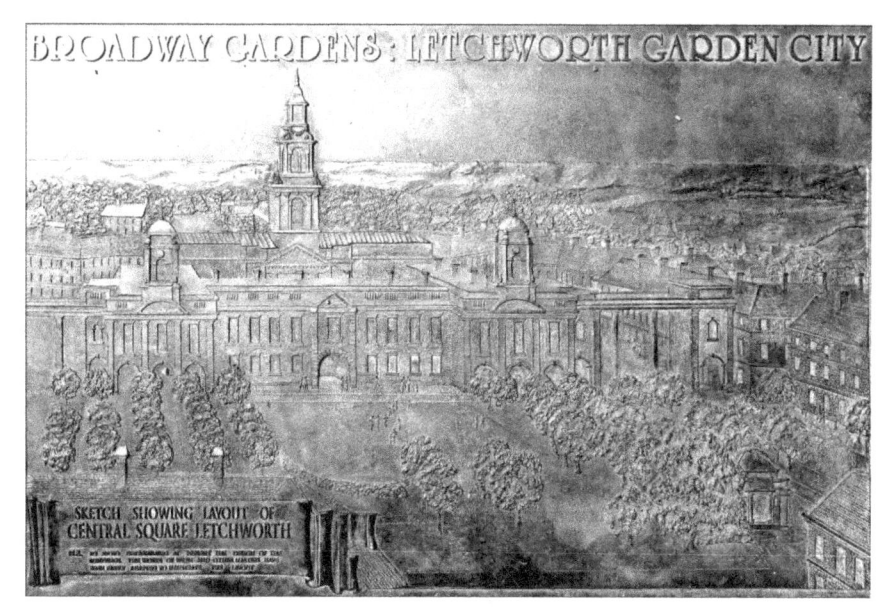

Unwin's conceptual layout for the Central Square, Letchworth.

the only reminder of the plan is a brass plaque at the junction of the Central Square's pathways.[232]

Unwin concluded that Greater London's road system did not require any major highway to be built through the Suburb's site, so arranged for the Hampstead Garden Suburb bill to be introduced in Parliament in February 1906 by Trust Director and Liberal MP, Henry Vivian. At this stage in the story, it is vital to remember that prior to 1909 there was no concept of town planning as we understand it today. Planning laws were in the gift of local authorities, yet they appear to have been ill-equipped to deal with the social changes large-scale industrialisation was creating.

Unwin had known of Vivian and his promotion of co-operative housing since he and Parker had planned New Earswick for Joseph Rowntree in 1902. Vivian had made a name for himself as a left-wing liberal and was convinced by the Garden City movement of the benefits of co-operative housing. The Bill Vivian introduced would lead in due course to the Housing, Town-Planning, &C. Act, 1909. The Hampstead

---

[232] Notwithstanding their differences in character, Unwin cited Lutyens in his 1937 acceptance speech of the Royal Gold Medal as one of the 'distinguished architects I have consulted'. *Journal of the Royal Institute of British Architects*, vol. 44, 3rd series, April 1937, p. 582.

Garden Suburb Act received Royal Assent on 4 August 1906. Its recital incorporated the Trust's aim to 'create for persons of all classes with gardens and open spaces and other special amenities and facilities for persons of the working class and others'. Section (2) provided that the average housing density was to be eight to the acre and that 'in every road in the Garden Suburb (whatever the width of the said road) there shall be between any two houses standing on opposite sides of the road a space of not less than 50 feet free of any buildings except walls fences or gates'.

Crucially, the Act gave the Trust powers to determine the width of roads. Under section 5(1) it could 'form and lay out roads of such width and in such manner and with or without footways riding tracks and grass margins as they may think fit' subject to certain provisos:

A. Any cul-de-sac whose primary purpose was to give access to houses that did not exceed five hundred feet in length was, subject to local authority approval, exempt from their by-laws relating to the width of new streets and footways, subject to its having a minimum width of twenty feet.

B. The Trust would be exempt from regulations as to the construction and maintenance of these roads so long as they were maintained 'to the reasonable satisfaction of the local authority'. However, it could consent to the local authority taking them over.

C. All other roads were to be of a minimum width of 40 feet.

D. If roads were constructed at a width greater than 40 feet, the additional width could be devoted to grass margins, grounds planted with trees or be laid out as gardens. So long as they were maintained 'in good order to the reasonable satisfaction of the local authority' the local authority could only take them over with the consent of the Trust.

E. Save for the provisions of (D), all roads other than cul-de-sacs were to be subject to local authority by-laws.

F. With the Trust's consent, the local authority could take over any road 'when such roads have been made up sewered drained levelled kerbed paved metalled flagged channelled made good and provided with proper means of lighting to the reasonable standard of the local authority notwithstanding that such roads may not be of the full width prescribed by or may not be otherwise in accordance with the by-laws relating to new streets and footways for the time being in force in the district of such local authority'.

G. The Local Government Board was to be appointed to arbitrate if either the Trust or the local authority required the other's consent and it was withheld.

HOW GARDEN SUBURBS CAME TO BE

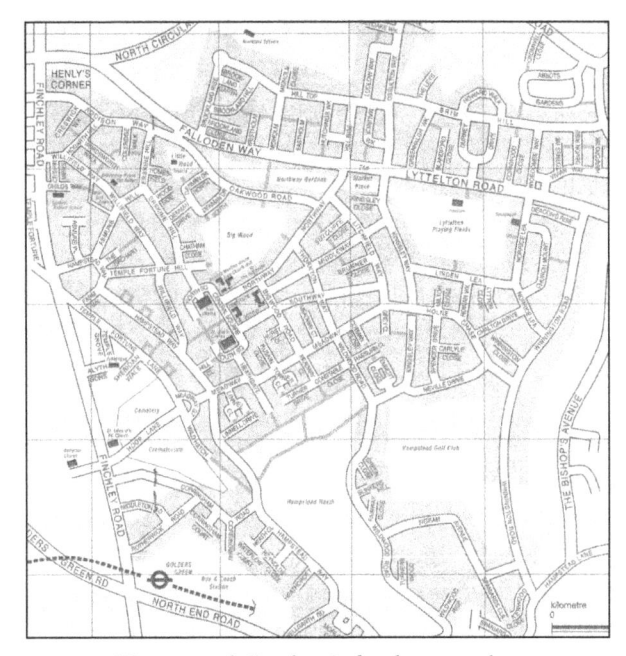

Hampstead Garden Suburb street plan.

The ultimate plan for the Suburb was published in August 1912, by which time the site had grown to 655 acres. The many cul-de-sacs are often joined to other roads by footpaths (shown as grey lines) known locally by their northern English name, ginnels. The street plan demonstrates Unwin's ideas for the formation of communities. The concept of respect for the site is amply demonstrated in this block of houses on Hogarth Hill where, to keep the roofline horizontal

Block of houses on Hogarth Hill.

105

throughout, the vertical distance between the ground and upper-floor window casements gradually increases from left to right, until the cottage at the right-hand end becomes three-storeyed.

Almost certainly due to his experiences in Letchworth, Unwin was responsible for passing every plan submitted by its architect or builder (at this time, an alien procedure, though it has now become standard planning practice). The group of young architects he assembled included (Thomas) Geoffry Lucas who, together with Courtenay Melville Crickmer and Michael Frank Wharton Bunney, would work with Unwin on housing schemes for munitions workers during the First World War.[233]

Whilst Hampstead Garden Suburb grew out of Parker and Unwin's creation at Letchworth, it made no attempt to be self-contained; there was no industry and few shops and services. Unwin moved to it in 1906 and lived there until his death in 1940. Nevertheless the ideas of both Mrs. Barnett and Unwin were based on a belief in the interdependence of architectural and social values. Canon Barnett summed it up: 'How hard it is to make a home of a dwelling exactly like a hundred other dwellings: how often it is the dullness of a street which encourages carelessness of dirt and resort to unhealthy excitement – how, in fact, it is the mean house and the mean street which prepare the way for poverty and vice'.[234] Fifty years later, on the occasion of the Suburb's Golden Jubilee, the combination of its integrated high-quality architecture and roads and open spaces reminiscent of country life caused Sir Nikolaus Pevsner to comment that it was 'the most nearly perfect example of the unique English invention and speciality – the Garden Suburb'.[235]

---

[233] Cobb and Saunders, p. 7.

[234] Cobb and Saunders, p. 8.

[235] Nikolaus Pevsner, 'A Master Plan', *Hampstead Garden Suburb Jubilee 1907-1957 Souvenir Booklet and Programme*. In: Mervyn Miller (2010), p. 30.

Town Planning Reaches the Statute Book: The Housing, Town-Planning, & C. Act, 1909

It will by now be clear to the reader that Raymond Unwin was a (quite possibly *the*) leading individual in the creation of town planning. The Hampstead Garden Suburb Act, 1906, taken through Parliament as a private member's bill by the Liberal MP Henry Vivian, was the first piece of legislation in Great Britain to address site layout. Unwin was closely involved with its drafting, because the Act's purpose was to allow him to build the Suburb's roads in a manner that otherwise would have offended existing by-laws governing the area. Thus began his decade-long transition from a partner in a successful architectural practice to a senior post in the civil service. He would be at the heart of town planning policy by the time the Government took the decision to build the Progress Estate as a wartime measure. To understand this, we need to look at the passage of legislative proposals that led to the Housing, Town Planning, &c. Act, 1909.

As we have seen, the story of housing legislation in the second half of the 19th century was driven by the need to improve public health and to bring some semblance of order to the suburbs as the demand for labour in factories created a need for large populations of workers to live within commuting distance of their locations. There was, however, the parallel problem – a rural housing shortage. By 1905, only four councils in the entire country had had plans to alleviate local housing shortages approved by the Local Government Board under the Housing of the Working Classes Act, 1890.[236] The problem was exacerbated by economics which were probably unforeseeable when this legislation was passed. Between 1895 and 1914, building costs increased by about a quarter,[237] whilst between 1900 and 1914 weekly wages for manual workers rose by only 6%.[238] For landowners, who at this time provided cottages for virtually all their workers, the rent that could be afforded did not justify the capital outlay and the same rationale stopped private sector builders and their investor clientele from filling the void.

---

[236] Swenarton (1981), p. 31.

[237] Maiwald's index of building costs 1845-1938. In: Powell, p. 92.

[238] Robert Price and George Sayers Bain, *The Labour Force*. In: Halsey p. 180.

Simultaneously, political change was also underway. The percentage of the population registered to vote at general elections increased from 5% to 18% between 1850 and 1910[239] as the Reform Act, 1867 and then, as noted earlier, the Representation of the People Act, 1884 and the Redistribution of Seats Act, 1885 came into effect.[240] The Independent Labour Party, formed in 1893, fielded 78 candidates at the 1910 general election and won 40 seats, an increase of ten in their parliamentary representation following the 1906 election.[241]

Rural housing was thus a live political issue in the decades either side of the turn of the century. In 1904, Dr. Frederick Mackarness and Sir Walter Foster, Liberal MPs, introduced 'a Bill to amend the Housing of the Working Classes Acts and to facilitate the buildings of houses for the working classes in rural districts'. It did not achieve a second reading. Foster introduced it again in 1908 and it was referred to a standing committee whose report was that it should be withdrawn. More radical bills had been introduced every year since 1901, initially by the Liberal MPs Dr. Thomas Macnamara and John Burns. Charles Bowerman, Independent Labour Party MP for Deptford and a regular parliamentary proponent of working-class interests, took up the cause once a year from 1906 to 1909. In May 1908 John Burns, now the Liberal government's President of the Local Government Board, introduced a Bill to amend the law relating to the housing of the working classes and to provide for town planning schemes. He told the House its object was:

> To provide a domestic condition for the people in which their physical health, their morals, their character, and their whole social condition would be improved; ... to secure the home healthy, the house beautiful, the town pleasing, the city dignified, and the suburb salubrious ...'

He added:

[239] Neil Johnston, *The History of the Parliamentary Franchise*, Research Paper 13/14, House of Commons Library, 2013, p. 4. researchbriefings.parliament.uk/ResearchBriefing/Summary/RP13-14, accessed 21 June 2016.

[240] The huge increase to 48% would not come about until the Representation of the People Act 1918 created universal male suffrage and the first female suffrage (Neil Johnston, *ibid.*, p. 44).

[241] David Butler, *Electors and Elected*. In: Halsey p. 302.

No one could go to Port Sunlight, or Earswick, ...without seeing the enormous schemes which had, during the last ten years, been undertaken ... What a few public-spirited owners, companies and corporations had done, without loss to themselves ... the Bill [will] enable a number of other people and associations to accomplish. ... They could see at Ealing, at Hampstead Garden Suburb, and at a number of other places, examples of what prescience, outlook and the development of estates according to a coherent and progressive plan were capable of doing.[242]

It had a second reading, was referred to a standing committee and, yet again, dropped at their behest. Walter Long, a long-standing MP with legislative experience in the housing arena who held seats for both the Conservatives and Irish Unionists and had been President of the Local Government Board from 1900 to 1905,[243] considered it to be so tortuous as to have left him with an 'appalling headache'. A revised Bill was re-presented in 1909 'to amend the law relating to housing of the working classes, to provide for the making of town planning schemes, and to make further provision for the appointment of medical officers and the establishment of public health and housing committees'. Burns had to fight hard for its proposed measures and it finally received Royal Assent on 3 December as the Housing, Town Planning, &c. Act, 1909.[244]

Part I of the Act dealt with Housing of the Working Classes,[245] Part II with Town Planning and Part III with County Medical Officers, County Public Health and Housing Committees &c. Its chief provisions were to:

- Outlaw back-to-back housing everywhere other than for previously approved developments.

[242] Swenarton (1981), p. 39. References to Port Sunlight and Ealing are to the estate built by William Lever in Cheshire exclusively for Lever Bros. employees, and Brentham Garden Suburb, respectively.

[243] en.wikipedia.org/wiki/Walter_Long,_1st_Viscount_Long#Political_career.2C_1880. E2.80.931911, accessed 21 June 2016.

[244] Gauldie, pp. 304-305.

[245] Under Section 76(1) of the Act, Part I, together with the Housing of the Working Classes Acts 1890-1903, may be cited collectively as the Housing of the Working Classes Acts 1890-1909. https://archive.org/details/housingacts00grea, accessed 5 July 2016.

- Take from landowners their right to develop subject only to local by-laws, which had the effect of also protecting them from poor-quality development on adjacent land.
- Bring the road widths permitted in the Hampstead Garden Suburb Act 1906 into general UK legislation.
- Provide for a systematic survey of rural housing to be obligatory.
- Grant local authorities additional powers to compulsorily purchase land for housing.
- Lower interest rates on Public Works loans.
- Allow local authorities to condemn or repair poor-quality housing.
- Empower the Local Government Board, upon receipt of a complaint, to compel local authorities to act if they failed to exercise their powers.[246]

The Act has been described as a minimal response by the Local Government Board to the demands for housing reform, and especially rural housing reform,[247] yet it may have been the best that, politically, was achievable. Firstly, the Conservative-dominated House of Lords was adept at overturning proposed Liberal legislation it did not like.[248] Secondly, the Liberal government that had won 400 out of 670 seats at the 1906 general election would see their majority wiped out on 14 January 1910, just six weeks after the Act received Royal Assent, whereupon their minority administration would become dependent on the votes of Labour and Irish Nationalist MPs to command a majority in the Commons.[249] Whatever its perceived faults, the Act's great achievement was to give the Local Government Board power to prod local authorities into action. Whereas between 1890 and 1908, 67 local authority schemes received sanctions for Public Works loans for housebuilding (3.7 per annum), the number increased between 1909

---

[246] Burnett, p. 138, Jackson, p. 101 and Anthony Sutcliffe, *Britain's first town planning act: a review of the 1909 achievement*. In: Town Planning Review, vol. 59 no. 3, July 1988, pp. 289-303.

[247] Swenarton (1981), p. 32.

[248] Lee, p. 40.

[249] Lee, p. 60.

and 1914 to 112 (22.4 per annum). The number of houses so financed rose from 78 in 1910 to 2,465 in 1914.[250]

The Act also removed from local authorities the requirement to sell or dispose of any lands or dwellings acquired or constructed by them. Although the Housing of the Working Classes Act, 1890 had empowered them to acquire land and erect houses, they were simultaneously obliged to sell their developments within ten years. This was a reflection, at the time, of the Conservative government's view that the state should not infringe on what was seen as an economic activity best carried out by the private sector. Opinion had changed in the ensuing two decades, courtesy of, for example, Booth's poverty maps, the work of social activists such as Octavia Hill and Samuel and Henrietta Barnett and the realisation that public health and poor housing had been instrumental in creating the substandard health of so many volunteering for military service during the Boer War. The enfranchisement of large numbers of the working classes and the consequent increase in the Left's parliamentary representation (Labour Party MPs as well as a number of Liberals who agreed with them on many social issues) had changed the political mood for all time. The principle of local authority housing, now on the statute book, would be seen after the First World War had ended – history that is beyond the remit of this book, although described in detail in many of the books listed in the bibliography.

---

[250] Local Government Board, Report (1913-14), p. xxxvii and xxxlx. In: Gauldie, p. 306.

Raymond Unwin Heads for Whitehall

Unwin and his family had moved to Wyldes Farm, Hampstead Heath, in 1907 and he would live there until his death in 1947. The original intention was to stay for the two years it was expected for Barry Parker to complete the houses their families would live in at Letchworth. However, the two partners decided to split the practice and work from the two sites. Wyldes comprised a 17th-century house, the family home, and a huge barn that became the office of his architectural practice where anything up to 40 architects, some of whom had come with him from Letchworth, worked, along with trainees, draughtsmen and assistants.[251]

There can be little doubt that Unwin's training as an engineer combined with his political views informed his contribution to the output of the Parker and Unwin partnership. In 1906 – the same year as Alexander Harvey had published *The Model Village and its Cottages: Bournville*, and in it described how, at a cost of £135, a cottage economically built could deliver its own uncluttered attractiveness[252] – Unwin had penned an article *Cottage Building in [Letchworth] Garden City*, recommending that buildings be arranged around greens or squares: 'Where groups of cottages must be kept absolutely simple, good results will depend largely on the arrangement of them'.[253]

It was at Wyldes that Unwin wrote *Town Planning in Practice* between 1908 and 1909. It was published in the latter year. This was the period during which the legislation that became the 1909 Act, discussed in the previous chapter, was making its way through Parliament. The book placed him at the forefront of the Town Planning movement.[254] It summarised everything he had learned in his career to date and was, in his opinion, the architectural profession's route to improving the lot of the working classes.

The Royal Institute of British Architects seems to have decided to claim the planning space as their own. They mounted the Town

---

[251] Jackson, p. 94

[252] Harvey, pp. 16-19.

[253] Unwin, 'Cottage Building in Garden City' *The Garden City*, News Series, vol. 1 no. 5 (June 1906), pp. 107-111. In: Swenarton (1981), p. 25.

[254] Jackson, pp. 101-109.

An imaginary irregular town from
Town Planning in Practice.

Planning Exhibition and Conference in London in October 1910 (following previous conferences held in America, Berlin and Vienna)[255] and attracted 2,000 architects and delegates, principally from Germany, America and Britain. Unwin, who had been appointed to its Exhibition Committee, presented his paper *City Development Plan*, advocating the growth of local centres of interest in place of zoning that would allow every part of the city to develop its own natural character. He drew this concept from French, German and Austrian cities where history, variety and tradition had determined their size and form.[256] He, like Charles Mulford Robinson,[257] an earlier speaker, stressed the importance of designing roads to fulfil their required function. A 50-foot by-law road cost three times as much as a properly finished carriage drive with a grass margin which, in many cases, was adequate.[258] Delegates visited Bournville and Hampstead Garden Suburb, Unwin himself leading the latter tour. At the age of 47, his international reputation was becoming established.

---

[255] *Town Planning Review*, vol. 1 no. 3, October 1910, p. 179.

[256] Jackson, p. 112.

[257] Charles Mulford Robinson (1869-1917), American journalist and writer, pioneer of urban planning, first Professor for Civic Design at the University of Illinois, preceded only by Harvard in offering a course on Urban Design. en.wikipedia.org/wiki/Charles_Mulford_Robinson, accessed 28 June 2016.

[258] *Town Planning Review*, vol. 1 no. 3, October 1910, p. 186.

Unwin's involvement in the Conference's organisation, which was by all accounts a great success, was rewarded when the RIBA awarded him a Fellowship and appointed him to the Town Planning Committee it had formed in 1907. The Institute also selected him as one of its three delegates to the Third National Conference and American City Planning Exhibition in Philadelphia in the spring of 1911. The other two were the architect Thomas Adams, Manager of Letchworth Garden City from 1903 to 1906 and, before that, Secretary to the Garden City Association, and T. H. Mawson.[259] A successful lecture tour followed the Conference and, upon his return to England, Unwin accepted an invitation to become lecturer in town planning at Birmingham University, a faculty newly endowed by George Cadbury at a fee of £400 per annum.[260]

In 1911, E. G. Bentley, LL.B. and S. Pointon Taylor, ARIBA (both members of the National Housing Council) published their book *A Practical Guide in the Preparation of Town Planning Schemes* with a foreword by Raymond Unwin in which he hints at the unavoidable complications inherent in town planning (the need for lawyers and architects to co-operate) and summarises his ambitions for this new professional skill:[261]

> The collaboration of a lawyer and an architect to produce a book on the preparation of Town-Planning schemes is peculiarly appropriate. The point of view is so entirely different, that each can contribute much that the other could hardly expect to know. The man of action in making the plan of a scheme is dependent on the man of law to tell him what he may and may not do, while the latter is dependent on the former to know what it is desirable should be done and how the doing of it may be facilitated or hindered, to tell

---

[259] Thomas Hayton Mawson (1861-1933), landscape architect, designed gardens and town planning schemes in America (1905-14) and Prussia, as well as Paris and The Hague. Author of *Civic Art* (1911) which discussed the principles of town planning. Non-conformist and ardent Liberal. Honorary member of the RIBA (1903). President of the Town Planning Institute (1923). Harriet Jordan, 'Mawson, Thomas Hayton (1861-1933)', rev. *Oxford Dictionary of National Biography*, Oxford University Press, 2004; online edn, Jan 2010 [http://www.oxforddnb.com/view/article/37748, accessed 28 June 2016].

[260] Jackson, p. 114.

[261] Pub: George Philip & Son, London. Available digitally at www.archive.org/details/housingtownplann00bent, accessed 21 June 2016.

HOW GARDEN SUBURBS CAME TO BE

him, in fact, just the points on which legal guidance would be valuable. The advantage of this combination will be apparent to all readers of the useful little volume which has resulted from it.

'Town Planning' has a prosaic sound, but the words stand for a movement which has, perhaps, a more direct bearing on the life and happiness of great masses of the people than any other single movement of our time. The relative proportion of people who dwell in cities to those who dwell in country villages has been rapidly growing, and while, as a result, much of the beauty of our old towns has been destroyed, little has been done to secure even a decent standard of health and comfort, much less to create any beauty in the new urban areas which have been developed to accommodate this rapidly-increasing population.

Town Planning simply represents the attempt of the community to control town development with a view to providing health, convenience and beauty. There have, in the past, been times when the City as the centre, has had predominating importance. Great and beautiful cities like Athens or Venice have resulted. They were the expression of what was best in the life of their citizens, and were planned to minister to its convenience and to enhance its glory. It is somewhat remarkable that in spite of the vast development of scientific organisation as an important element of industrial life throughout the last century, we should have failed entirely to apply this organisation to our city development.

We have allowed our towns to grow in such a haphazard manner that we find the banks of our canals and the margins of our railway sidings crowded with rows of cottages, while the materials of our industry, for want of immediate access to these very canals and sidings, have to be carted long distances at great expense and often with much resulting congestion of traffic. Town Planning when fully carried out, means the reservation for industrial uses of the areas most valuable for the purpose by reason of having immediate access to rail, road or water conveniences. It means arranging for the most convenient communication by road or railway between these industrial regions and the most healthy and attractive areas, which again would be reserved and most carefully laid out for residential purposes. It also means providing the most convenient means of access possible between both these areas and the great centres of exchange, of wholesale and retail business, all which would enormously add to the efficiency of the population, facilitating their industrial activities and rendering their dwellings more healthy and attractive.

The movement which has brought into being Mr. Burns' Town Planning

Act, and which is seeking to find through that Act the means of realizing its aims, indicates a great development of the civic spirit; and if this continues to grow it is not too much to say that Town Planning will prove to be the first step in the creation of a new type of beautiful cities expressing what is best in modern life.

As is clear from the plans for New Earswick and Letchworth, the Hampstead Garden Suburb Act, the 1909 Act and his speech at the 1910 Conference, Unwin saw the rethinking of roads as critical to the development of high-quality working-class housing. The difference between the first two developments and Hampstead was that the local authorities for these areas had not adopted by-laws governing roads, so he and Parker were free to build the roads they wanted. Hampstead was different, because it had been in the Metropolis since 1844. It was thus subject to London's by-laws and these included minimum road widths. The only way Unwin could build the roads he wanted was to have the law changed. Hampstead's Act achieved that for Hampstead but nowhere else. These regulations applied nationally when the 1909 Act was passed.

The remaining issue was one of economics. Apart from the work of a few garden city and garden suburb planners, developers as a whole had been building suburbs on grids of by-law roads with high-density housing in and around London since 1844.[262] Elsewhere, local authority areas that had promoted their own Acts of Parliament since 1877 were required to build new streets over 100 feet in length to a width of at least 36 feet.[263] The task of Unwin and like-minded planners was to demonstrate that the opportunities planners were offered by the 1909 Act were economic.

To this end, Unwin published *Nothing Gained by Overcrowding!* in 1912.[264] Its subtitle was: *How the Garden City type of development may benefit both owner and occupier*. The introductory paragraphs remind the reader of the garden city's principle of organic development.

---

[262] The Metropolitan Building Act 1844 required new roads in the metropolis to be 40 feet wide or as wide as the highest building along them was tall, whichever was the greater. John Nelson Tarn, *op.cit.* p. 8.

[263] Local Government Board, model by-laws, 1877. In: Burnett, p. 159.

[264] Unwin (1912).

As a town grows, it becomes surrounded by 'a federation of groups constantly clustering around new subsidiary centres, each group limited to a size that can effectively keep in touch with and be controlled from the subsidiary centre, and through that centre have connection with the original and main centre of the federated area'. Satisfactory environments will not be created by allowing towns 'to swallow up and obliterate the country all round, like the spreading of flood water over a shallow valley'.

Most of the pamphlet (it ran to just 23 pages) was devoted to explaining why garden city/suburb housing to lower densities than typical by-law housing was an economic option.

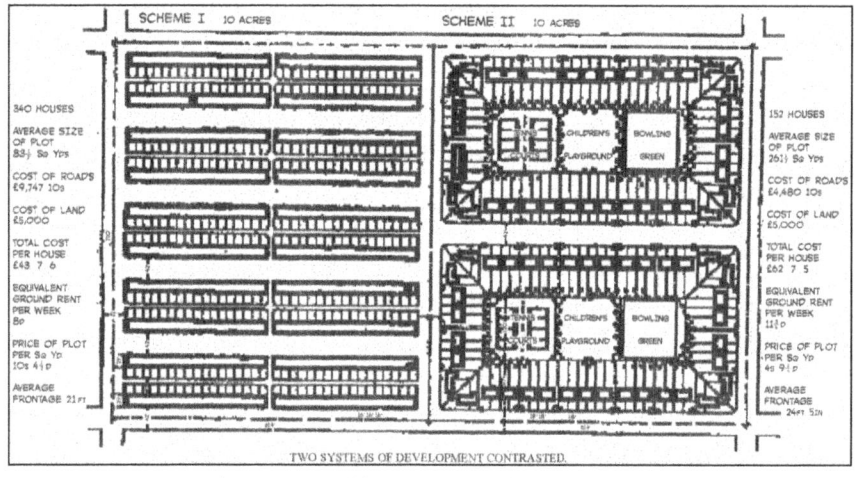

Nothing Gained by Overcrowding! *Diagram I.*

This diagram compares ten acres of by-law housing with a similar area of Garden City housing. In each case, the capital outlay (land, sewers, roads and housebuilding costs) is expected to return 4% per annum. Given a common cost of land of £500 per acre, by-law development provides 340 homes with plots of 83½ square yards at a ground rent of 8d. per week and garden city-style development 152, each with 261½-square yard plots at 11¾d. per week. The major saving is in the cost of roads and the argument is that a 47% increase in rent (from 8d. to 11¾d.) provides the homeowner with a plot that is 213% larger. A second example, with land at £300 per acre, increases rents from 8d. to 9½d. (19% more) and plot size from 98 to 398 square yards

(306% larger). A further example describes how a landowner who has discovered coal under his land can develop garden city-style housing to accommodate the people needed to exploit the resource without reducing his absolute profit if he is willing to dispose of sufficient acreage.

Unwin's calculations were based on two presumptions that were arguably problematic. Firstly, not all members of the working classes had the income to afford increased rents. Thus, pre-1914 garden cities and suburbs rarely housed the lowest wage earners and their families. Governments resisted state-subsidised housing, hoping instead that higher wage earners would move into better accommodation, thereby vacating their less desirable homes which would then become available to the lowest earners.[265] Secondly, it presumed landowners would not attempt to squeeze the last ounce of profit from their land were they to be offered the financial opportunity of speculative housing development.

The reality is that Unwin and other like-minded people were, in their time, the flag-bearers of social reform stretching back to the mid-1800s. Unwin's publication was a signpost along this road and remained oft-quoted.

In February 1912 Walter Runciman, then President of the Board of Agriculture, appointed Raymond Unwin and Cecil Harmsworth, Chairman of the Garden Cities and Town Planning Association, to a committee charged with reporting on buildings for smallholdings. Its findings, published in March 1913, led to the Board launching a major cottage-building programme the following autumn. It reflected Unwin's previously expressed views such as the importance of aspect, ventilation and the availability of light in the most-used rooms.[266] It reiterated his and Barry Parker's 1905 view, also held by the vast majority of architects working in the field of working-class housing, that a parlour, undeniably desired by more or less all tenants, should only be provided 'where economy is a less urgent consideration'.[267]

John Burns, the Liberal MP who had steered the Housing, Town Planning, &c. Act, 1909 through Parliament, was transferred by Prime

---

[265] Swenarton (1981), pp. 40-42.

[266] Swenarton (1981), p. 42.

[267] B. Parker and R. Unwin, 'The cheap cottage: What is really needed'. In: *The Garden* City, vol. 1 no. 4, July 1905 pp. 55-58. In: Swenarton (1981), p. 42.

Minister Asquith from President of the Local Government Board to the Board of Trade on 12 February 1914. His skill was as an administrator rather than a legislator and the Board needed someone to bed down the radical legislation put on the statute book by his predecessors, Winston Churchill and Lloyd George.[268] Burns had always thought there were too few skilled town planners to extend the new competence very far beyond a narrow architectural remit, but when he was replaced by the distinctly left-of-centre Liberal Herbert Samuel,[269] who already had good relations with the Town Planning Institute, the door opened for planners to move into government.[270] Thomas Adams, one-time occasional nemesis of Unwin's at Letchworth, had been appointed Town Planning Assistant to the Local Government Board in 1910[271] with responsibility for implementing the 1909 Act, whereupon he had qualified as a surveyor and guided the emerging profession through its early years. In April 1914 George Pepler was appointed by Samuel to assist Adams with the administrative work.[272] Pepler, by profession a surveyor and town planner, had joined the Garden City Association by 1910 and had been actively advocating the garden city concept and the powers local authorities had been granted under the 1909 Act.[273] Unwin and Pepler had formed a friendship,[274] quite probably through the Association and their shared professional convictions.

Adams left the Board in September 1914 to take up a similar post with the Canadian Government, whereupon Pepler was promoted to

---

[268] Kenneth D. Brown, 'Burns, John Elliot (1858-1943)', *Oxford Dictionary of National Biography*, Oxford University Press, 2004; online edn, April 2016 [http://www.oxforddnb.com/view/article/32194, accessed 28 June 2016].

[269] Bernard Wasserstein, 'Samuel, Herbert Louis, first Viscount Samuel (1870-1963)', *Oxford Dictionary of National Biography*, Oxford University Press, 2004; online edn, May 2011 [http://www.oxforddnb.com/view/article/35928, accessed 28 June 2016].

[270] Jackson, p. 121.

[271] Michael Simpson, 'Adams, Thomas (1871-1940)', *Oxford Dictionary of National Biography*, Oxford University Press, 2004 [http://www.oxforddnb.com/view/article/63125, accessed 22 June 2016].

[272] Jackson, p. 121.

[273] F. J. Osborn, 'Pepler, Sir George Lionel (1882-1959)', rev. Catherine Gordon, *Oxford Dictionary of National Biography*, Oxford University Press, 2004 [http://www.oxforddnb.com/view/article/35469, accessed 29 June 2016].

[274] Jackson, p. 121.

Chief Technical Planning Officer. Samuel's appointment of Unwin as Town Planning Inspector to assist him was announced on 11 December 1914.[275]

Unwin had swapped a lucrative private practice for a civil service salary of £800 a year.[276] A relative, Freda White, wrote that 'he was willing to give endless pains to gaining a small advance, if it was in the right direction ... because he knew that if nobody who knew and cared for reform in housing was in the civil service, that absolutely nothing would be done'.[277] Another biographer has noted that 'after the passing of the 1909 Act, his chief ambition became to create a national planning framework for imaginative, low-density housing [based on his] pamphlet *Nothing Gained by Overcrowding!*'.[278]

Parker and Unwin formally dissolved their partnership in May 1915 although their professional and family friendships endured. Their ambition to design housing which fostered a sense of community was evident from at least the early days of Letchworth. Thereafter, their joint contribution to Britain's housing was, undoubtedly, the promotion of garden suburbs. At least eighteen were constructed between 1906 and 1915 and one, other or both as a partnership had input into at least ten of them.[279] As the story of the Estate moves on, it is fitting to recall extracts from the paper Unwin presented at the Royal Institute of British Architects' International Congress in 1906, describing how the design of towns should be from the site upwards:

> It is important, first of all, to prepare a contour plan of the ground; it will usually suffice if the contour lines represent five feet variation in level. It is impossible properly to lay out the roads to the best advantage without such a plan. To some owners the cost of this may seem an extravagance, but such cost may be saved many times over in one of the roads by its direction being

---

[275] *Municipal Journal*, vol. xxiii (11 December 1914), p. 1343. In: Swenarton (1981), p. 54.

[276] Jackson, pp. 121-2.

[277] Sir Raymond Unwin Collection, Department of Town and Country Planning, University of Manchester, Freda White notes, pp. 2-3. In: Jackson, p. 121.

[278] Andrew Saint, 'Unwin, Sir Raymond (1863-1940)', *Oxford Dictionary of National Biography*, Oxford University Press, 2004; online edn, Jan 2008 [http://www.oxforddnb.com/view/article/36613, accessed 29 June 2016].

[279] Analysis derived from Sarah Rutherford, *Garden Cities*, Shire Publications, 2014.

more thoroughly adapted to the contour. A survey should then be made of all the trees and other features on the estate that may be worth preservation. The cutting down of fine trees may in some rare cases be justified where they would stand in the way of some necessary lines of development. On the other hand, where the plan can be made to work in the existing trees as features, the cutting of them down becomes a positive crime, for the decoration they can afford can only be reproduced after many generations. It is even possible at times to make effective use for street or garden decoration of well-grown existing hedgerows. Anything, in fact, in a suburban district that will redeem or break the bare naked newness which for the first twenty or thirty years generally characterises such a district should be seized upon and made the most of. Not only must the site be studied for its characteristics, but the direction of the roads … should also be studied on the site rather than in the office. The plan, in fact, should be largely made in the fields and committed to paper afterwards.[280]

---

[280] Unwin (1908), p. 420.

Charles Robert Ashbee and Frank Baines

Charles Robert Ashbee (1863-1942) grew up in the family home in Bloomsbury whilst his father's wealth as a merchant rose. He, Charles, read History at King's College, Cambridge where he met the Socialist and homosexual Edward Carpenter during the latter's visit to the university city for a few days in July 1886. When Carpenter returned to his home in Millthorpe – a village less than ten miles south of Sheffield where Raymond Unwin began to attend Edward Carpenter's Sheffield Socialist Society in March 1886 – he wrote to 'Dear Charlie', inviting him to visit him at Millthorpe at the end of August.[281] He did. Their friendship helped Ashbee come to terms with his own sexual proclivities and whilst on the visit he made Unwin's acquaintance at the Society's meetings.

Being good at drawing, Ashbee developed an interest in art and a study of Ruskin's writings linked this to his social concerns. He had decided to train as an architect and, in 1886, became articled to George Frederick Bodley. Having fallen out badly with his father over his decision to go to Cambridge – he would give him £1,000 to finish his precious education and that was the last penny he was to expect[282] – he chose to live not at home but at Toynbee Hall, the settlement house set up by Canon Samuel and Henrietta Barnett, in London's East End.

We have seen that Bodley was in the chronological line of architects that ran unbroken from Ruskin's time, through Morris to the end of the 19th century. William Bidlake, William Alexander Harvey's architectural tutor, had been employed by Bodley and Garner (the partnership Bodley formed for health reasons)[283] from 1885-6. Raymond Unwin and Ashbee were both born in 1863; Carpenter was nineteen years their senior and his biographer states that Ashbee was amongst 'the Cambridge elite that were attracted to [the Sheffield

---

[281] Crawford, pp. 21 and 23.

[282] Felicity Ashbee, p. 16.

[283] Michael Hall, 'Bodley, George Frederick (1827-1907)', *Oxford Dictionary of National Biography,* Oxford University Press, 2004; online edn, Jan 2016 [http://www.oxforddnb.com/view/article/31944, accessed 29 June 2016].

Socialist Society]'.²⁸⁴ Whilst it is not possible to conclude, on the basis of the research for this book, whether Ashbee was a major influence on Unwin or vice versa, the extent to which there was a chain of not dissimilarly thinking social reformers, architects and (in due course) town planners from Ruskin's time right through to the beginning of the 20th century would seem incontrovertible.

Residents at Toynbee Hall were expected to do some educational or social work in the East End. This, in Ashbee's case, led him to open the Guild and School of Handicraft in Commercial Street, next door to Toynbee Hall, on 23 June 1888. His somewhat undefined notion 'was that the men in the workshop should be the teachers in the school, and that the pupils in the school should be drafted into the workshop as it grew in strength and certainty'.²⁸⁵ The organisation moved to Essex House at 401, Mile End Road in 1891. Although the Guild prospered, the School was closed in 1895; it is the latter that causes the enterprise to be part of the story told here. Of the 576 pupils it taught during its nine years of operation, nineteen were architects or architects' pupils. One of these was Frank Baines.

Ashbee encouraged his clientele to award decorative commissions to the Guild. Most of his buildings were in Chelsea, where, by the dawn

72-75 Cheyne Walk, Chelsea.

²⁸⁴ Chushichi Tsuzuki, 'Carpenter, Edward (1844-1929)', *Oxford Dictionary of National Biography*, Oxford University Press, 2004; online edn, Sept 2012 [http://www.oxforddnb.com/view/article/32300, accessed 29 June 2016].

²⁸⁵ Charles Robert Ashbee, p. 2.

of the 20th century, he lived. His houses were designed to bring a sense of the urban village to the city with regular references to old London and the illusion of piecemeal development.[286] Unfortunately, nearly all were either destroyed by enemy action during the Second World War or demolished during post-war redevelopment. He designed the four houses in the photograph on page 123 in 1897.[287]

Frank Baines (1877-1933) was born at 1, Maria Terrace, Stepney on 7 December 1877,[288] just ¾ mile west of Ashbee's Guild and School of Handicraft and 1½ miles east of Toynbee Hall. He studied at the People's Palace School, Mile End (now the Queens' Building, part of the University of London) and, whilst there, joined the Boys' Club that Ashbee and others had set up at the Hall. In his final year, 1892, he was awarded the Governors' Prize for free-hand drawing and mathematics. Upon leaving, as was apparently not uncommon for pupils from his school,[289] he became apprenticed to Ashbee.

Ashbee and other like-minded contemporaries were appalled by the actual and threatened destruction they witnessed as the City's charms gave way to industrialisation. Spurred on by the demolition of a 16th-century hunting lodge in Bow to make way for a modern school building, he founded the Survey of the Memorials of Greater London in 1894. Researchers used standardised forms to provide information, thereby minimising emotional input to their selection.[290] Although Baines left Ashbee in February 1895, about a year before the Survey published its first monograph (a study of the 17th-century Trinity almshouses on Mile End Road that were threatened with demolition), he must surely have known about the study whether or not he was a member of its research team.

Baines left Ashbee to join the Office of Works as an assistant

---

[286] *Building Design*, 23 January 1981, p. 2.

[287] Crawford, p. 246.

[288] C. C. Pond, 'Baines, Sir Frank (1877-1933)', *Oxford Dictionary of National Biography*, Oxford University Press, October 2014; online edn, Jan 2015 [http://www.oxforddnb.com/view/article/60657, accessed 5 July 2016].

[289] Alan Crawford, p. 37.

[290] Thurley, p. 59.

Investiture group in City Levée dress civil uniform at the Investiture of the Prince of Wales at Caernarfon Castle in 1911. Frank Baines is second from the left.

draughtsman in the royal palaces section[291] at 15/- per week. The Office always carried a large pool of draughtsmen who, technically, were employed on a temporary basis. In reality, these people were the group from which individuals were invited, through a process of selected competition, to apply for the post of Assistant Architect;[292] they often remained in the Office's employ for many years.[293] Thus, in 1911, Baines was promoted to Assistant Architect, second-class, and was made a Member of the Victorian Order for his work at Caernarfon Castle in connection with the Investiture of the Prince of Wales in July of that year.[294]

[291] Thurley, p. 86. The Office of Works Staff List, 1914-15, p. 10, to which the author refers could not be found by the staff of Historic England, the successor organisation of English Heritage Archives in July 2016.

[292] Port, p. 77.

[293] Parliamentary Papers 1914 [Cd 7416] xlix, *Report of Committee of Enquiry into the Architects and Surveyors' and Engineering Divisions of H.M. Office of Works, London*, paras. 79-81. In: Port, p. 77.

[294] The Royal Victorian Order, established by Queen Victoria in 1896 for the monarch to award to people for distinguished personal service to themselves or the royal family. When he retired in 1927 Baines was made a Knight Commander of the Victorian Order for his work for the latter. A KCVO has the accolade of knighthood and is thus referred to as 'Sir'. Baines, however, had already been knighted in 1918 for his work with the Ministry of Munitions, the Ministry of War and the Air Ministry, and so became known to colleagues as 'twice a knight Baines'. Thurley, p. 86.

Previous chapters have described how, as the second half of the late-19th century wore on, the prevailing attitude amongst legislators that the owners of property – be that land, buildings or both – had a more or less absolute right to do with it as they wished was gradually whittled away. Somewhat similarly, the idea that the future of ancient buildings should not be at the whim of their owners gained statutory recognition with the passing of the Ancient Monuments Protection Act, 1882. Under section 5, 'The Commissioners of His Majesty's Treasury shall appoint one or more inspectors of ancient monuments, whose duty it shall be to report to the Commissioners of Works on the condition of such monuments, and on the best mode of preserving the same …'.[295] As with early housing legislation, it was permissive and thus of limited effect.

In 1912, Premier Herbert Asquith appointed Sir Lionel Earle (1866-1948) as Permanent Secretary to the Office of Works[296] and new legislation was passed in 1913 – the Ancient Monuments Consolidation and Amendment Act. It established the Ancient Monuments Board, whose initial members were drawn from learned societies, to advise the Office of Works, and introduced the scheduling of ancient monuments.[297] Earle became a member of the Board. The Ancient Monuments Department, then the foremost division of the Office of Works, was headed by Charles Peers, Inspector of Ancient Monuments, who, in turn, was supported by his Principal Architect, Frank Baines.[298] The rise of Baines from Assistant Architect only two years earlier had been meteoric.

By 1912/13, H.M. Office of Works, measured by its salary roll of £127,600, was the fourth-largest government department. It absorbed 14% of the total salaries of the ten principal ministries and was comparable in size to the Board of Agriculture (£127,000) and the Local Government Board (£132,400).[299] It reorganised itself in early 1914,

---

[295] www.unesco.org/culture/natlaws/media/pdf/gb/uk_act_1882_orof.pdf, accessed 5 July 2016.

[296] Eric de Normann, 'Earle, Sir Lionel (1866-1948)', rev. Mark Pottle, *Oxford Dictionary of National Biography*, Oxford University Press, 2004 [http://www.oxforddnb.com/view/article/32955, accessed 5 July 2016].

[297] www.theheritagealliance.org.uk/update/ancient-monuments-act-1913-a-triumph-for-independent-heritage-movement, accessed 5 July 2016.

[298] Thurley, p. 86.

[299] Port, p. 35.

following the retirement the previous December of Sir Henry Tanner, Principal Architect and Surveyor, who had held the post since 1898.[300] It now had three principal architects, one dealing primarily with post offices and a second with art and science buildings, labour exchanges and overseas properties. The third, Frank Baines, was responsible for Monuments – royal palaces and public buildings.[301] Under these three served 9 Architects, 20 First-class Assistant Architects – six of whom were ARIBA and four FSI[302] – and 26 Second-class Assistants, of whom 11 were ARIBAs. Most of these, in accordance with the Office's modus operandi, had been recruited as temporary draughtsmen. They were assisted by 39 clerks of varying grades, 33 Architectural Assistants First- and Second-class, 2 lady typists and a shorthand writer, 3 sanitary assistants, 1 building inspector and 21 clerks of works (in charge of specific buildings). There were also 200 'temporary' draughtsmen, and 74 clerks of works employed on building sites.[303] The total payroll was therefore 240 full-time staff and the 200 (technically) temporary draughtsmen.

So for Baines, trained by someone to whom the preservation of buildings was a passion (Ashbee), then being attached to the Office's royal palaces section when he joined it as an assistant draughtsman in 1895, everything fell into place as Monuments became his civil service vocation. Now in his mid-thirties and his career rising fast, he undertook projects at Buckingham Palace, Hampton Court and Eltham Palace, and at the medieval religious abbeys of Tintern, Byland, Rievaulx, Jedburgh, Melrose, and Dryburgh. His greatest achievement was his proposal for the restoration of the roof of Westminster Hall at the Palace of Westminster. Upon inspecting it in 1913, he had found the wooden structure to be seriously decayed by beetle larvae. His June 1914 report proposed the insertion of steel reinforcements weighing,

---

[300] M. H. Port, 'Tanner, Sir Henry (1849-1935)', *Oxford Dictionary of National Biography*, Oxford University Press, 2004; online edn, Jan 2008 [http://www.oxforddnb.com/view/article/63423, accessed 15 July 2016].

[301] Respectively, W. Pott, R. J. Allison and F. Baines. Harcourt MS 459. 1914/15 staff list. Parliamentary Papers 1914 (Cd 74160 XLIX, para. 17). In: Port, p. 79.

[302] Respectively, Associates of the Royal Institute of British Architects and Fellows of the Surveyors Institution.

[303] Other contemporary government reports quote slightly different numbers for First-class and Second-class – Assistant Architects – Port, fn. 163).

in aggregate, 350 tons which would be invisible from the ground and would minimise the removal of medieval material. The war intervened so the project started in the early 1920s and was concluded in 1922. It brought him international recognition.[304]

Baines was an inspiration to his colleagues. Earle claimed: 'No one did more to win the war in a civilian capacity than this man: his energy and determination was remarkable and his power of work Napoleonic'.[305] Contributing to Baines's obituary in 1933, Mr E. H. Bright, former Principal Clerk at the Office of Works, a colleague for over 25 years and a personal friend for even longer, said: 'From his first entry into His Majesty's Office of Works [he] began to impress his virile personality on his colleagues and to imbue the Department with his own sense of the responsibility of service to the State. One of his earliest acts was to ascend the Nelson Monument in Trafalgar Square to ascertain that the work thereon for which the country was paying had been satisfactorily carried out ... He organised a complete department for dealing with the special technique of preserving historic buildings'.[306]

Clearly the Office of Works was not to be unaffected by the outbreak of war in August 1914. The work of its Ancient Monuments Department began to wind down as resources were transferred to the war effort. The Office was given responsibility for the construction of arms factories and the associated housing estates for their workers, as well as for the workers at naval bases. It was also made responsible for the tens of thousands of civilians in internment camps.[307] Baines's Principal Architect's job of looking after royal palaces and ancient buildings was replaced with responsibilities for the war effort. Earle probably thought Baines's characteristic energy and determination were just what his department needed to deliver the required results. Baines became, in effect, the CEO of a business responsible for about £80ml of construction work during the four-year wartime period, of which £10ml was spent on housing schemes for government and municipal

---

[304] C. C. Pond, 'Baines, Sir Frank (1877-1933)', *Oxford Dictionary of National Biography*, Oxford University Press, Oct 2014; online edn, Jan 2015 [http://www.oxforddnb.com/view/article/60657, accessed 5 July 2016].

[305] Lionel Earle, *Turn Over the Page*, Hutchinson & Co., London, 1935. In: Thurley, p. 100.

[306] 'Sir Frank Baines: The Care of Public Buildings', *The Times* obituary, 27 December 1933.

[307] Thurley, pp. 99-100.

authorities. At the end of the war, he received formal thanks from Lord Colwyn's Committee of Enquiry for the manner in which the work was conducted[308] and was granted a knighthood in the 1918 New Year Honours list[309] for his work with the Ministry of Munitions, the Ministry of War and the Ministry of Air.[310]

Since 1914 inflation has increased prices by about 100 times, so in today's values the 'business' for which Baines was responsible had a turnover of some £800ml during the war years. The £10ml spent on housing schemes probably represented the construction of 25-30,000 homes.[311] Even a man of his undoubted ability to absorb work could not have had day-to-day responsibility for delivering any one project. He must have spent much of his time in high-level negotiations with the Munitions, War and Air Ministries, not to mention the Treasury. In 1917, the Office was described as a handmaid of the latter ever since its creation in 1851. 'The First Commissioner operates and is by statute under practically complete Treasury control, less in any case he has express liberty to act by statute, which cases are most rare'.[312] By 1915, for works expected to cost more than £6,000, the Office was only allowed to exceed estimates by up to 5%. As will be discussed in due course, it is now clear that once the principles for the Estate had been established, his staff worked incredibly hard to deliver its 1,298 homes within an extremely short period of time. There is, however, one more issue to be explained in order for its development to be described in context.

---

[308] E. H. Bright in 'Sir Frank Baines: The Care of Public Buildings', *The Times* obituary, 27 December 1933.

[309] en.wikipedia.org/wiki/1918_New_Year_Honours, accessed 19 July 2016.

[310] Thurley, p. 86.

[311] Derived from Swenarton (1981), pp. 54-55.

[312] Public Record Office, Work 22/30, memo. 1917. In: M. H. Port, p. 81.

The Housing Act, 1914

Once again, it is important to remember the political climate of the time. The legislature's acceptance of the idea of publicly financed housing in an age when the vast majority of people rented their homes from private landlords only came about as huge numbers of troops returned from the trenches and the outer reaches of the Empire demanding better housing. 'Homes fit for Heroes' came to describe Lloyd George's 1918 general election promise. As with the issue of housing provision for agricultural workers discussed in the chapters about Letchworth Garden City and the Town Planning Act, 1909 (as the Housing, Town-Planning, &C. Act came to be known) the problem was that the rise in building costs had made it impossible for private developers to build houses whose rents were affordable by the average working-class family.[313]

Work had begun in 1909 on a new naval base at Rosyth on the Firth of Forth.[314] Probably as a result of publicity given to garden cities, the Admiralty had engaged Raymond Unwin as a consultant in 1909 yet, five years later, had done nothing about providing the three thousand houses they estimated would be required for its civilian employees. Neither they nor Dunfermline Borough Council, the local authority, wanted to finance the houses and the only non-governmental offers had been contingent upon levels of financial assistance that would have required parliamentary approval. Thus, at the beginning of June 1914, the Admiralty stated that unless a bill was introduced before the summer recess, 'it will be impossible to provide in time for the housing of the men to be employed at Rosyth'. Similar, though smaller problems were on the horizon at the Admiralty's base at Crombie in Fife and the War Office's aircraft factory at Farnborough. The political problem thus highlighted was how the government could best avoid being seen as not providing housing for its own employees.

The Treasury opined that 'the whole question is tied up with the general housing policy of the Government and it is important to lay down a general and consistent policy at the outset'. The Admiralty's already-expressed view was that 'the State [should recognise its duty] of

---

[313] University of the West of England: fet.uwe.ac.uk/conweb/house_ages/council_housing/section3.htm, accessed 20 July 2016.

[314] Swenarton (1981), pp. 1 and 44-47.

seeing that a relative standard of comfort and convenience is secured in the housing of the working classes'.

The Housing Bill as introduced to Parliament in July 1914 offered identical financing solutions for both rural housing and the housing of government employees. The former may have been a distracting tactic because Walter Runciman, the President of the Board of Agriculture, was not reluctant to give up the rural clauses during the second reading debate on 20 July in order to secure the passage of the latter (and thus a solution to Rosyth's particular problem). The Bill, in its final form, reached the statute book six days after Great Britain had declared war on Germany:

> An Act to make provision with respect to the Housing of Persons employed by or on behalf of Government Departments where sufficient dwelling accommodation is not available. [10 August 1914.]
>
> 1. – (1) The Local Government Board shall have power, with the approval of the Treasury, to make arrangements ... for the purpose of the provision, maintenance, and management of dwellings and gardens and other works or buildings for or for the convenience of persons employed by or on behalf of Government departments or Government works where sufficient dwelling accommodation is not available for those persons, and the Commissioners of Work shall have power for the same purpose, with the consent of the Treasury, given after consultation with the Local Government Board, to acquire and dispose of land and buildings, and to build dwellings and do all other things which appear to them necessary or desirable for effecting that purpose.

Thus everything was in place for the Estate to be financed by the government at the beginning of the following year, starting with the acquisition of the site.

THE EVOLUTION OF THE ESTATE

Cecil Henry Polhill and the Site for the Estate

The Polhill family fortune was founded by Cecil's great-great-grandfather, Nathaniel Polhill (1723-1782).[315] He became an eminent tobacco merchant, a brewer and a banker in the City of London with Langston, Polhill, Towgood and Amory of 29 St. Clement's Lane, Lombard Street. He was elected a Whig Member of Parliament for Southwark in October 1774 and again in 1780. He sold his brewery business in 1781 and purchased Howbury Hall at Renhold, 60 miles north of London on the A1 and just north of Bedford, for £17,500. When he died the following year, his property also included estates in Sussex, Surrey, Kent and Middlesex. Successive generations pursued military and political careers. Frederick Polhill, Cecil Henry's grandfather, unfortunately lost a very considerable sum of money in various theatrical ventures that included ownership of the Theatre Royal, Drury Lane and the Covent Garden Theatre. These failures contributed, in 1834, to the breakdown of his marriage to Frances Margaretta, whereupon he settled his various manors and estates for life on her and her children at his decease. Howbury no longer had any attraction for him and he moved to London. The second child and eldest son of the marriage, Frederick Charles Polhill, inherited his father's diminished estate in 1848.

On 10 February 1852 Frederick Charles married Emily Frances Barron, daughter of Sir Henry Winston Barron, 1st Bt. (1795-1872)[316] and Anna Leigh Guy Page-Turner (?-1852). Anna Leigh was the daughter of Sir Gregory Page-Turner, 3rd Bt. and Frances Howell. On 21 February 1853 Frederick Charles assumed the additional surname of Turner by Royal Licence in compliance with the testamentary injunction of his mother-in-law, Frances. Their three sons (they also had three

---

[315] www.all-saints-church-renhold.org/polhillfamilyhistory.html, accessed 21 July 2016.

[316] www.thepeerage.com/p11964.htm#i119636, accessed 25 July 2016.

daughters) were Frederick Edward Fiennes, born 10 June 1858, Cecil Henry, born 23 February 1860 and Arthur, born 7 February 1862. The marriage went some way to restoring the fortunes of Howbury, Anna Leigh being a scion of the Page dynasty.

Sir Gregory Page, 1st Bt. was a merchant of vast wealth and a director of the East India Company. When he died in 1720[317] virtually all his estate passed to his eldest son, Sir Gregory Page, 2nd Bt. It comprised investments worth about £600,000 and landed property that produced an income of some £24,000 per annum.[318] Today's equivalents would be, respectively, some £87ml and £3½ml per annum.[319]

Sir Gregory, 2nd Bt. spent a large part of his fortune on the purchase, in 1725, of the vast estate of Wricklemarsh in Blackheath, then in Kent and now in South-East London. He pulled down the old manor house and engaged the architect, surveyor and carpenter John James[320] to design a magnificent structure that was built at a cost of £90,000. Its walls were hung with over a hundred valuable paintings, including works by Rubens, van Dyck, Titian and other Old Masters. He died without issue in 1775 and bequeathed Wricklemarsh and its collections to his great-nephew Sir Gregory Turner, 3rd Bt. (1748-1805)[321] who subsequently changed his surname to Page-Turner. Sir Gregory Page-Turner, as he had thus become, married Frances Howell in 1785.[322] Upon his death, the bulk of his estate, which included the Battlesden

[317] en.wikipedia.org/wiki/Sir_Gregory_Page,_1st_Baronet, accessed 25 July 2016.

[318] *The Gentleman's Magazine*, vol. 97, January to June 1805, p. 278, https://babel.hathitrust.org/cgi/pt?id=nyp.33433081674404;view=1up;seq=302, accessed 25 July 2016. One of the deceased's investments was £10,000 of South Sea stock. His executors sold it before the bubble burst, thereby more or less doubling the value of the investments from the £310,000 the magazine stated as their value.

[319] www.johnowensmith.co.uk/histdate/moneyval.htm, accessed 4 August 2016 updated post 1998 from http://inflation.stephenmorley.org.

[320] Sally Jeffery, 'James, John (c.1672-1746)', *Oxford Dictionary of National Biography*, Oxford University Press, 2004; online edn, Jan 2008 [http://www.oxforddnb.com/view/article/14609, accessed 21 July 2016].

[321] *The Gentleman's Magazine*, vol. 45 (1775), p. 407, accessed at http/babel.hathitrust.org/cgi/pt?id=mdp.39015012326784;view=1up;seq=441, 27 July 2016 and Charles Sebag-Montefiore, 'Page, Sir Gregory, second baronet (1689-1775)', rev. *Oxford Dictionary of National Biography*, Oxford University Press, 2004 [http://www.oxforddnb.com/view/article/37829, accessed 27 July 2016].

[322] www.thepeerage.com/p26692.htm, accessed 25 July 2016.

Park estate, Bedfordshire that he had inherited from his great-aunt in 1780,[323] passed to his eldest son, Sir Gregory Osborne Page-Turner, 4th Bt. (1785-1848). Reverting to the second paragraph of this chapter, their daughter Anna Leigh Guy Page-Turner's marriage to Sir Henry Winston Barron, 1st Bt. in 1852 produced two children, Emily Francis Barron (died 1913) and Sir Henry Page-Turner Barron, 2nd Bt. (1824-1900). Sir Henry (the son) died unmarried and without issue on 12 September 1900.[324]

Sir Henry Page-Turner Barron, 2nd Bt. worked in the diplomatic service from 1840 until the year of his death. He had become a very wealthy man. The probate value of his estate was £306,473/5/1d. This included about 4,680 acres of land, apparently principally in Ireland. He bequeathed his real estate in England together with half his investments to his nephew Cecil Henry Polhill-Turner, the second son of his sister Emily and Frederick Charles Polhill-Turner. Cecil's inheritance comprised this unspecified acreage of real estate in England, as well as investments that might have been worth about £72,500.[325] Thus Cecil became, in his fortieth year, an affluent man with an income of around £11,500 per annum.[326] Today, these figures would be around £8½ml and £1.3ml per annum, respectively.

Cecil's elder brother, Frederick Edward Fiennes, had inherited the Howbury estates on the death of their father in 1881. An Army man, he gave up residence at the Hall in the 1890s before dying, unmarried,

---

[323] www.thepeerage.com/p26692.htm#i266919, accessed 25 July 2016

[324] en.wikipedia.org/wiki/Barron_baronets, accessed 23 July 2016.

[325] Will of Sir Henry Page-Turner Barron, London Probate Office, made on 9 July 1897. The gross value of Sir Henry's estate for probate purposes was £306,473/5/1d. He left his English real estate to his nephew Cecil Henry Polhill and his Irish real estate to his cousin Edward Winston Barron. The will does not specify their individual values. English agricultural land prices at the time were about £20/acre, so if Irish values were the same the land would have been valued at £93,600. By deduction, this implies a value of about £213,000 for his other investments that comprised securities, stocks, shares, bonds and bank balances. This was divided equally between his nephew and cousin after the deduction of specific legacies totalling £62,000 and £6,000 to build a church (substantially a family mausoleum). Given this assumption about land values, £145,000 was therefore divided equally between them. (For land values, see Bethanie Afton and Michael Turner, 'Rent and Land Values'. In: Joan Thirsk, ed. *The Agrarian History of England and Wales*, Vol. VII (Part II), 1850-1914, Cambridge University Press, 2000, pp. 1914-19).

[326] Usher, p. 50.

in 1903. The Howbury estates thus became the second inheritance of his younger brother, Cecil. Whilst the probate declaration of Frederick's estate proscribes it a nil net value, the Howbury assets would almost certainly have been held in trust. Real estate assets of landed families were often owned by trusts, their *tail male* provisions ensuring the eldest surviving male heir possessed them for his lifetime. However, the Howbury assets were worth a fraction of the wealth Cecil derived from his share of the Page-Turner Barron estate. In 1902, he dropped the second part of his surname becoming, by deed poll, Cecil Henry Polhill.

Cecil is famous for two reasons. Firstly, he became a national figure as a result of his contribution to Eaton Cricket Club's achievements whilst a pupil at the school and continued to excel in the sport after going up to Cambridge.[327] The second was due to the influence of his younger brother Arthur that resulted in Cecil's conversion to Christianity in 1884. The following year, they both went to China as missionaries with five other Cambridge graduates, the group becoming collectively known as 'the Cambridge Seven'. Other than for a short interlude on the Indian/Tibetan border, Cecil remained in China until poor health caused him to be sent home in 1900. His interest in missionary work in the country continued, however, and he revisited it on a number of occasions. In 1908, he returned from one such trip via Los Angeles, which marked the beginning of his involvement with the Pentecostal movement. In 1909, he became a joint founder of the Pentecostal missionary movement which sent its first missionaries to China the year after.[328] He continued to be involved with the movement until 1925. His personal account books reveal a wide range of financial donations to Pentecostal causes. Many were, individually, relatively small – the cost of hall hire for meetings, for example – although others were substantial.[329] Between 1902 and 1925 he gave a total of £57,915 to the movement.[330]

---

[327] Robeck, p. 288. For his cricketing scorecards, see http://cricketarchive.com/Archive/Players/237/237144/Miscellaneous_Matches.html, accessed 24 July 2016.

[328] Centre for the Study of World Christianity, ref. GB 3189 CSCNWW10, http://archiveshub.ac.uk/data/gb3189-cscnww10, accessed 24 July 2016.

[329] Usher, p. 50.

[330] Usher, p. 56.

THE EVOLUTION OF THE ESTATE

The significance of Cecil Polhill to this book is that his estates included land in Eltham. In 1903, the Metropolitan Borough of Woolwich was involved in acquisitions of real estate that would enable it to build a tramway from Woolwich to Eltham. On the Eltham side of Shooter's Hill this had to do with, firstly, widening and straightening the existing road running between Shooter's Hill and Well Hall railway bridge (the bridge next to what is now Eltham railway station) and, secondly, acquiring the necessary land to construct a new section of road between the bridge and St. John the Baptist church on Eltham High Street.[331] Both required the purchase of land controlled by Cecil Polhill and his trustees and he had agreed to give up as much of it as was necessary, subject to certain non-onerous conditions, and to contribute £5,000 towards the cost of the road.[332] Presumably these vendors calculated that the value of a road frontage across his land was at least equal to this outlay. The strips of land required to widen and straighten the section north of the railway bridge are implied on the conveyance plan drawn up for the indenture recording the subsequent sale of land to build the Estate; to the east of the improved road, cross-hatched strips of land mark its previous route (see illustration on page 141).

The land for the construction of the Estate was a much larger transaction. Cecil was either a willing seller of his land, patriotic (unlike many Pentecostals, he was not against the war[333]) or both. The decision to build the Estate as a Government Housing Scheme was taken at a meeting of representatives from the War Office, the Treasury, the Local Government Board and H.M. Office of Works on 12 January 1915[334] and, less than a month later on 10 February, Woolwich's Town Clerk reported that 'he had been informed that the Principal Architect of His Majesty's Office of Works has …purchased [land] from Mr. Polhill-Turner, amounting to about 90 acres, on either side (but mainly on the

---

[331] At this time, Well Hall Road south of the railway bridge followed old field boundaries, turning west at the Bridge along what is now Sherard Road and joining Eltham High Street at its western end. In due course, 'Well Hall Road' included the new road and the London County Council issued an order for the re-naming and renumbering of the original road (MBW, November 1906 to October 1907, p. 104, Works Committee, minute no. 2, 26 November 1906).

[332] MBW, November 1902 to October 1903, p. 588, minute no. 3, 9 July 1903.

[333] Author's notes form his conversation with John Usher, August, 2016.

[334] Swenarton (1981), pp. 53-54.

east side) of Well Hall Road, Eltham, between the cinder path and the Co-operative Stores'.[335] There were three reasons for the site's selection. Firstly, the Bexleyheath railway line from Dartford to Blackheath, where it interconnected with the North Kent to London line, had opened on 1 May 1895,[336] thereby permitting the rapid transport of building materials to the site. Secondly, the aforementioned tram service (route 44) had opened on 23 July 1910,[337] which would enable residents to commute to and from the Royal Arsenal munitions factories in Woolwich. Thirdly, all other potential sites nearer to Woolwich of sufficient acreage for the required number of houses were either common land or under the Army's control.

It is of course possible that contingent negotiations had been carried out in the background between Cecil Polhill and either the Borough, the War Office, the Local Government Board or the Office of Works before the 12 January meeting. Even if this was so, events had moved fast. Although Polhill was the beneficial owner of the land it was held by three trustees because, on his death, beneficial ownership was to pass to other (defined) heirs, so the trustees would have needed to agree to the sale, its consideration and its conditions.[338] The consideration for the arable land, chiefly used for market gardening,[339] was £38,260/10/-, and the terms of the sale are recorded in an Indenture dated 9 November 1915.[340] The land to the east of Well Hall Road comprised 65 acres, 2 roods and 25 perches and, to the west, 30 acres. There are four roods to the acre and 40 perches to the rood, so the total area of the land was 95.65625 acres 'or thereabouts'. Barring 24.2 square yards, the price

---

[335] MBW, 1914-1915, p. 588, Public Health and Housing Committee, minute no. 12, 10 February 1915. The Town Clerk appears not to have been informed of Polhill-Turner's dropping 'Turner' from his surname by deed poll in 1902.

[336] Gus White, pp. 1-2.

[337] Kennett (2007), pp. 8 and 12.

[338] Will of Sir Henry Page-Turner Barron, London Probate Office, made on 9 July 1897. Unfortunately the majority of H.M. Office of Works records dealing with the estate were apparently lost in the Second World War (Beaufoy (1952), p. 143). The author also understands that Polhill's post-1914 private papers have not come to light.

[339] Jones, introduction.

[340] Indenture dated 9 November 1915 made between Cecil Henry Polhill for the first part, Sir Arthur Dryden, Edward Winston Barron and Frederick Wolfe for the second part, and the Commissioners of His Majesty's Works and Public Buildings for the third part.

works out at precisely £400 per acre. Whilst it is very hard to establish pre-First World War land values with any great certainty,[341] it appears as though they were virtually unchanged since 1898 when, as already noted, Ebenezer Howard had stated that £40 per acre was the average price for agricultural land in England. Even allowing for higher prices near the Metropolis, it seems unlikely Polhill and his trustees would have been disappointed with the price the acreage achieved.

One interesting aspect of this transaction is that it leaves unanswered the question as to how these lands in Eltham came to be in the beneficial ownership of Cecil Polhill. They almost certainly formed part of the English real estate of Sir Henry Page-Turner Barron, because the three trustees involved in the sale as its legal owners were the executors and trustees of Sir Henry's will. Furthermore Polhill, in his ledgers, describes his entire inheritance from his uncle as 'the Page estate',[342] and Woolwich's Borough Engineer is recorded as having said 'a considerable amount of [my] time is now being occupied in connection with the Government Housing Scheme on the Page Estate, Well Hall Road, Eltham'.[343] However, as mentioned above, the biographer of Sir Gregory Page, 2nd Bt. stated that he bequeathed Wricklemarsh in Blackheath and its collections to Sir Gregory Page-Turner, 3rd Bt. Page-Turner did not live there and sold it in 1784,[344] so this physical asset would not have formed part of Sir Gregory Osborne Page-Turner, 4th Bt.'s inheritance when his father died in 1805. The 3rd Baronet's daughter Anna Leigh Guy Page-Turner married Sir Henry Page-Turner Barron, in 1882 and predeceased him on 22 November 1852.[345] The first possibility is that the Eltham assets Polhill inherited formed part of Sir Henry Page-Turner Barron's real estate in England either because his mother had left them to him, or they had been inherited by her husband when she died and he in turn had bequeathed them to his son. The second is that when Wricklemarsh was sold, other lands in the area were retained.

[341] Bethanie Afton and Michael Turner, 'Rent and Land Values', In: Thirsk, pp. 1914-1919.

[342] Usher, p. 42.

[343] MBW 1914-1915, p. 248, Works Committee, minute no. 7, 30 January 1915.

[344] Charles Sebag-Montefiore, 'Page, Sir Gregory, second baronet (1689-1775)', rev. *Oxford Dictionary of National Biography*, Oxford University Press, 2004 [http://www.oxforddnb.com/view/article/37829, accessed 27 July 2016].

[345] www.thepeerage.com/p26692.htm#i266918, accessed 27 July 2016.

The apparently odd shape of the Progress Estate is probably due to a convergence of Government edict, the field boundaries on Polhill's land and the desirability of Well Hall Road's tram route to run through it. The Estate comprises 1,298 homes, of which 212 are two-storey buildings split into ground- and first-floor flats.[346] A total of 1,192 two-storey buildings were, therefore, to be constructed. All construction under the Housing Act, 1914 was the responsibility of the Local Government Board. The Treasury was informed that Herbert Samuel, the President of the Board, 'hoped that care will be taken to ensure that any site is laid with due regard to the best practice in connection with the planning of estates'. The Board also told the Office of Works that the Estate was to follow 'best town-planning lines' with twelve houses to the acre and that the opportunity was to be taken to show what a scheme of this nature should be under Government auspices'.[347] Raymond Unwin's 1912 pamphlet *Nothing Gained by Overcrowding!* had chiselled '12 houses to the acre' into the subconscious of every town planner and Samuel had announced his appointment to the Board as Town Planning Inspector only a few weeks earlier. To construct the 1,192 buildings would require 99⅓ acres of land. The ratio could be increased to a fraction under 12½ to the acre because the 1914 Act only permitted the construction of homes; a typical new private estate of this size would have included community buildings such as churches, schools and shops.

Because travel to and from Woolwich was a prerequisite, all the Estate's houses needed easy access to the no. 44 trams running along Well Hall Road. This argued for the Estate being built on either side of it. The vendors conveyed six fields to its east in their entirety.[348] Collectively, these comprised just over 65 of the required 95 acres. To the west of the road, he sold the whole of the triangular field bounding onto Well Hall Road plus sufficient of the adjacent fields to form a plot containing the required balance of 30 acres. Thus the Indenture refers to the western

---

[346] Government Housing Scheme at Well Hall, Eltham, Kent.

[347] Baines (1917), p. 947. Also *Official History of the Ministry of Munitions*, vol. 5 part 5, p. 83. In: Swenarton (1981), p. 54.

[348] The apparent straightening off of the north-east boundary – almost certainly before the sale was agreed – is shown on OS Map London Sheet P, revised in 1914 and published in 1920.

THE EVOLUTION OF THE ESTATE

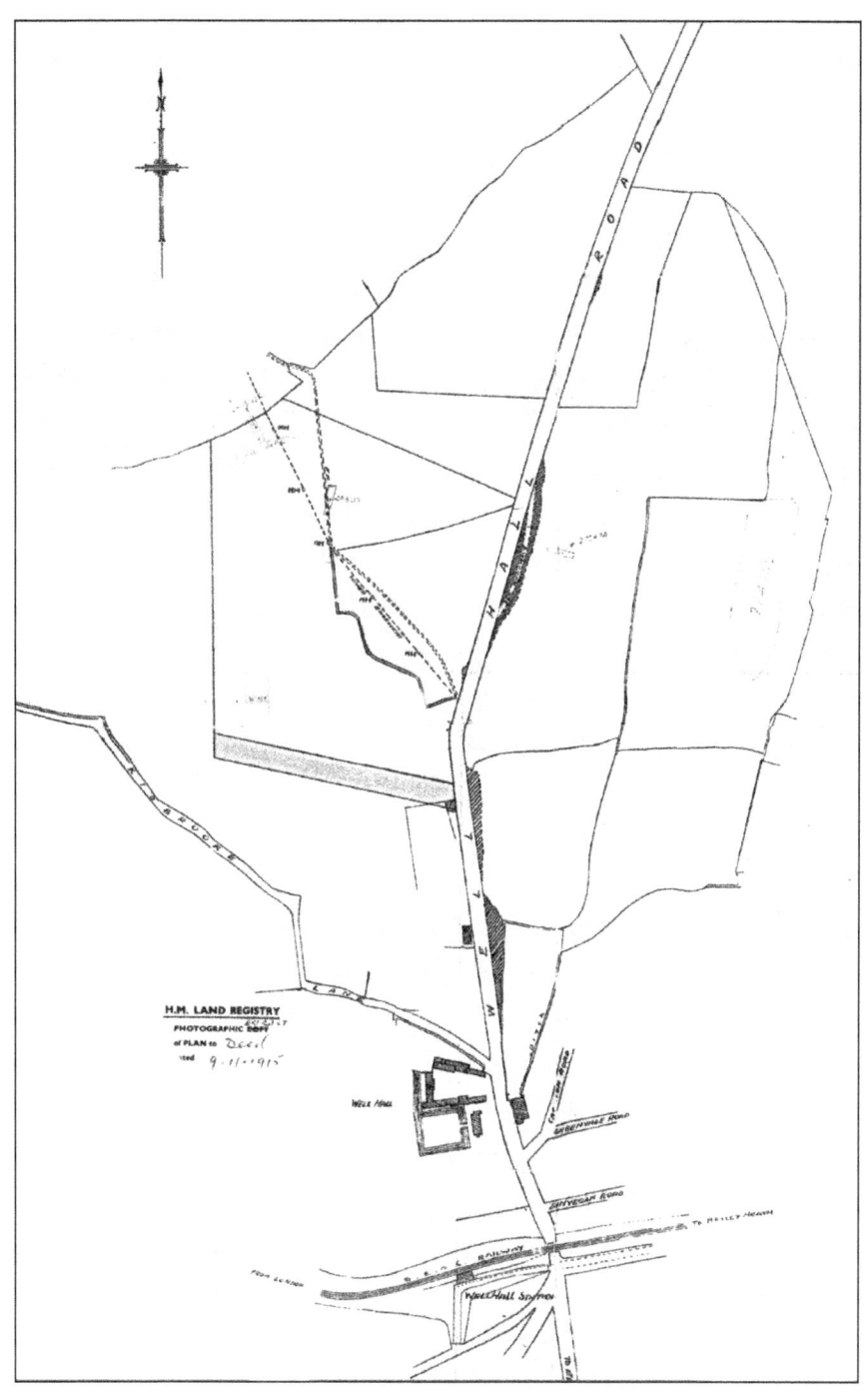

Plan of the Estate incorporated in the Indenture of 9th November 1915.

portion of the Estate as 'that piece of land as now staked out'.[349] The wide strip of land along the southern border of this western portion, coloured light grey in the illustration on page 141, was included in the conveyance. Three other features are noteworthy.

The double-dotted line that enters the western portion of the conveyed land through its northern boundary is the southern end of a public footpath. Part of the northern portion was re-routed during construction. It enters the Estate at the same point, but its direction was moved slightly to the west, joining Phineas Pett Road some 65 feet west of the line of the original path. The historic name of the path, Kakehill Lane, was restored in 2013 as a result of an Eltham Society study of the Survey of Eltham, 1605.[350] The remainder of the path disappeared during the building of the Estate; although Franklin Passage, the footpath between Phineas Pett Road and Dickson Road, might appear to be an extension of the original footpath, it is not. The latter swung to the south-east just south of Phineas Pett Road, heading for what is now the junction of Dickson Road with Well Hall Road.

The single-dotted line marks a sewer easement. The north-western boundary of the conveyed land, either side of where it is crossed by the sewer, marks the 1914 boundary of the civil parishes of Charlton & Kidbrooke to the west and Eltham to the east. These were then, respectively, in the Metropolitan Boroughs of Greenwich and Woolwich.[351]

The two parallel solid lines mark the course of a ditch. This became apparent from a comparison between the conveyance plan and the western site layout plan drawn up by the Office of Works.[352] A footbridge over it is probably marked by the gap in the lines just before the sharp turn to the east in the centre of the conveyed land. It seems

---

[349] See fn 340. Other than for an apparent amalgamation of two fields to the eastern boundary of the estate, those conveyed in whole or part are clearly marked on the Ordnance Survey Second Edition 1897, surveyed in 1862-63 and resurveyed and revised in 1893-94: Kent sheet 11.13/London sheets CVI, CVII & CXX (Parts of), Kent sheet 11.14/London sheets CVII & CVIII (Parts of), and Kent sheet VIII.I/London sheets CXXI & CXXX (Parts of).

[350] Email correspondence between the author and Laurie Baker, Secretary, The Eltham Society, November 2016.

[351] London Sheet P, Ordnance Survey, 1920 (1914 revision).

[352] Map nos. 545 & 546, Greenwich Heritage Centre, Woolwich.

THE EVOLUTION OF THE ESTATE

as though this plan, and the one for the east side, were annexed to the Indenture: the Commissioners covenanted that the land 'shall be laid out and developed and built upon not otherwise than in accordance with the large scale Plan[s] ... annexed hereto or with such variations only in detail as the Vendor may approve'. These plans are discussed in greater detail later on in this book.

The conveyed land formed part of the catchment area of the River Quaggy, a watercourse that is now substantially carried through culverts and, at Lewisham, drains into the Ravensbourne. The clay subsoil was covered by spongy topsoil, full of pebbles and inclined to be damp.[353] A valley begins in the northern corner of the Estate, clearly marked by the 200-foot contour on the map on page 168, and falls south-south-west, becoming shallower as it descends and crosses Well Hall Road at its junction with Downman Road. It continues behind the houses on the east side of Downman Road before changing to a westerly course to go behind the houses on the north side of Dickson Road. It then heads south-west, leaving the Estate to the west of Whinyates Road just north of the Dickson Road/Whinyates Road junction.[354] Any water running down the valley (it may have been a winterbourne) might have drained into the Lower Kidbrook River, a tributary of the Quaggy, some 500 yards further west and near today's junction of Briset Road and Rochester Way.[355]

The conveyed land had been used for market gardening. The photograph on page 144 was taken around 1905 and is of Well Hall Road, looking north, before it was widened and straightened as a precursor to the building of the tramway from Woolwich to Eltham discussed earlier. The cottages, quaintly known as Nell Gwyn's Cottages and possibly shown on the map John Rocque engraved in 1746, were demolished in 1923 to make way for a parade of shops.[356] They were opposite the junction of Well Hall Road and Admiral Seymour Road, and thus some 170 yards south of the Rochester Way/Well Hall Road roundabout. As can be seen, trees were sparse as one might expect given

[353] Jones, introduction.

[354] Determined from contours on Explorer Map 162, Edition A1, Ordnance Survey, 2001 (1998 revision with selected changes in 2001).

[355] Ken White, p. 54.

[356] Kennett (Progress Estate).

THE ORIGINS AND EVOLUTION OF THE PROGRESS ESTATE

Well Hall Road looking north, circa 1905.

its agricultural usage, although it is recorded that none were felled during the laying out of the site.[357]

The published plan for the west side of the Estate (see page 152) includes thirty-five trees growing to the west of Well Hall Road. Other than for two on the edge of this road just north of its boundary with Dickson Road, one at the eastern end of Ross Way and one in Sandby Green, all grew along ditches whose courses are shown on the site layout plan and are implied by the lines of the trees in the published plan. This photograph shows one such row in Dickson Road.

Elms trees growing in Dickson Road, looking east.

The density of trees in the west was 2.7 times that on the east: thirty-five as opposed to twenty-eight (excluding those on the boundary) on

[357] Government Housing Scheme at Well Hall, Eltham, Kent.

THE EVOLUTION OF THE ESTATE

just under half the acreage. That the ground on the west was somewhat flatter and thus probably damper might have been a contributory factor. None of the trees on the western side exist today. As is evident from the two illustrations opposite, English Elms (*Ulmus procera*) made up a very high proportion. There is an at least ninety per cent. probability that any remaining in the late-1970s were killed or severely affected by Dutch elm disease.[358] These were generally felled for reasons of sanitation, safety or aesthetics.[359] There were no boundary trees on this side of the Estate. As noted earlier, nealy all the conveyed land here did not comprise entire fields but was staked out across parts of fields.

The illustration on page 153 is the published plan for the east side of the Estate. Unlike that for the west, the site layout plan does not include any ditches although lines of trees to the south of Boughton Road (subsequently incorporated into Rochester Way) and around the southern end of Admiral Seymour Road imply their presence. Other than for one or two dotted around, the rest of the trees are on or immediately over the eastern boundary.

The trees in Boughton Road were elms[360] so, again, probably died in the late-1970s even if they had not been removed earlier. That those at the southern end of Admiral Seymour Road are in two lines forming a right angle may well indicate they, too, were elms growing along ditches.

Ecologically, the eastern boundary comprises two parts, dividing east of the intersection of Cornwallis Walk (the short road connecting Arsenal and Granby Roads that is unnamed on the published plan) with Granby Road. The straight-edged northern section appears to have predated the sale of the land by, at most, only a few years and the lack of trees actually on the boundary probably indicates it was demarcated by a fence rather than being hedged.[361] Trees growing in hedges along old boundaries are a not uncommon English topographical feature.

The east side published plan shows eight or nine trees growing

---

[358] Rackham (1986), pp. 244-245.

[359] Gibbs, Brasier and Webber.

[360] *View of Gilborne Way looking West*, file no. 1, Box Eltham G-L, Greenwich Heritage Centre, Woolwich.

[361] Comparison between OS maps Kent II.SW, revised 1893-94, published 1898, and London Sheet P, revised 1914, published 1920. National Library of Scotland, http://maps.nls.uk, accessed 8 September 2016.

exactly on the line of the southern/eastern boundary. This was probably an ancient field boundary. A further three are only a few feet east of the line. Interestingly, an Ordnance Survey map drawn up between 1862 and 1873[362] shows all the trees at field corners in exactly the same positions; trees marking changes in the direction of hedgerows were often kept alive for hundreds of years by regular pollarding. Although the architect(s) who drew up the site layout plans might not have illustrated the size of trees with individual accuracy, an estimate of the diameter of their canopies can be ascertained by comparing them with the widths of gardens. This indicates that their crowns were 10-15 feet across, so they were reasonably mature specimens in 1915. Like the 1862/73 Ordnance surveyors, H.M. Office of Works architects surveying the site would only have documented trees that were of sufficient size to be of landscape value, so it is likely that the few large trees visible today were but small saplings in 1915 and went unrecorded. A general rule for native species is that non-woodland trees put on one inch of girth at breast height for every year of their age,[363] implying a diameter of 32 inches for a 100-year-old specimen. This may well explain why the large ash tree growing on the edge of the path behind 33-43 Granby Road is not included on the east side layout plan. Including this specimen, there are now seven boundary trees visible from the public highway. The diameter of the bowl of this tree, an oak behind 99A Granby Road and an ash behind 38 Moira Road – each approximately 30 inches – suggests they were probably saplings when the Estate was built. There can be less certainty of the age of the three sycamores behind 192 Well Hall Road and a fourth behind 113A Granby Road. Sycamores, Central European natives of mountainous regions, are likely to exhibit a faster growth rate in the warmer, moister and more hospitable climate of England.[364] It has also not been possible to form an opinion about the two trees behind what is now 532 Rochester Way. One or two tall trees are there, but only the very tops of their crowns are visible from the highway.

Oak and ash trees seed successfully, so whilst it is probably wrong to conclude that any of these boundary trees were those plotted by the architects of 1915, they could well be their progenies.

---

[362] Ordnance Survey, Essex LXXXI (includes: Borough of Greenwich; Poplar Borough; West Ham) pub. 1870 to 1882.

[363] Rackham (1990), p. 13.

[364] Oliver Rackham (1986), p. 56.

His Majesty's Office Goes to Work

The 1914-18 war was on a scale that the world had never witnessed before and the second chapter of this book has described the enormous expansion that was required in the output at the Royal Arsenal munitions factories in Woolwich. A nation that now expected decent homes for its workers had its chief armaments manufacturer situated in a town with insufficient houses for the people it needed to employ. At the end of 1914, its Director anticipated having to recruit a further 3-4,000 employees 'in the next few months'[365] which probably proved to be an underestimate; the total number of employees rose by just over 23,000 in 1915 as a whole, an average of extra 1,900 every month. The Metropolitan Borough of Woolwich, with the help of Will Crooks, the town's Member of Parliament had, apparently without much difficulty, persuaded the Government that the solution lay with the national authorities and Herbert Samuel, the left-of-centre President of the Local Government Board had expressed his opinion that the Estate of 1,298 homes should be constructed 'with due regard to best practice',[366] apparently within six months.[367] They were expected to accommodate 6,490 people.[368]

This then was the project that landed on the desk of Frank Baines, at the time one of the three Principal Architects at H.M. Office of Works.[369] There is no evidence that he had previously designed houses, let alone an estate of this size to be built at breakneck speed on a greenfield site. It seems as though the Office was given responsibility for anything to do with 'building' that did not sit conveniently with an alternative Ministry. For example, after the war it took on responsibility for the Commonwealth War Graves Commission and for British war memorials across Europe.[370] When it was given the job of erecting the monument that would became the Cenotaph in London's Whitehall,

---

[365] Public Record Office T161/68 s5222/1 (War Office to Local Government Board, 30 December 1914). In: Swenarton (1981), p. 53.

[366] Swenarton (1981), p. 54.

[367] MBW 1914-1915, p. 240, Public Health and Housing Committee, minute no. 12, 10 February 1915.

[368] Government Housing Scheme at Well Hall, Eltham, Kent.

[369] Swenarton (1981), p. 56.

[370] Thurley, p. 99.

Baines called upon Edwin Lutyens, whom he would have met through the Commission, to design it.[371] One of Baines's strengths seems to have been his readiness to call upon available expertise.

The initial site survey was completed on a Saturday, either 9 or 16 January 1915 by Baines and A. J. Pitcher, the architect reporting immediately to him with responsibility for new building works. À la the methodology pronounced by Raymond Unwin in his aforementioned 1906 speech, it resulted in their indicating on an Ordnance Survey map the position of the principal features such as ditches and groups of trees. Others, possibly on the same day, surveyed its contours and a team was selected to prepare the site layout and house plans. It was fortunate that there were four architects in the Office's employ with previous domestic architectural experience. Pitcher was one of them and the three others were George Edward Phillips, James Albert Bowden and Gerald Parker.[372] There is very limited biographical information available about them[373] and the destruction of many of the Office's London-based records during the Second World War means that the verifiable information about the part each played is generally limited to interviews conducted in the early 1950s.[374]

The day after the initial survey, Baines instructed Pitcher, Phillips, Bowden and Parker to produce a site layout plan apiece based on the Baines/Pitcher initial survey. Pitcher was the only one who had seen the site. Phillips spent the day contemplating the challenge and, by 8:00 p.m., had concluded the Estate should look 'as if it had grown and not merely been dropped there'. He worked through the night and by 8:00 on the Monday morning had completed the layout that Baines

---

[371] Tim Skelton and Gerald Gliddon, *Lutyens and the Great War*, Francis Lincoln, London 2008, p. 45. Lutyens's sketch for the Cenotaph is held by the Imperial War Museum, London. He was one of the three Principal Architects to the Commonwealth War Graves Commission, for which he was not remunerated.

[372] Beaufoy (1950), p. 260.

[373] The British Architectural Library's Grey Books have brief notes about Pitcher and Parker. The training and qualification dates for Phillips and Bowden are included in *Directory of British Architects 1834-1914*, Royal Institute of British Architects, 2001. Bowden's obituary states that 'During the 1914-18 War he built munition factories, and resumed private practice on his own account when the war ended [by when he would have been 40 or 41], dealing mostly with industrial and commercial concerns. ... (*The Builder*, vol. 177, 14 October 1949, p. 496).

[374] Beaufoy (1952), p. 143.

decided to take forward.³⁷⁵ Houses would need to be carefully sited for his vision to become a reality. He designed in views of the then open countryside, visible between houses as one walked through the Estate.

Baines sent plans for the proposed Estate to the London County Council's Superintending Architect on 19 January 1915, stating in his covering letter that the matter was one of extreme urgency. The Woolwich Arsenal would be unable to turn out munitions sufficient for both [the Army and the Navy] unless the requisite number of workmen could be obtained.³⁷⁶

Baines had stated in his letter that the London Building Acts did not apply because the Estate was to be built as a Government Housing Scheme. The purpose of the Acts (the first had been passed in 1894) was to give the London County Council powers to regulate building across the whole of London; hitherto a fragmentary and ill-working system had allowed each local authority within the Council's area do so under their own by-laws.³⁷⁷ The Superintending Architect disagreed with Baines, arguing that to accept this interpretation would (a) set a 'dangerous precedent' that other government departments might choose to follow; and (b) upset builders developing, privately, land in the immediate vicinity of the Estate.³⁷⁸ The Acts obliged private developers to build roads to a minimum width of 40 feet, whereas Baines was proposing a minimum of 30 feet. London's biggest builder of artisan houses before the war, Corbett, had been developing the nearby Eltham Park Estate since 1900.³⁷⁹ The firm was run by the Glaswegian Cameron Corbett who was also the Member of Parliament for Glasgow Tradeston. He had taken the Liberal Whip when first elected in 1885, changed his allegiance to the Liberal Unionists from 1886 to 1908 and then crossed the floor to rejoin the Liberals in 1908. He was created first Baron Rowallan when he retired from the Commons in 1911.³⁸⁰ Upsetting such a man was

---

[375] Beaufoy (1950), p. 260.

[376] Minutes of the LCC Building Acts Committee, 25 January 1915, p. 533, para. 35. In: Hills, p. 9.

[377] Tarn, pp. 127-129.

[378] Hills, p. 9.

[379] Wingham, p. 13.

[380] en.wikipedia.org/wiki/Archibald_Corbett,_1st_Baron_Rowallan, accessed 2 August 2016.

unlikely to have been a priority for the Superintending Architect; road-building was an expensive component in estate development.

A week after Baines had written his letter he met, on 26 January, the Chairman of the London County Council's Building Acts Committee and the Superintending Architect at their request. Agreement was reached on all the Committee's points other than road widths. The Office of Works sent revised plans to the Committee and, at its 8 February meeting, the Superintending Architect was able to report that these amendments resolved their concerns.[381] Baines's elegant solution to the lack of 40-foot roads reflected a combination of Unwin's approach at Hampstead Garden Suburb and the national necessity for the speed and economy of construction.[382] The metalling of the roads was to remain at 30 feet, but the houses were to be set back for later widening (without specifying who would pay for it). Additionally, provision was made for an 80-foot arterial road to be constructed at a later date.[383] The Committee resolved to send a letter to Baines expressing complete satisfaction at the attention he had given, although a further letter was to be sent to H.M. Office of Works stating the Committee could not agree that the scheme was not subject to London Building Acts, but due to its urgency they would not further oppose it subject to their agreement being 'without prejudice'.[384]

The Office of Works involved Woolwich Borough Council in the planning of the Estate's infrastructure from the very start, because the latter would be asked to adopt its roads and sewers once it was completed. On 22 January 1915 Baines wrote to the Council asking whether it would help 'in regard to the construction and supervision of the road-making and sewering'. It would be impossible for him to obtain consent for remuneration for such services. The Council resolved that the Borough Engineer would render advice as to construction of sewers and roads, with periodical inspection and checking, as long as it

---

[381] Hills, p. 10.

[382] Hampstead Garden Suburb Act 1906, s2: 'In every road in the Garden Suburb (whatever the width of the said road) there shall be between any two houses standing on opposite sides of the road a space of not less than 50 feet free of any buildings except walls fences or gates'.

[383] Rochester Way, opened in 1932.

[384] Minutes of LCC (Building Acts Committee), 8 February 1915, p. 788 para. 39. In: Hills, p. 10.

did not interfere with their own work or interests.[385]

The architects' site layout plans and some of their drawings for individual houses, known to have been in the Woolwich Local History Collection,[386] were discovered in the Greenwich Heritage Centre's archive in 2016. The site layout plans for the east and west sides of the Estate show the roads as numbered rather than named and each block of houses is identified by the number of its detailed drawing. Altogether, the Estate's 1,192 dwellings were built from 106 detailed drawings, representing 575 dwellings. One, for a block of four houses, was used fourteen times whilst at the other extreme fifty-five were only used once. Some of the latter are for very long groups of houses such as 56-80 Congreve Road and 16-52 Admiral Seymour Road. These drawings take account of the roads' gradients, the changes in the height of roofs' ridge lines being precisely visible in the front elevation of the houses today. A few drawings were reversed to be used on the opposite sides of the roads. Thus 99-123 Congreve Road was built as a mirror image of 56-80 and the block of three houses now numbered 45-47 Prince Rupert Road/485 Rochester Way is the mirror image of the block opposite, 58-60 Prince Rupert Road/487 Rochester Way.

The collection's detailed drawings are entirely for houses on the east side of the Estate and represent 18½% of all the houses situated there (counting ground- and first-floor flats as one house).

Construction began on the east side of the Estate and thirteen of the sixteen detailed plans that have come to light are dated between January and March 1915 (the other three being undated). According to its minute book, the detailed road layout for the site west of Well Hall Road was not presented to the Borough of Woolwich's Works Committee until 19 July 1915.[387] As soon as Baines had decided to adopt his plan (sent to Woolwich Borough Council on 22 January) Phillips continued to develop his initial layout. He worked on the siting of houses and the sketching of their elevations whilst Pitcher worked on detailed designs for those facing Well Hall Road, the first that would be built.[388] The Woolwich Town Clerk, when making his report to the

[385] MBW 1914-1915, p. 248, Works Committee, minute no. 7, 30 January 1915.

[386] Hills, p. 30 and Pepper and Swenarton, p. 369.

[387] MBW 1914-1915, p. 655, Works Committee, minute no. 19, 19 July 1915.

[388] Beaufoy (1950), p. 260.

THE ORIGINS AND EVOLUTION OF THE PROGRESS ESTATE

Public Health and Housing Committee on 10 February said: 'it appears that the houses are to be erected on garden city lines [and] erected in blocks of 4 and 6, and not in terraces'.[389] However, the outcome was that 39% of the dwellings were in blocks of 7 or more.[390] Whether this was due to an attempt by H.M. Office of Works to economise subsequent to the Town Clerk's report, or to a misunderstanding on his part, is a moot point. It does, however, indicate that the site layout plan for the east side was not finalised at that time. The reproductions of

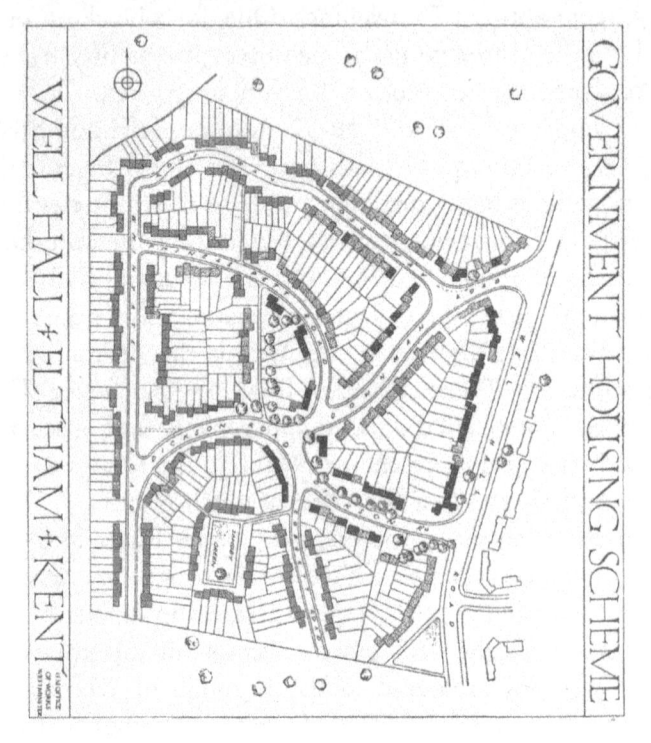

West (ABOVE) *and East* (OPPOSITE) *sides of the Estate.*

the Estate's final appearance included here are the two aforementioned site layout plans (a) with road names added (proposed by the London County Council in a letter to the Woolwich Borough Council dated 22

---

[389] MBW 1914-1915, p. 240, Public Health and Housing Committee, minute no. 12, 10 February 1915.

[390] Calculation counts ground- and first-floor flats as one house and are based on an analysis of the site layout plans (maps no. 545 and 546, Greenwich Heritage Centre, Woolwich).

THE EVOLUTION OF THE ESTATE

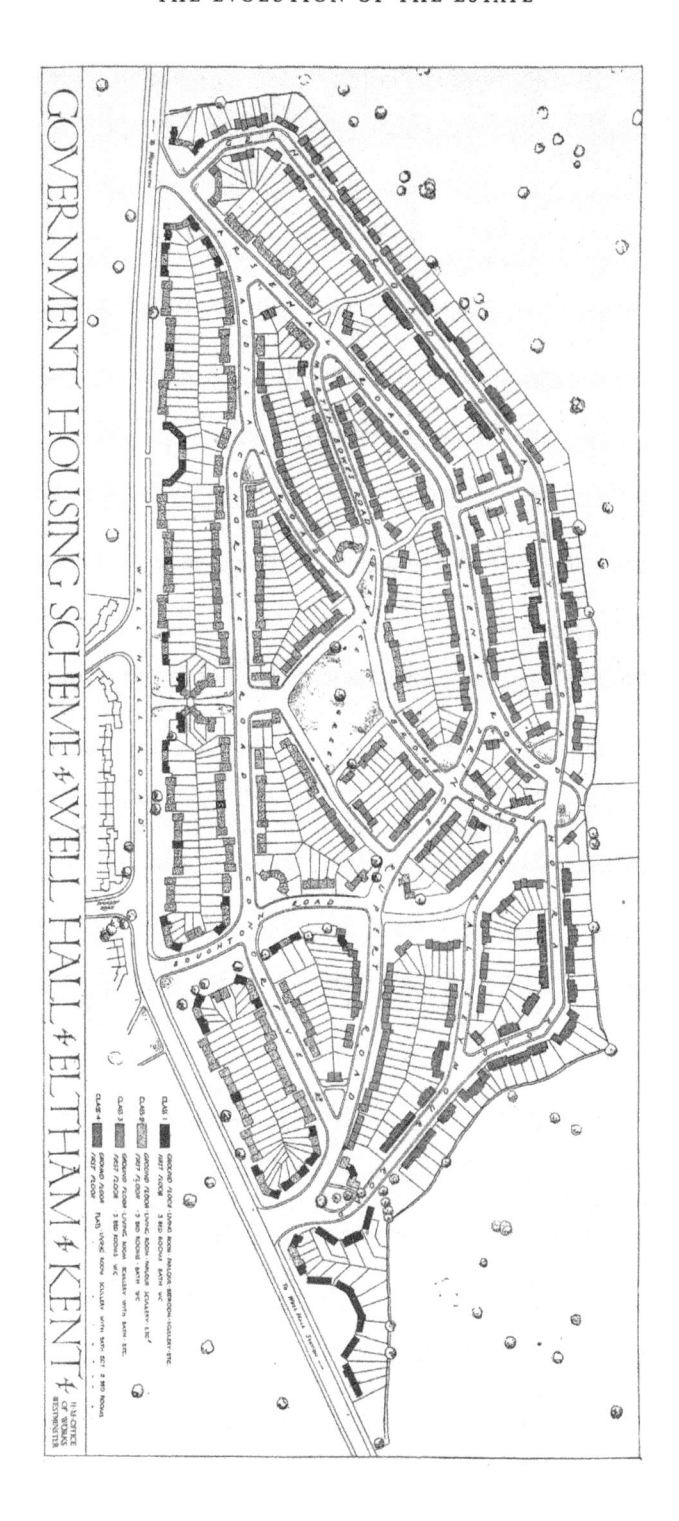

June 1915)[391] and (b) with the colour-coding of dwelling types replaced with a black and white key for printing. Three roads are unnamed due to a lack of space:

- On the west side, Franklin Passage, a non-vehicular path joining Dickson Road and Phineas Pett Road.
- On the east side, Cornwallis Walk, which connects Granby Road and Arsenal Road roughly halfway along each.
- Again on the east side, Gilbourne Way, the road connecting the east end of Boughton Road with Admiral Seymour Road.

The reader should also bear in mind that the houses in Boughton Road, Gilbourne Way and the northern section of Admiral Seymour Road that ran from the end of Gilbourne Way to the eastern boundary of the Estate became addresses in Rochester Way when this relief road was opened in 1932.

Roads are most economically built when excavation is minimised and the way to build a flat road is to follow the natural contours of the site. This is generally how communities that grow piecemeal have developed and the technique would help to satisfy Phillips's desire that the Estate should look 'as if it had grown and not merely been dropped there'.

To the east of Well Hall Road, the site slopes with gentle concavity from north-north-east to south-west. The overall gradient is about 1:25 although at the northern end of Granby Road it reaches 1:10. The top third of Granby Road, including the westerly turn it makes to join Arsenal Road, runs broadly parallel to and just below the 65m contour. Other than for the first 100m as it falls away from Well Hall Road, Arsenal Road tracks the 60m contour for about 200m and then slopes gently to the south as it moves towards the flatter ground.

The western half of Ross Way forms the steepest part of the site west of Well Hall Road and again exactly tracks a contour – this time 50m – until about 60m before its junction with Whinyates Road. Phineas Pett Road, to the south of Ross Way, closely follows the 45m contour. Forming the western boundary of the site, the northernmost 50m of Whinyates Road between these two unavoidably goes down a 1:10

---

[391] MBW 1914-1915, p. 666, Works Committee, minute no. 20, 19 July 1915 and p. 742, Works Committee, minute no. 9, 27 September 1915.

Raised pavement in Ross Way.

gradient before flattening out south of its junction with Dickson Road.

The raised footway in Ross Way was largely the work of Charles Mole[392] who had joined H.M. Office of Works in 1911.[393] Mole was said to be 'constantly on the job, altering or changing the position of houses as might be necessary to overcome site difficulties or effect economies'. Presumably this elevation was to avoid the houses on the north side of the road's western half having particularly steep back gardens. So when were the site layout plans, which are undated yet detail precisely the plan number of each block of dwellings, produced? Of the sixteen detailed drawings in the Greenwich Heritage Centre, two are dated February 1915, ten March and three are undated. One dated January was not used for reasons that will be explained in the next chapter.

The site layout plans for the east and the west sides were drawn to a scale of 32 feet to the inch (1:384).[394] A plan for the east side was submitted to Woolwich Borough Council in time for their meeting

---

[392] Beaufoy (1952), p. 143.

[393] Obituary, *The Times*, 6 December 1962. Sir Charles Mole, KBE MVO FRIBA, born 1886, died 4 December 1962. Entered H.M. Office of Works in 1911. Architect to the Coronation of King George VI MVO 1937. Director of Works 1944. As Director General 1946 until retirement in 1958, responsible for a programme of Government building and maintenance, including defence and research establishments, which amounted to about £40-£50ml per annum.

[394] Map nos. 545 & 456, Greenwich Heritage Centre, Woolwich.

on 30 January 1915[395] and, as noted previously, for the west side on 19 July. H.M. Office of Works had asked the Council to provide space for a public exhibition showing the proposed accommodation shortly before their meeting on 11 March.[396] Just over five months later, on 20 August, Baines wrote to the Council 'expressing the sincere thanks of his Department for the help and assistance afforded by the Borough Council in connection with the Exhibition'.[397] Although the minutes do not say when the exhibition opened and closed, one might presume it ran from late-March until maybe shortly after the date of Baines's letter; the Borough Treasurer had been sent accounts for supplying and erecting stands for the exhibition (£7/15/2d) and for the cost of lighting and attendance (£8/9/6d) sometime prior to the Works Committee meeting held on 27 September.[398] The road names for the Estate were 'under consideration' by the London County Council by 22 June[399] (so they had presumably seen the site layout plan for the west side at least four weeks before it was submitted to the Council) and they confirmed their adoption to the Council on 5 August.[400]

As the graph on page 157 illustrates, Mowlem, one of the two main contractors for the Estate, had incurred about 75% of its total wage bill for the contract by early August,[401] so whilst it is possible that site layout plans for the entire Estate could include the numbers of detailed drawings by the time the exhibition closed, it is most unlikely they were available when it opened. Exhibits were probably amended and added during the time it was open. Therefore, speculatively, one might conclude that (a) the site layout plan for the east side was included from the start of the exhibition; (b) that for the west was added during the second half of July; and (c) the selection of detailed drawings now in the Greenwich Heritage

[395] MBW 1914-1915, p. 248, Works Committee, minute no. 7, 30 January 1915.

[396] MBW 1914-1915, p. 376, Establishment Committee, minute nos. 12 & 13, 11 March 1915.

[397] MBW 1914-1915, p. 742, Works Committee, minute no. 8, 27 September 1915.

[398] MBW 1914-1915, p. 739, Works Committee, minute no. 2, 27 September 1915.

[399] MBW 1914-1915, p. 666, Works Committee, minute no. 20, 19 July 1915.

[400] MBW 1914-1915, p. 742, Works Committee, minute no. 9, 27 September 1915.

[401] Analysis book, analysis of contracts from H.M. Office of Works, *H.M. Office of Works Well Hall Housing Scheme*, pp. 516-518, 531-532 and 550, London Metropolitan Archive, ACC/2809/12.

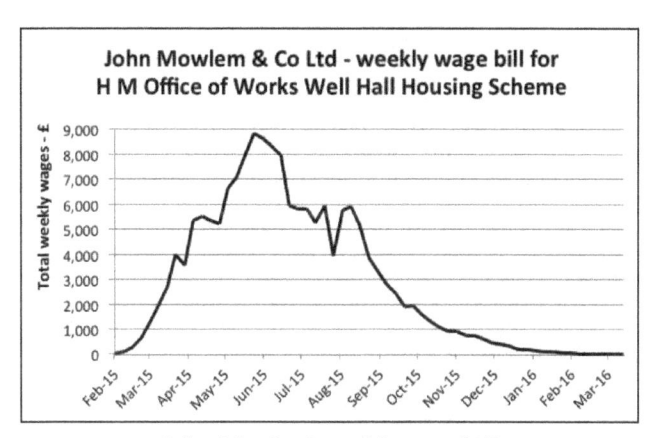

John Mowlem's weekly wage bill.

Centre were those selected for public display in Woolwich. It would also explain why the collection does not contain detailed plans for houses on the west side; its construction began, at the earliest, in the second half of July, by which time the majority of the houses on the east side would have been structurally complete with, at most, only internal work and finishing remaining.[402] The first residents, Mr. and Mrs. Sidney Aylward, had moved into their home in Well Hall Road on 22 May[403] and on 19 July Woolwich Borough Council's Works Committee minuted that houses on the new roads behind it would soon be occupied.[404]

The four classes of accommodation (see page 158) were defined by their internal rooms and not, save for the flats, by their external appearance. The layout of the accommodation is described as 'general' because there are occasional variations; the detailed drawings show a few of the Class II houses as having externally accessed ground-floor WCs (typical in Class III homes), and the occasional Class III house has an upstairs bathroom and WC (usual only in Class I and II homes). Some of the WCs in ground-floor flats were accessed internally and others externally. In a general review of designing small houses, Baines recorded that the two-storey flats proved to be very popular, particularly with

---

[402] The first residents, Mr and Mrs Sidney Aylward, moved into their house on the eastern side of Well Hall Road on 22 May 1915. In: Kennett (Progress Estate).

[403] Kennett (Progress Estate).

[404] MBW 1914-1915, p. 668, Works Committee, minute no. 26, 19 July 1915.

CLASSES OF ACCOMMODATION

Class	Key on plans	General layout of accommodation		Weekly rent	No. built
I	Black	Ground	Living room, parlour, spare bedroom or dining room, scullery	14/6d to 16/6d	116
		First	Three bedrooms, bathroom (hot and cold water laid on), WC		
II	Dotted	Ground	Living room, parlour and scullery	12/- to 13/6d	357
		First	As Class I		
III	Hatched	Ground	Living room, scullery with a bath, WC with external access	10/- to 11/6d	613
		First	Three bedrooms		
IV	Cross-hatched	Flat	Living room, scullery with a bath, two bedrooms, WC (accessed externally for some ground floor flats)	7/- to 7/6d	212

Source:: *Houses for Workers*, Technical Journals Ltd., undated, p.60.

young, married couples and people with one or two children.[405] They represented 16% of the homes on the Estate and one of their features was that each had its own back garden. This called for a sometimes complex design of rear boundaries, as the plan of Moira Road on page 159 shows.

As the table states, Class I and II houses had parlours. These had been a bone of contention between architects and the artisan classes for years. The former favoured one large living room over two smaller ones. They considered parlours would either turn into somewhere to show off useless ornamentations[406] or – worse still – be reserved for impressing Sunday teatime visitors and for the laying-out of the dead. As one commentator riled, of Bolton in 1899, 'The women are proud when they can exhibit a parlour to Sunday visitors. It is shut up six days a week, and is only kept for brag. Ostentatious superfluity in the idea of the artisan's wife is, as with those in higher grades of society, a sign of superiority'. The fact that a room could be so set aside for deliberate under-use, though perhaps irrational, was an indication of the ability to afford a surplus.[407] Even Frank Baines

[405] Baines (1918), p. 205.

[406] Harvey, p. 31.

[407] Allen Clarke, *The Effects of the Factory System*, 1899, p. 134. In: Burnett, p. 172.

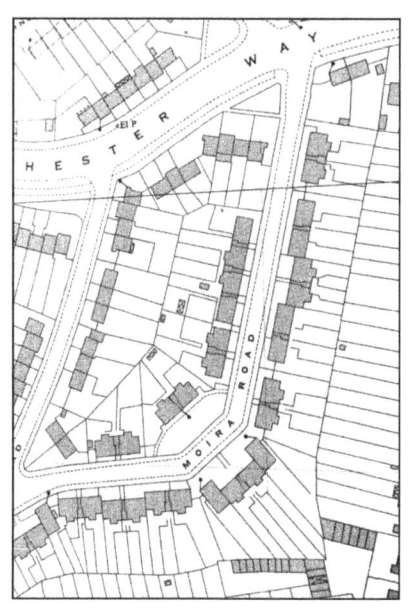

Moira Road flats.

felt it necessary to address the matter. Adopting more measured tones in 1918, he wrote: 'The parlour question is a very difficult one. On the one hand, people prefer to have a large, pleasant living room, rather than a small pokey room and a small parlour. On the other hand, people urge that the parlour is absolutely necessary for the purpose of the children studying and doing their lessons in quiet, for accommodating the piano, and the household gods, and for placing the coffin, in the event of a death in the family. Further, when visitors call, and the head of the household has just returned from work, the only place where the visitors can be introduced is the living room, and the necessity of a parlour is urged as being the only way of giving the householder some sort of privacy before he has changed his clothes after return from work'.[408]

The rents were fixed by H.M. Office of Works after consultation with a valuer and the Chief Superintendent of Ordnance Factories, who knew the wage-earning capacity of the men likely to occupy the houses.[409]

---

[408] Baines (1918), p. 204.

[409] MBW 1914-1915, p. 597, committee of the whole council, minute no. 2, 30 June 1915.

How to Build 1,298 Homes Fast – Frank Baines-Style

It was thanks to the intervention of the Ministry of Munitions that the Well Hall Estate was built by H.M. Office of Works and not the Woolwich Arsenal Engineering and Building Staff.[410] As we have seen, Frank Baines was apparently a master of getting things done. His supercharged work rate might not have endeared him to all his staff all the time, yet they rose to the task in hand and were individually modest about their individual roles in achieving a desired outcome.[411] Pitcher and Phillips concentrated on the designs and Bowden and Parker on the execution of the scheme.[412] Baines believed the demand of the working classes to live in conditions better than those which obtained prior to the war was a just one. The Office's scheme endeavoured to meet this aspiration and he considered that only the best was good enough.[413]

Visualising the rate at which the Estate was built remains a challenge. The setting out of the roads, sewers and houses began on 3 February 1915 and 312 days later, on 11 December, everything was finished.[414] Parts of this chapter will give some idea of how this was achieved.

In about the third week of January, tenders were invited to build the first 40 houses on the basis of H.M. Office of Works' drawings and specifications. One of these is drawing no. 8A (design G) in the Greenwich Heritage Centre Collection. Dated January 1915, it is for a pair of Class II semi-detached houses, and the annotation allows for the later addition of a contract number. The Office's internal estimate had been for an average of about £450 per house over all 40, but when the tenders arrived at the end of the month it became apparent that builders wanted at least twice as much.[415] The Office had run into the same problem that caused the Royal Arsenal to rely on direct labour.

[410] Beaufoy (1950), p. 259.

[411] Beaufoy (1952), p. 143.

[412] Beaufoy (1950), p. 260.

[413] The Inter-Allied Housing and Town-Planning Congress, *The Builder*, 18 June 1920, p. 727.

[414] *Houses for Workers*, Technical Journals, 1917 or 1918, p. 59. *The Building News* no. 3334, 27 November 1918, p. 358 stated that setting out commenced on 1 February – a Monday.

[415] Beaufoy (1950), p. 260.

Tendering only worked if all the details were available *ab initio*, whereas direct labour allowed them to be finalised as work proceeded. Bills of quantities had not been issued with the drawings. Unit prices would decline if the Office controlled the Estate's construction.

The government abandoned competitive tendering for building works as a whole during the war and instead let contracts on the basis of paying cost plus an agreed percentage for overheads and profit, a system that became known as 'cost-plus'.[416] As will be explained shortly, Baines took this a step further for the building of this Estate.

Most of the 252,327 tons of materials delivered to the site[417] arrived by rail. New sidings were constructed at Eltham Well Hall railway station (shown almost at the foot of the Indenture plan on page 141) to accommodate it. At the peak of construction (May to July 1915) 75 wagons were being offloaded per day,[418] each trainload's materials totalling between 1,800 and 2,430 tons.[419] Mr. (later Sir) Eustace Missenden, Traffic Superintendent at the Bricklayers Arms Depot on the Old Kent Road, the main freight yard of South Eastern Railways, provided valuable assistance in overcoming the scarcity of wagons.[420] A narrow-gauge railway was built to transport materials from the station to the site.

House construction showing narrow-gauge railway.

[416] Cooper, p. 48.

[417] Government Housing Scheme at Well Hall, Eltham, Kent.

[418] Gus White, p. 15.

[419] Hills, p. 11.

[420] S. G. L. Beaufoy (1952), p. 143. Eustace Missenden became the first chairman of the Railway Executive following the nationalisation of the railways in 1947 (en.wikipedia.org/wiki/Eustace_Missenden, accessed 28 September 2016).

Given the existence of the tramline along Well Hall Road, and the fact that the east side was almost certainly substantially completed before the west, one might suppose it ran to the west of and more or less parallel to the Road. As can be seen from the photograph, the line branched along its route through the site.

Having decided against tendering H.M. Office of Works needed to appoint main contractors, although their own staff would control the site. John Mowlem Ltd was selected for the roads, and they and N. Leslie Ltd shared the house construction work equally. A further 36 subcontractors were involved at one time or another.[421]

Mowlem had been contracted by H.M. Office of Works for major government building works on seven occasions since 1884, four times as main contractor and three for the construction of foundations. The main contracts were for two separate extensions to the Admiralty (£146,000 and £350,000), the refronting of Buckingham Palace (£50,000) and, between 1907 and 1910, work of unspecified value for the Office of Woods and Forests (the government department responsible for revenue-earning Crown lands). The foundations works were for the National Gallery (North) in 1884/85 and 1887/88, new public offices in Great George Street (off Parliament Square) between 1899 and 1908 and at the War Office in Whitehall in 1899/1900 and 1907/08.[422] Writing the firm's history, Baines described Mowlem as 'London's jobbing builders'.[423] On 27 November 1910, Sir John Mowlem Burt and Mr George Burt[424] trading as Messrs John Mowlem & Co. Ltd, were granted a warrant entitling them to use the Royal Arms in connection with the business as Builders and Contractors to His Majesty.[425]

Leslie had built the foundations for the completion of South Kensington Museum in two stages, 1899/1900 and 1910/11.

Baines's approach to building the Estate was to take the process to

---

[421] Government Housing Scheme at Well Hall, Eltham, Kent.

[422] M. H. Port, Appendix 3.

[423] Baines, (History of John Mowlem & Co).

[424] John Mowlem lived from 1788 to 1868. George Burt (1816-1894) was his principal partner. Sir John Mowlem Burt (1845-1918) was George's elder son and John Mowlem's godson. www.oxforddnb.com/view/article/51893/51897, accessed 31 March 2016.

[425] London Metropolitan Archives, file no. ACC/2809/69, framed certificate from the Lord Chamberlain's Office.

industrial proportions, as somewhat intimated by his building of the light railway from Well Hall station to the heart of the site. Whereas under a typical prime-cost contract the contractors would purchase materials and add an agreed percentage before billing the developer, here H.M. Office of Works itself ordered all the timber and supplied baths and fireplaces, checking the correct quantities were delivered before being housed in a large onsite store. Their staff also did all the timekeeping, prepared wage sheets and supervised the payments. They also set out all the foundations and put in all the levels, including those for roads and sewers.[426] (This does not conflict with the previously-mentioned minutes of the Metropolitan Borough of Woolwich; they had resolved that their Borough Engineer 'would render advice as to construction of sewers and roads, with periodical inspection and checking'.) It is also probable that the Office controlled the supply of backing bricks.[427]

Traditionally, brick-making had been a seasonal activity. Suitable clay would be dug in the autumn and left exposed to be broken down by the frosts over winter. Come springtime, it would be soaked, kneaded and placed in moulds until their contents had dried out sufficiently to be handled. The bricks were then stacked in 'walls' with spacers to allow the air to complete the drying process.[428] Finally, they were baked in a kiln. The first problem with bricks was that, being heavy, they were expensive to transport. Thus brickfields were plentiful around all communities; Ebenezer Howard's plan for Garden City (see page 69) allowed for brickfields on the left-hand side of its outskirts. The second was that their quality, especially the degree to which they were non-porous, was highly variable.

In the 1880s brick-makers who had leased parcels of land surrounding Fletton Lodge in Huntingdonshire started to make bricks not out of clay at ground level but from the Lower Oxford Clay beneath. It had three advantages over surface-dug clay. Firstly, the formations were of a consistent quality, depth and uniformity. Secondly, the clay did not need to be broken down and then re-soaked; it could be ground to a powder and squeezed into moulds before being stacked in the kiln to dry in recycled heat. Finally, it contained a high proportion of carbonaceous

---

[426] Beaufoy (1952), p. 143.

[427] Government Housing Scheme at Well Hall, Eltham, Kent.

[428] Hillier, pp. 8-9.

material so the bricks, once heated, virtually fired themselves. All this significantly reduced the coal required and so lowered the cost of production,[429] thereby moving brick-making from an agricultural to an industrial process and providing a product whose non-porosity was far more reliable.

Thus H.M. Office of Works chose flettons for backing bricks and trains of 50 wagons delivered them from Peterborough, a dispatch point for the industry, to Well Hall Station every day.[430] Facing bricks were obtained from a large number of traditional, and probably more local, brickfields, the variety amongst those not rendered providing an aesthetically pleasing result.[431]

Roofs were finished either with tiles or slates. Tiles, whose colour and tone varied from dark brown to light red, and dark blue to light grey, also came from many individual brickfields and some old tiles were introduced as well. The majority of the slates were obtained from the Carnarvon district – 'Greenarvon', Welsh Green 'rustic randoms', 'Vaingaled' and Abergynolwyn Welsh greys – along with Old Delabole of the rough-faced, stout, grey-green variety. The timber used for the half-timber work was mostly pitch pine treated with the then quite new preservative Solignum.[432] Some of the weatherboarding was oak. Floorboards and rafters had standardised dimensions. Most of the rough-cast was applied in one coat.[433]

The variety of materials added to the variation in the Estate's houses compared to those of garden suburbs built before or after it. Whilst satisfying Phillips' ambition of building an Estate that should look 'as if it had grown and not merely been dropped there', it also allowed materials to be sourced from many different suppliers, thereby greatly increasing the total volume that could be acquired in a given period of time and thus maximising the rate of building.[434] Sourcing materials

---

[429] Hillier, pp. 14-15.

[430] Beaufoy (1952), p. 143.

[431] Government Housing Scheme at Well Hall, Eltham, Kent.

[432] 'Founded on over 100 years of tradition …', www.solignum.co.uk, accessed 10 October 2016.

[433] Government Housing Scheme at Well Hall, Eltham, Kent.

[434] Baines (1918), p. 205.

THE EVOLUTION OF THE ESTATE

as locally as possible also served to reduce transport costs. Thus, for example, Woolwich's Borough Engineer was able to report on 15 March that he had offloaded considerable amounts of building material from his stock.[435]

- 2,250 yards of concrete channelling for kerbside drainage at his usual price of 1/- per yard.
- Clinker bricks for building manhole covers at 27/- per 1,000, thereby clearing the stock, H.M. Office of Works paying for haulage.
- All the accumulated clinker at the Woolwich and Plumstead Dust Destructors.[436] It was free from Woolwich, collection to be by the contractors, which saved the Borough the cost of disposing of it themselves. At Plumstead, the Office agreed to pay 6d. per ordinary load up to 1,000 loads and 4d. per load thereafter, or free at the door of the destructor where it was hot, receipts going to the Electricity Department.
- Surplus accumulations of gravel at 2/- per load for large and 2/6d for small material at the gravel pits; 'several loads' had already been taken away by tractor.
- Old tar paving at 1/- per load for blinding[437] on hardcore.

Although the soft and spongy surface of the site added vastly to the preliminary work, the ditches that intersected it were dammed up and served as a water source until a piped supply was laid on.[438]

The Estate has 2⅞ miles of roads on the east side and 1⅜ miles on the west.[439] Of these, 40% in the east, and only 24% in the west, matched London's legal minimum width of 40 feet. However, 90% in the east and 63% in the west had widths of either 30 or 40 feet. Boughton

---

[435] MBW 1914-1915, p. 742, Works Committee, minute no. 1.2, 15 March 1915.

[436] Incinerators fed by collected household waste. The Plumstead incinerator powered steam engines for the production of electricity. Ramsey (Greenwich Industrial History). The construction industry used its clinker as ballast, for example as a base for roads.

[437] A thin layer of coarse material to stop wet concrete running into the hardcore. www.constructiontermsx.com/blinding-definition, accessed 29 September 2016.

[438] Government Housing Scheme at Well Hall, Eltham, Kent.

[439] Hills, p. 13.

Road, Gilbourne Way and the eastern end of Admiral Seymour Road had especially wide verges to make provision for the Shooters Hill bypass road that, as Rochester Way, would be opened in 1932.[440]

There are 4.85 miles of sewers, including a 600-foot 15-inch sewer passing under Well Hall Road that reaches a maximum depth of 30 feet.[441] In the interests of economy, H.M. Office of Works decided not to provide separate sewers for soil and surface drainage[442] save that some of the ditches across the site were piped for the drainage of surface water from roads and roofs prior to them all being filled in.[443] All are gravity-fed and thus many run in a broadly north-north-east to south-west direction rather than under the lines of the roads.

One of the contemporary descriptions of the Estate states that 'the oak fencing, of which there is 27½ miles on the Estate, is also an interesting study in variety'.[444] Much renewal will have taken place over the last 100 years, so the original variety may no longer be there to see. Although the length of fencing initially strikes the readers as massive for the size of the Estate, it does stand up to analysis.

The total road length, 2⅞ miles on the east side and 1⅜ miles on the west, was 4¼ miles. Whilst the communally-maintained gardens the lengths of Well Hall Road are well known, as to a lesser extent are those in Whinyates Road and Admiral Seymour Road, contemporary photographs[445] show that front gardens elsewhere on the Estate did not have dividing fences. Nearly, if not all, the Estate's roadside fences were built in a castellated style (see illustration of Dickson Road on page 144) although houses along the raised section of Ross Way were not provided with front fences until 1938 (see illustration on page 216). The few fences one sees today dividing houses' front gardens that are in this style were, almost without doubt, built subsequently. Some in Ross Way, away from the raised section, appear to be original but either have been moved from the front of houses or are good subsequent replicas;

---

[440] MBW 1914-1915, p. 742, Works Committee, minute no. 12, 15 March 1915.

[441] Government Housing Scheme at Well Hall, Eltham, Kent.

[442] Hills, p. 13.

[443] MBW 1914-1915, p. 742, Works Committee, minute no. 12, 15 March 1915.

[444] Government Housing Scheme at Well Hall, Eltham, Kent.

[445] Eltham photographs, Greenwich Heritage Centre.

almost all have posts with squared-off tops and not the rounded tops of the original fence posts. Many other wooden dividing fences are of differing and varied styles. A few gardens are divided by wire or brick structures and hedges have proliferated. Front fencing was therefore only erected parallel to the roads and at the returns at the end of blocks next to footpaths, so both sides of the new roads accounted for around 8½ miles of the total.

The boundary fencing on the west side of Well Hall Road extends for about ¼ mile and, on the east side, some ¾ mile.

The next element derived from one of the covenants contained in the Indenture recording the sale of the site, discussed in the chapter about Cecil Henry Polhill. This obliged the Commissioners [of Works] to construct by [9 December 1915]:

> and forever thereafter maintain a close split oak park pale fence not less than six feet six inches high or other fence approved by the Vendor upon the boundary of the land hereby conveyed so far as adjoining any part of the Vendors ... Estates ...so as to sever and divide the same from such adjoining parts of the ... Estates except where ... the Vendor may require access to and from his adjoining estates over and along any roads made or to be made by the Commissioners ...

Less than half of the Estate's boundaries adjoin land owned by the Vendor.

The map on page 168 shows that Craigton Road and Grangehill Road, immediately to the east, were developed by 1914[446] so the Estate's houses between its southern end in Well Hall Road and the junction with Admiral Seymour Road, all those along Admiral Seymour Road and those in Granby Road almost up to its junction with Cornwallis Walk would have backed onto this existing development. On this side, therefore, boundary fencing was only necessary along the northern half of Granby Road to its junction with Well Hall Road. This extends for about a ½ mile.

The longest portion was required on the western boundary, where the acquired land cut across the Vendor's fields (see illustration on page 141). Its length was approximately 1⅛ miles.

---

[446] Ordnance Survey, London (1915-Numbered sheets) X.11 revised 1914, pub. 1916. Also London Sheet P, revised 1914, pub. 1920.

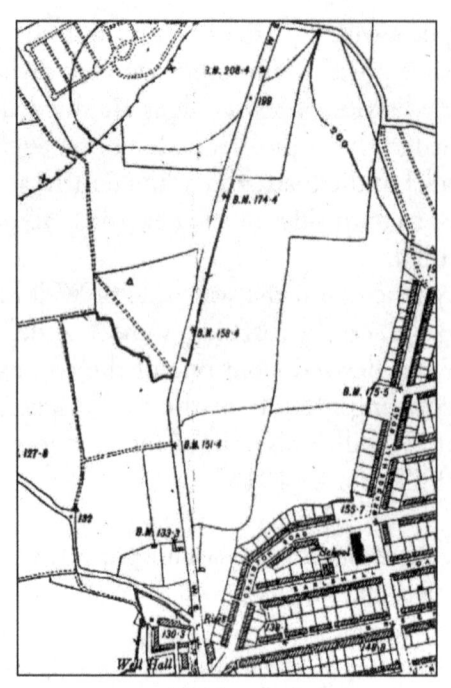

*Part of Ordnance Survey
London Sheet P (revised 1914).*

The appearance of the original boundary fence cannot be ascertained. Progress Estates Ltd., who purchased the Estate from H.M. Office of Works in 1925, replaced it with a close-boarded fence during 1957-58 at a cost of £2,464/6/3d[447] and this is probably the concrete-posted, approximately 5-foot high feather-boarded pine fence visible behind parts of 1-99 Granby Road today. Glimpses of a similar structure are visible at the end of gardens in Whinyates Road from Appleton Road, the road subsequently constructed to its west.

So, in summary, front fences along most of the Estate's new roads (8½ miles), Well Hall Road (¼ mile plus ¾ mile) and boundary fencing (½ mile plus 1⅛ miles) accounted for 11⅛ of the 27½ miles of fencing. What took the remaining 16⅜ miles? The answer is back gardens.

The minimum size of back garden provided was 1,100 square feet,[448]

---

[447] PEL, 1 November 1957, minute no. 2.

[448] 'The Inter-Allied Housing and Town-Planning Congress: The Well Hall Housing Scheme', *The Builder*, 18 June 1920, p. 727.

although many were much larger; sample sizes in a review of the Estate range from 1,426 to 2,850 square feet.[449] 16⅜ miles of fencing works out at an average of 67 feet per home over the Estate's 1,298 houses. Houses away from the Estate's boundaries would have shared the fence at the foot of their garden with the house behind and a side fence with a neighbour. Ignoring the 'extra' fence each block of houses required at one end, this 67-foot average would have built one side fence and half a rear fence, which sounds reasonable. Given the inevitable approximations in an analysis such as this, the total length of fences claimed appears to be borne out by evidence verifiable today.

The text on the detailed drawings for the Estate's houses describes their scale as 1¼ inches to 10 feet,[450] more generally referred to in the building trade as ⅛ inch to the foot. As can be seen from the illustration on the front cover, the architects laid out the internal design of each house. Assuming the drawings in the Greenwich Heritage Centre are representative of the Estate as a whole, it is clear that they also specified the external finishes – hung tiles, wood, brick, render or some combination of these materials. Comparing them with the frontages of the houses one sees today, it is also clear the drawings were followed meticulously; 99% of the mismatches are obviously later alterations. The major change is to the entrances to those flats where four share a common entrance. The architects specified a single front door, inside which two doors provided access to each ground-floor flat and a third to the staircase leading to the two first-floor flats. On-site, the front door leading to the outside was omitted and the three doors leading off the external vestibules are seen today. The other fairly common change is to the positioning of chimney stacks. Many that were designed to rise from the rear roof slopes were repositioned to sit symmetrically across the ridges of roofs and in a few cases additional stacks were also incorporated.

On-site decisions would therefore generally have been to do with the choice of materials for the interior of houses, the layout of gardens for the flats and possibly the choice of roof tiles or slates. Mr W.T. Bowman was H.M. Office of Works' Principal Resident Officer on the site. He had

---

[449] Government Housing Scheme at Well Hall, Eltham, Kent.

[450] Greenwich Heritage Centre, Woolwich, *Government Housing Scheme Woolwich, design C.C.C.* drawing no. 127, H.M. Office of Works.

joined the Office in about 1890, some five years before Baines. By 1904 he was working in its section that was responsible for post offices[451] and presumably transferred to Baines's section when the war effort began. He appears to have been responsible for overseeing the Office's day-to-day involvement in the supply of materials and timekeeping whilst Charles Mole, the architect referred to in the previous chapter, liaised between him and those who had designed the site, altering layouts and possibly changing the position of some houses. Although precise information has not come to light, it seems clear that much detail was decided on-site, albeit the Office's four architects assigned to the project were given the opportunity to comment. Bowman remained in post until the last house was finished.[452]

The need for decision-making to be devolved to site level if all 1,298 homes were to be built at the expected rate is clear when one considers the numbers of people employed in its construction. One of Mowlem's surviving financial records is the analysis book whose entries formed the basis of the graph on page 157. Payments under the contract totalled £339,787/18/6d (ignoring £9,192/10/- of sundries) of which £166,655/17/10d was for wages and £173,132/0/8d for materials. By way of comparison, accounts rendered to Parliament under the Housing Act, 1914 for the fiscal year 1915-16 included £700,603/4/9d for the erection of buildings and £57,239/9/6d for roads, sewers, etc.[453] Half the building costs plus all the charges for roads and sewers (the two elements of Mowlem's contract) amount to £407,541/1/10d, 20% more than Mowlem's payments. Although the records do not say what their prime cost mark-up was, they do show the contract accounted for the greater part of their increase in turnover to £1,043,475 for 1915, up from £616,980 in 1914.

From this data it is possible to estimate the average weekly earnings of workmen on the site before cross-checking the conclusion with national data for contemporary wages in the building trade.

---

[451] 'The Post Office Extension', *Norwich Mercury*, 2 April 1904, www.britishnewspaperarchive.co.uk/viewer/print/bl/0001669/19040402/081/0005.

[452] S. L. G. Beaufoy (1952), p. 143.

[453] 1916(149) Housing Act 1914, Account, 1915-16, 1916 session, House of Commons papers; accounts and papers, 20 Century House of Commons Sessional Papers vol. XVII, page 177.

The maximum number of men simultaneously employed on the construction of the Estate was 5,637[454] and one might assume this was close to the time when Mowlem's wages bill peaked at £8,833 for the first week of June 1915. Gangs of labourers were brought over from Ireland and two special trains were laid on each day to transport men from Cannon Street to Well Hall station.[455] If Mowlem was employing half the people on the site their average employee was earning around £3/2/6d per week. Overtime accounted for a quarter of the wage bill,[456] so stripping this out indicates average basic weekly wages of about £2/10/-.

In 1914, for the United Kingdom as a whole, carpenters, masons, bricklayers and plasterers were estimated to earn an average 8/7½d for a 10-hour day and plumbers 9/-. Labourers earned 6/- for a 9-hour day.[457] Bricklayers normally worked in set gang sizes, five typically being supported by three labourers carrying hods of bricks to 'the trowels' and mixing mortar.[458] These gangs probably represented a high proportion of the Estate's labour force when employment peaked. The average wages per gang member for a six-day week at these rates works out at £2/5/10d. The wages paid to carpenters, plasterers and plumbers would have increased this somewhat, so one can say with reasonable certainty that the average wages derived from Mowlem's records (£2/10/-) is a reflection of national wage rates for the building industry.

Baines's group of four architects worked an average of eleven or twelve hours per day and seven days a week with frequent all-night sessions to avert threatened delays[459] and many of those employed onsite worked similarly long hours and weeks. Overtime and Sunday working were common-place and night-work was also undertaken. Over and above those commuting from Cannon Street, many others travelled

---

[454] Government Housing Scheme at Well Hall, Eltham, Kent.

[455] S. L. G. Beaufoy (1952), p. 143.

[456] 'The Inter-Allied Housing and Town-Planning Congress: The Well Hall Housing Scheme', *The Builder*, 18 June 1920, p. 727.

[457] R. W. Postgate, *The Builders' History*, The National Federation of Building Trade Operatives, London, 1923, p. 455.

[458] Email correspondence between the author and Peter Haywood, London South Bank University, December 2015.

[459] S. L. G. Beaufoy (1950), p. 261.

from other parts of London and public transport was not that good at weekends and night-time.[460]

Despite these pressures, there were only two short labour disputes during the construction of the Estate. The second was the easier to settle. It lasted for a day in late-July or early August, was caused by an unpopular foreman and resolved by his being moved to another part of the site.[461]

The first, in late-April or early May, was more complicated. It concerned wage levels and the aforementioned transport difficulties. The men argued that the Office of Works' degree of involvement in managing the prime cost contract for the site meant that they were employed by the government. Men working at the Royal Arsenal factories had just been awarded a 4/- per week pay rise and, as *de facto* war workers, they should receive the same. They wanted 1d per hour plus various travel facilities. Mowlem and Leslie claimed they were the employers and thus London building rates applied.[462] Mr. Bowman obtained a settlement 'with a proper mixture of persuasion and good basic English'.[463] The men settled for 3/- per week (about three farthings per hour) provided they lost no more time than three hours per week, excluding Sundays, through travel delays.[464]

The Office of Works introduced economies wherever possible, yet the overriding consideration was the rapid completion of houses. One can imagine the pressure Baines was subjected to by the War Office, and then from June 1915 Lloyd George's newly formed Ministry of Munitions, as it became clear that the Estate was unlikely to be completed by the initially (and probably unreasonably) promised time of mid-August,[465] whilst on the other hand the Treasury would have been forever expressing their concerns about the steeply-rising costs.[466]

---

[460] Alan Hills, p. 15.

[461] Alan Hills, p. 15.

[462] Alan Hills, pp. 14-15.

[463] S. L. G. Beaufoy (1952), p. 143.

[464] *The Pioneer*, 7 May 1915 p. 5 and 14 May 1915, In: Alan Hills, p. 15-16.

[465] MBW 1914-1915, p. 240, Public Health and Housing Committee, minute no. 12, 10 February 1915.

[466] Swenarton (1981), p. 54.

That he managed his way through this, representing as it did the Office's first major wartime project for something that was outwith its pre-war sphere of activities, adds to his previously-noted organisational talent an insight into his political aptitude. Five years after the Estate was finished, he stated the final cost of homes was: Class I – £713; Class II – £606; Class III – £465; and Class IV – £399.[467] Taking the numbers of each class shown on page 158, this gives a cost for the entire Estate of £668,683, whereas the total in the government accounts was £806,660/16/11d.[468] What accounted for the difference of £137,977? Maybe Sir Frank (as, by then, he was) omitted some of the infrastructure costs. One hundred years after the event, we will probably never know. Based on the Government's accounts, the average home cost £621.

The Estate's new roads (that is, all except Well Hall Road) were gravelled, as were the pathways. The pathways likely to be the most used had staggered concrete slabs laid down the centre,[469] as can be made out in the lower of the two illustrations on page 144 from the central, lighter portion of the pavement in Dickson Road. Thanks in part to footpaths on the east side that connect north-south roads in an east-west direction, no house on the Estate is more than 400 yards from Well Hall Road.[470]

Tenants were given the choice of electricity or gas. The former was produced by Woolwich Borough Council whose Plumstead incinerators of household waste powered the steam engines that generated it.[471] They claimed it ensured cleanliness, a pure atmosphere, would not damage decorations and was by far the cheapest illuminant. The South Metropolitan Gas Company responded that 'one penny spent on gas buys twice as much light and three times as much heat as a penny spent on electricity'.[472] Their advertising also offered their customers 'modern gas fittings throughout the house, a gas cooker and a gas fire (if desired)'.

---

[467] 'The Inter-Allied Housing and Town-Planning Congress: The Well Hall Housing Scheme', *The Builder*, 18 June 1920, p. 727.

[468] 1916(149) Housing Act 1914, see fn 453.

[469] Government Housing Scheme at Well Hall, Eltham, Kent.

[470] Jones, p. 9.

[471] Ramsey (Greenwich Industrial History).

[472] Kennett (Progress Estate).

Tenants could apply for the service at the Company's showrooms, 36, Powis Street, Woolwich or 1, Park Place, Eltham.[473]

Although street lighting was installed, it was sparse. Whilst electricity was supplied to houses, it was not available for public street lighting. Mr. Talbot, the Superintendent of Lighting to the South Metropolitan Gas Company told the Deputy Borough Engineer when they met to discuss the installation in early July that H.M. Office of Works had suggested that a column more ornamental in design than the ordinary pattern should be used in the Estate roads. Approximately 70 lamps would be required on the east side and 50 on the west. The Borough's Works Committee was, however, of the opinion that the ordinary column, fitted with a Metro lantern and a No. 2 burner, as used in the majority of side streets in the district, was quite suitable for the roads on the Government Estate.[474] The cost would be £691, which was approved by the Finance Committee on 28 July 1915.[475] The same Finance Committee meeting also approved a loan of £2,172 for the laying of electricity mains and wiring for 'certain houses'; wiring in houses remained the property of the electric company.[476]

The only worker killed during the construction of the Estate was Harry Steward Crook, a 53-year-old bricklayer living at 47 Duke Road, High Road, Chiswick. He fell 16 or 17 feet from scaffolding into the well of a staircase. At the inquest held in Woolwich, Charles Fletcher of Eastney Street, Greenwich said he saw the deceased's head strike a plank just before he reached the ground which corresponded with the certifying doctor's cause of death – a coma, following a fracture at the base of the skull and concussion of the brain. Mr. Fletcher said the scaffold was slippery as it had been raining. The jury returned a verdict of accidental death and a representative of the War Office expressed the sympathy of the staff with the relatives of the deceased.[477]

Sir Frank Baines CBE MVO (knighted for his war work in 1918 and, by now, Director of H.M. Office of Works) looked back on

---

[473] *The Pioneer*, Friday, 7 May 1915, p. 7.

[474] MBW 1914-1915, p. 668, Works Committee, minute no. 26, 19 July 1915.

[475] MBW 1914-1915, p. 678, Finance Committee, minute no. 1, 28 July 1915.

[476] PEL, 22 July 1925, minute no. 6.

[477] *The Kentish Independent and Kentish Mail*, Friday, 9 July 1915.

the development in June 1920. The Office had been asked by the Government to provide accommodation for the enormous increase in the local population in a hurry in 1915, and had to rush through a housing scheme. The scheme did not include provision (usually made in town planning schemes) for playgrounds, schools or public buildings; the problem with which they had to deal was the accommodation of workers in the shortest possible time. There were, however, two large, open spaces for recreation. It was decided to try to produce something which would be of permanent assistance in the housing problem, modelled on the lines of the old English village and representative of the best traditions of English domestic architecture, with gardens to each house and as many open spaces as possible. He thought they had achieved this aim.[478]

Notwithstanding the initially-declared ambition of the President of the Local Government Board that the project should be completed in six months, it is hard to disagree with Sir Frank's summary. From a roadless site (save for Well Hall Road) with no services laid on, first surveyed in February 1915, the first block of houses was finished and tenanted on 22 May, 800 were ready for occupation by 20 July and 1,000 by 15 September.[479] At the height of activities, one house was being completed every two hours.[480] All 1,298 were finished by the end of the year and only 50 were without tenants.[481] There was a waiting list of 3,700 by Christmas[482] and the Estate's popularity continued; in his remarks in June 1920, Sir Frank reported that the London County Council (whom the Office had appointed to manage the Estate in July 1915)[483] still had a waiting list of 1,700 families.

---

[478] 'The Inter-Allied Housing and Town-Planning Congress: The Well Hall Housing Scheme', *The Builder*, 18 June 1920, p. 727.

[479] *The Building News*, no. 3334, 27 November 1918, p. 358.

[480] Hills, p. 12.

[481] Jones, p. 5.

[482] *The Pioneer*, 23 December 1915, p. 1. In: Hills, p. 19.

[483] MBW 1914-1915, p. 674, General Purposes Committee, minute no. 4, 20 July 1915.

The Estate's Road Names

The only road on the Estate that preceded its construction was Well Hall Road, the highway connecting Woolwich with Eltham. As for the rest, H.M. Office of Works suggested to the London County Council that the new streets should bear the names of famous men who had lived in Woolwich and held high office at Woolwich Arsenal or the Dockyard. Their wish was more or less carried out by the LCC although whether one or two, important men though they were, could be described as having held 'high office' in the usual sense of the phrase in either of these theatres is questionable. The LCC wrote to Woolwich Borough Council on 22 June 1915 listing the names under consideration. Whilst the Borough asked that Martin Bowes Road, Admiral Seymour Road and Prince Rupert Road be abbreviated to Bowes Road, Seymour Road and Rupert Road, respectively, and also that Gordon Road be substituted for Phineas Pett Road, the Council's proposed list was adopted with just one alteration (Ross Way replacing their initial suggestion of Ross Green) because there were already a number of roads in the London postal area that had the Borough's suggested shortened names.[484]

The lives of sixteen of the twenty-six people remembered in the Estate's roads span, collectively, the 18th and the first half of the 19th centuries. A number from the military were appointed to the Order of the Bath. This order of chivalry was founded in 1725 by George I and its members are, in order of seniority, Knight Grand Cross (GCB), Knight Commander (KCB) and Companion (CB).[485]

This chapter is somewhat based on W. T. Vincent's *The Records of the Woolwich District*,[486] and the notes on the people are, mostly, limited to their military or naval careers insofar as they were linked to Woolwich. Some, for example Cobbett, had memorable civilian lives as well, and anyone interested in finding out more about them might like to study the sources listed in the footnotes. The *Oxford Dictionary of National Biography* is particularly well-referenced.

---

[484] MBW 1914-1915, pp. 666 and 742, Works Committee, minutes nos. 20, 19 July 1915 and no. 9, 27 September 1915.

[485] en.wikipedia.org/wiki/Order_of_the_Bath, accessed 28 November 2016.

[486] Published in two volumes by J. P. Jackson, Woolwich and J. S. Virtue & Co., London, 1890.

Admiral Seymour Road

Thomas Seymour was born in or before 1509, the fourth of six sons of Sir John Seymour, landowner and courtier of Wolf Hall in Wiltshire. Sir John and his wife Margery also had four daughters, one of whom, Jane, became the third wife of Henry VIII on 30 May 1536. It was as a result of this marriage that Thomas rose to prominence. He became a gentleman of the privy chamber on 2 October 1536 and was knighted on 18 October 1537, six days after Jane had given birth to Edward, Prince of Wales. He was further rewarded with grants of former monastic lands in Essex, Hampshire and Berkshire.

In the summer of 1543 he was marshal of the English Army in the Low Countries, which experience may explain his appointment as Master of the Ordnance for life on 18 April 1544, a striking mark of royal favour. He took part in the capture of Boulogne on 14 September of the same year. The following month he was appointed an Admiral of the Fleet, and was much involved in naval action in 1545. By the end of Henry's reign, Seymour's annual income was £458/6/8d. He was sworn onto the Privy Council on 23 January 1547, five days before the King's death. The King had named Seymour as one of the assistants to the executors of his will and left him £200. Sir William Paget, the King's Principal Secretary, believed the King had wished Seymour to be ennobled and thus, on 16 February 1547 he was created Baron Seymour of Sudeley and granted additional lands valued at £500 per annum. He was nominated Knight of the Garter and appointed Lord High Admiral the following day.

Notwithstanding the social status and wealth that royal patronage had laid upon him, Seymour was dissatisfied with his position vis-à-vis the Regency Council of Edward VI. He embarked on a series of intrigues and dalliances that were to be his downfall, despite his sister Jane being the King's mother and the Council being led at the time by his brother Edward, Duke of Somerset. He secretly married the King's widow, Katherine Parr, in May or June 1547. Katherine had cherished the hope of their marrying after her second husband, Lord Latimer, died in March 1543, but Henry's desire to do likewise thwarted the idea; to refuse the King would have been to defy God's will.[487] The

---

[487] Susan E. James, 'Katherine [Katherine Parr] (1512-1548)', *Oxford Dictionary of National Biography*, Oxford University Press, 2004; online edn, Jan 2012 [http://www.oxforddnb.com/view/article/4893, accessed 26 January 2017].

marriage was nevertheless in open defiance of the Privy Council. Katherine, at the age of 36, died on 5 September 1548 shortly after giving birth to their daughter, Mary Seymour. Seymour had begun to flirt with the fifteen-year-old Princess Elizabeth (daughter of Henry VIII and Anne Boleyn and the future Elizabeth I) before Katherine's death. He was arrested on 17 January 1549, examined on 18 and 23 February and beheaded at Tower Hill on 20 March. On hearing of his execution, Elizabeth, who might not have been reluctant to receive his advances only a few months earlier but was aware of the political sensitivities, said, 'This day died a man with much wit, and very little judgement'.[488]

Arsenal Road

Woolwich Dockyard can be traced back to 1512 and the Government works, now known as the Arsenal, is at least as ancient as this. In 1558, a battery of seven guns was erected (along with similar installations at Erith, Greenhithe and Gravesend) to protect the capital should Spanish ships attempt to journey along the Thames to attack it. Woolwich Ropeyard was erected on Crown property in 1573-76 to supply cordage to the Navy, and continued to be an important hive of industry for three centuries. For about a hundred years thereafter, the Ropeyard and the Warren, a piece of land later known as Woolwich Green and used to prove and test newly-cast guns, were jointly controlled by the Board of Admiralty. In 1667, Prince Rupert (see page 192) was ordered by the King 'to raise works and batteries at Woolwich and build in the Warren a platform with 60 guns upon it as a defence against the Dutch'. Gun manufacturing first took place in 1683, at which time the Government had full control over 'all the wharfs, magazines, cranes &c' and provided a dwelling for the Master Gunner of England and lodgings for ten field gunners and 'such Ordnance labourers as might be necessary'.

The Arsenal Football Club moved north of the Thames before the Estate was built. It was formed as the Royal Arsenal Football Club in 1893. Its name was subsequently changed to the Woolwich Arsenal

---

[488] G. W. Bernard, 'Seymour, Thomas, Baron Seymour of Sudeley (*b.* in or before 1509, *d.* 1549)', *Oxford Dictionary of National Biography*, Oxford University Press, 2004; online edn, May 2015 [http://www.oxforddnb.com/view/article/25181, accessed 16 November 2016].

Football Club and then, in 1914, to the Arsenal Football Club. It played its last match at its South London ground in Plumstead on 26 February 1913. The club then moved to Highbury and played its first game there on 6 September 1913.[489]

Boughton Road

This is one of the two roads that became completely incorporated in Rochester Way (see page 194).

Sir Edward Boughton was King Henry VIII's confidential clerk and local agent at Woolwich and Plumstead. He was also the owner of considerable lands and a manorial dwelling in Plumstead and had managed the estates the King had confiscated from the monks of Lessness (now Lesnes) Abbey. When the monastery of St. Augustine at Canterbury was dissolved, on 30 July 1538, the manor and the church at Plumstead became vested in the Crown, but on 20 January 1539 the King granted to Sir Edward 'the manor and parsonage, tythes, &c., within the parishes and villages of Plumstead, Bostall, Wickham, Welling, Woolwich, Bexley, Lesseness, Erith, Yard alias Crayford, and the advowson of the vicarage of Plumstead, and the chapel of Wickham thereunto annexed'. (An advowson is the right to present to the diocesan bishop a nominee to fill a vacancy for a parish priest.) About three years later he also granted to him 120 acres of marshland, then covered with water, in Plumstead, to the north of 50 acres owned by Martin Bowes (see page 188). In 1545, Sir Edward either sold or relinquished the tenancies of two parcels of land known as 'Bowton's' (or 'Boughton's') to the King and, subsequently, two more parcels named 'Sandhill' and 'Our Lady's Hill'. All were included in the earliest limits of the infant dockyard.

Brome Road

General Joseph Brome was three times Commandant of Woolwich Garrison (portions of 1790-91, 1792 and 1793). He began his career as a drummer in the Royal Artillery in about 1726 and is described as a

[489] Tony Attwood, Andy Kelly and Mark Andrews, *Woolwich Arsenal FC: 1893-1915*, Hamilton House, 2012.

very small man, very reserved and strict as to duty. He died on 24 April 1796 at the age of 84 and was buried in Plumstead churchyard, the last resting place of many military and naval men associated with Woolwich.

Cobbett Road

William Cobbett was born on 9 March 1762 in Farnham, Surrey. He enlisted at Chatham in a line regiment in 1784 and was posted to Nova Scotia from 1785 to 1791. There he met his future wife, Anne Reid, then a girl of thirteen. She was the daughter of a sergeant major in the artillery and he of the same rank in his foot regiment. Six months later the artillery battery was sent home to Woolwich and his Love went with them. He gave her his life savings of £150, telling her to use them as her own. Two years later his foot regiment returned to Woolwich and he found his girl working as a servant to Captain Brisac for £5 a year, yet she put in his hands the entire £150. They married at Woolwich Church on 5 February 1792 and were said to have thereafter lived a life of uninterrupted married bliss.

After returning to Woolwich, Cobbett became a politician, radical journalist and agriculturalist. He was famous, under the *nom de plume* 'Peter Porcupine', as the most vehement critic of one-time fellow Woolwich resident Tom Paine (1737-1809). Paine was the author of, most famously, *The Age of Reason* (1793-95) and, as a serial pamphleteer, a leading advocate of republicanism in the age of the American and French Revolutions, in which countries he resided for long periods of time. Cobbett, formerly a Tory but by now turned radical, apologised for his literary attacks on Paine after the latter's death in 1809 and, in 1819, had his bones dug up and brought back to England where they subsequently disappeared.[490] He established a plant nursery at Kensington in 1820 where he and his son developed a dwarf strain of maize that grew well in the shortish English summer. He died in Farnham on 18 June 1835 and was buried in the parish church of St Andrew's churchyard in Farnham, Surrey.[491]

---

[490] Mark Philp, 'Paine, Thomas (1737-1809)', *Oxford Dictionary of National Biography*, Oxford University Press, 2004; online edn, May 2008 [http://www.oxforddnb.com/view/article/21133, accessed 16 Nov 2016].

[491] en.wikipedia.org/wiki/William_Cobbett, accessed 16 November 2016.

Congreve Road

Lieutenant General Sir William Congreve (4 July 1742 to 30 April 1814) served with honour in several battles and had much influence on the progress of artillery science. In 1778 he organised the school of instruction which has been known ever since as the Royal Military Repository at Woolwich, and in due course all his energies became concentrated on the Office of Comptroller, Royal Laboratory, which was conferred upon him in 1783. He also founded the gunpowder factory at Waltham Abbey after he had successfully lobbied for the government to run its own gunpowder mills, these leading to improved artillery strength as a result of experimentations with gunpowder. He was made a Baronet on 7 December 1812.

His eldest son, also Sir William Congreve (20 May 1772 to 16 May 1828), the second Baronet, invented the Congreve rocket. He was known by the courtesy title of Colonel Congreve. His rocket resulted from the establishment of a military rocket programme at the Royal Arsenal, Woolwich. After their invention, they were manufactured near Waltham Abbey and first used in Royal Navy attacks on the French fleet at Boulogne in 1805. They continued to be used by the United Kingdom until the 1850s. He continued to invent both military and civilian machines throughout his life, examples being a gun-recoil mounting and a process of colour printing. In 1814, he became Comptroller of the Royal Laboratory at Woolwich, the same post his father had held, and continued in it until his death.[492]

Cornwallis Walk

Charles Cornwallis, 5th Baron Cornwallis and his wife Elizabeth, a niece of Sir Robert Walpole, had three sons. The eldest, Charles, born on 31 December 1738, was styled Viscount Brome in 1753 whilst his father was still alive. There is no connection with General Joseph Brome, after whom Brome Road was named; the Cornwallis hierarchy had been established at Brome Hall near Eye in Suffolk in the 14th

---

[492] en.wikipedia.org/wiki/Sir_William_Congreve,_2nd_Baronet, accessed 16 November 2016.

century and the family's position had been established through its exceptional loyalty to the Crown, a trait that Charles continued.[493]

Charles joined the Army in 1757. Upon his father's death in 1762, he became Earl Cornwallis and took his seat in the House of Lords. He received his military education primarily on the Continent. From 1766 to 1805 he was Colonel of the 33rd Regiment of Foot and, from the date of his attaining this rank until 1781, was one of the leading British generals in the American War of Independence. He was knighted in 1786 and appointed Governor-General and Commander-in-Chief in India. Upon returning to Britain in 1794, he was appointed aide-de-camp to the Marquess of Granby (see page 186) whom he served for a year until being given the post of Master-General of the Ordnance. In 1798 he was appointed Lord-Lieutenant and Commander-in-Chief of Ireland where he was instrumental in bringing about the political union of Great Britain and Ireland in 1800-01. He was reappointed to India in 1805 where he died not long after his arrival.[494]

The fourth son of Baron Cornwallis and Elizabeth was William Cornwallis (10 February 1744 to 5 July 1819). He entered the Navy, aged eleven, in 1755. The ships upon which he served took part in many battles which, collectively, gave the Royal Navy almost complete dominance over the world's oceans for more than a century, leading Horace Walpole to remark: 'our bells are worn threadbare ringing for victories'. His first command, in July 1762 (at the age of eighteen) was of the eight-gun sloop-of-war HMS *Wasp*. He commanded many ships of increasing firepower, as well as squadrons that saw several engagements before being promoted, in 1796, to Rear-Admiral of Great Britain (of the United Kingdom after the 1801 Union of Great Britain with Ireland). He was further elevated to Vice-Admiral of the United Kingdom in 1814. He served as Member of Parliament for Eye on four occasions between 1768 and 1807 and for Portsmouth from 1782 to

---

[493] C. A. Bayly, Katherine Prior, 'Cornwallis, Charles, first Marquess Cornwallis (1738-1805)', *Oxford Dictionary of National Biography*, Oxford University Press, 2004; online edn, Sept 2011 [www.oxforddnb.com/view/article/6338, accessed 18 November 2016].

[494] en.wikipedia.org/wiki/Charles_Cornwallis,_1st_Marquess_Cornwallis, accessed 18 November 2016 and Andrew Lambert, 'Cornwallis, Sir William (1744–1819)', *Oxford Dictionary of National Biography*, Oxford University Press, 2004; online edn, Jan 2008 [http://www.oxforddnb.com/view/article/6346, accessed 4 May 2017].

1790. He was a friend of Lord Nelson's and served as commander-in-chief of the Channel Fleet during the Napoleonic Wars (1803-1815).[495]

The third son, James (25 February 1743 to 20 January 1824) took Holy Orders. The boys' uncle on their father's side, Frederick, became Archbishop of Canterbury in 1768 and James was Dean of Canterbury from 1775 to 1781.[496]

It is probably Charles who lent his name to Cornwallis Walk for having been Master-General of the Ordnance from 1795 to 1801; William's associations were with Eye and Portsmouth, not Woolwich.

Dickson Road

Major General Sir Alexander Dickson GCB (3 June 1777 to 22 April 1840) began his career as a gentleman cadet in the Royal Military Academy, Woolwich on 5 April 1793 and became second lieutenant Royal Artillery on 6 November 1794. He was Superintendent of the Royal Gun Factories in Woolwich from 1822 to 1827. He rose through the ranks and was made up to Colonel on 1 July 1836 having, along the way, been a major and then lieutenant colonel in the Portuguese Army. Dickson excelled himself under the command of the Duke of Wellington and the glory he gained during the wars against Napoleon was followed by distinguished service in other parts of the world. In 1825, he became the first Royal Military Officer to receive the GCB. He was made Director-General of the Royal Artillery's field training department in 1838, combining it with the duties of Deputy Adjutant-General of the Royal Artillery until his death in 1840. His remains were interred in Plumstead churchyard, a notable resting place for heroes. He had a magnificent funeral and his regiment went into mourning for him for one month. A very stately monument was erected, by regimental subscription, in the Royal Military Repository in 1847 to record his many and distinguished services.[497]

---

[495] en.wikipedia.org/wiki/William_Cornwallis, accessed 18 November 106.

[496] en.wikipedia.org/wiki/James_Cornwallis,_4th_Earl_Cornwallis, accessed 18 November 2016.

[497] H. M. Chichester, 'Dickson, Sir Alexander (1777-1840)', rev. Gordon L. Teffeteller, *Oxford Dictionary of National Biography*, Oxford University Press, 2004; online edn, Jan 2011 [http://www.oxforddnb.com/view/article/7612, accessed 18 November 2016].

Although Dickson Road is almost undoubtedly named in remembrance of Sir Alexander Dickson, it is worth mentioning his third son, General Sir Collingwood Dickson (1817-1904) who also had a distinguished career in the Royal Artillery that began with his education at the Royal Military Academy, Woolwich. He served in many campaigns including the Crimea and was wounded at Sebastopol. He was Inspector-General of Artillery from 1870 to 1875 and was made a KCB on 20 May 1871. He reached the rank of general on 1 October 1877. He was President of the Ordnance Committee from 1881 until his retirement on 20 November 1884.[498] He inherited the methodical and extremely detailed notes his father had written about artillery activities during the Peninsular sieges along with letters his father had written to General Macleod at the same time. He subsequently lent them to Colonel Francis Duncan whilst the latter was writing his *History of the Royal Regiment of Artillery*.[499]

Downman Road

The military career of General Sir Thomas Downman (1776-11 August 1852) began and ended at Woolwich. He was commissioned second lieutenant, Royal Artillery on 24 April 1793 and joined the Army in The Netherlands upon completing his education at the town's Royal Military Academy. He saw distinguished service with the Royal Horse Artillery in France, the West Indies and Spain, where Wellington mentioned him for bravery in his dispatch from Celada. He was made Director General of Artillery in 1843-4 before being appointed to command the Woolwich Garrison in 1848. He was made KCB on 6 April 1852 and died at the Royal Arsenal whilst still in his post as Woolwich's commander.[500]

Vincent also mentions a Lieutenant General Sir C. Downman, KCB KCH, saying he distinguished himself in many engagements under the

---

[498] E. M. Lloyd, 'Dickson, Sir Collingwood (1817-1904)', rev. James Falkner, *Oxford Dictionary of National Biography*, Oxford University Press, 2004 [http://www.oxforddnb.com/view/article/32820, accessed 18 November 2016].

[499] pub: John Murray, London, 1879.

[500] H. M. Stephens, 'Downman, Sir Thomas (1776-1852)', rev. Roger T. Stearn, *Oxford Dictionary of National Biography*, Oxford University Press, 2004 [http://www.oxforddnb.com/view/article/7985, accessed 22 November 2016].

Duke of York, Marquess of Anglesey, and Duke of Wellington. He does not say when he was born or died, or whether he was related to Sir Thomas Downman.

Franklin Passage

Sir John Franklin (16 April 1786 to 11 June 1847) was a Royal Navy seaman who became an Arctic explorer. The Navy resumed Arctic exploration after the end of the Napoleonic Wars, looking for the Northwest Passage. A sea route linking the Pacific and Atlantic Oceans was seen as important to the expansion of the British Empire and could be investigated now there were many idle seamen at home. Her Majesty's ships *Erebus* and *Terror* were placed under Franklin's command and fitted out under his direction at Woolwich in the summer of 1845. They were powered by high-pressure steam engines with the latest boilers. Their keels were extended to increase their vertical alignment and to protect their interiors. Their sterns were redesigned to allow for the raising and lowering of new propellers. This was to be Franklin's fourth Arctic voyage and its aim was to circumnavigate America. Both the ships had been engaged in the South Polar expedition under the command of Captain Sir James Ross (see page 198) in 1839-43 and the *Terror* had visited the Arctic in 1836, then attempting to trace the northern boundary of America but forced to turn back by the ice. Franklin's was to be the 58th Arctic expedition from England and the two ships, carrying supplies for a long voyage that included ten live oxen to be killed and their flesh frozen once the ships found ice, set sail on 17 May 1845. Save for a sighting by whalers in Baffin Bay on 26 July 1845 the crews – 135 men – were never seen again.[501] It was ascertained by a subsequent voyage that the two ships were beset by ice on 12 September 1846. Franklin had died on 11 June 1847 and the ships were abandoned on 22 April 1848. All the officers and crew are believed to have perished before the end of that year.

---

[501] B. A. Riffenburgh, 'Franklin, Sir John (1786-1847)', *Oxford Dictionary of National Biography*, Oxford University Press, 2004; online edn, Sept 2012 [http://www.oxforddnb.com/view/article/10090, accessed 22 November 2016].

Gilbourne Way

This is the second road that became completely absorbed into Rochester Way (see page 194).

The Gilbourne family came into possession of the Manor of Woolwich in 1580. In 1663, Dr. Gilbourne leased property to the Admiralty, for seventeen years at a premium of £1,200 together with a rent of £132 per annum for the first six years and £182 per annum for the remaining eleven years. It was described as two ballast quays, two ballast pits, two limekilns and two tenements (the legal description of permanent buildings).

Granby Road

The military career of John Manners, Marquess of Granby (2 January 1721 to 18 October 1770) was launched when his father, the third Duke of Rutland, raised the Leicester Blues in support of the Hanoverian dynasty during the Jacobite rising and made his son its colonel. After the rebellion ended (his regiment never saw action) he decided to make the military his career and served on the Duke of Cumberland's staff in Scotland where he was present during operations at Strathbogie, a prelude to Culloden. He campaigned in the Low Countries in 1747. During the 1750s, his reputation as a racegoer and gambler gradually gave way to that of a parliamentarian (he was elected Member for Cambridgeshire in 1752). In May 1758 he was promoted to Colonel of the prestigious Royal Horse Guards (Blues). His reputation as a battlefield commander greatly increased during the Seven Years' War when he led many successful actions. However, his resulting public popularity exceeded his reputation amongst the military who were concerned that someone responsible for the welfare of 25,000 troops had so few administrative skills. The very large number of public houses called the Marquess of Granby is probably testimony to his having set up disabled non-commissioned officers as publicans.[502]

Granby reorganised the Military Academy in 1764 when he augmented the Cadet Company, increasing the daily allowance from

---

[502] Alastair W. Massie, 'Manners, John, Marquess of Granby (1721-1770)', *Oxford Dictionary of National Biography*, Oxford University Press, 2004; online edn, May 2006 [http://www.oxforddnb.com/view/article/17958, accessed 22 November 2016].

1/4d to 2/6d, appointed superior professors and introduced qualifying examinations. In 1766, he introduced two gold and two silver medals as prizes to honour the gentlemen cadets. He was appointed Master-General of the Ordnance on 1 July 1763 and Commander-in-Chief of the Army on 13 August 1766.

His aversion to party politics continued as he supported a small number of individuals he considered to be public-spirited. The resulting lack of institutional parliamentary support led to political difficulties, despite his continuing popularity with the public at large, and he resigned as both Commander-in-Chief and Master-General of the Ordnance on 17 January 1770. The resulting loss of salaries totalling £4,500 per annum caused consternation amongst his many creditors. He died intestate in Scarborough on 18 October 1770 from a sudden attack of gout in the stomach. His debts were around £60,000 and his assets only £23,000.

Lovelace Green

The Lovelace family was associated with Woolwich for several generations and many of the male line were named William. Sir William the younger, baptised in 1584, was knighted by James I in 1609. He held an estate in, and was a resident of, Woolwich. He apparently died during the Siege of Groll on 12 August 1627, prior to which he had, as noted by his widow Anne, née Barnes, 'served about thirty years in the warres' in the Low Countries. Their eldest son and the second of eight children, the poet and Army officer Richard Lovelace (9 December 1617 to 1657) followed the family tradition of military service and also, for a period, lived in The Netherlands. He fought in the Scottish expedition of 1639, after which he retired to his estate at Bethersden, near Canterbury, which brought him an income of £500 a year. His military exploits are largely unrecorded, and it was his poetry that brought him lasting fame.[503] His grandfather Sir William Lovelace the elder had been knighted by the Lord-Lieutenant of Ireland during Essex's 1599 Irish campaign; other forebears further justified the contemporary reputation of the Lovelaces as 'a Race of Gentlemen ...

---

[503] Raymond A. Anselment, 'Lovelace, Richard (1617-1657)', *Oxford Dictionary of National Biography*, Oxford University Press, 2004; online edn, Jan 2010 [http://www.oxforddnb.com/view/article/17056, accessed 22 November 2016].

who have in Military Affairs achieved Reputation and Honour, with a prodigal Losse and Expence'.[504]

Martin Bowes Road

Sir Martin Bowes (1496/7-4 August 1566) was described by the historian Stow as 'a great and worthy citizen, Lord Mayor of London, and a benefactor of the first size'. He was apprenticed to the court supplier and future Master of the Jewels, Robert Amadas, in 1513 who taught him the assaying skills that were to be the foundation of his highly successful career. He became perhaps the most prominent member of the Company of Goldsmiths in Tudor times. He was elected Fourth Warden in 1532-3, third in 1534-5 and second in 1535-6 before being elected Prime Warden firstly on 17 September 1537, then twice during 1540-2 (during which time he was knighted) and on a further ten occasions in the periods 1549-51, 1553-7 and 1558-62. Even after he had finally retired, his successors sought his views before taking their decisions.[505] He endowed the Goldsmiths' almshouses in Cannon Row, one of the most valuable of the Woolwich charities. The almshouses were abolished in 1888, and the charity's income, which had amounted to £252/18/- in 1867-8, was converted into pensions. He was four times Lord Mayor of London and, as the Master of the Mint, flourished in the reigns of Henry VIII and Edward IV. Henry VIII, in 1541, granted him a dwelling house in Woolwich, the property also possessing a garden and a wharf.

Maudslay Road

Henry Maudslay was born in Woolwich on 22 August 1771. He began work at the age of twelve as a 'powder monkey', making and filling cartridges. He joined his father in the carpenter's shop two years later but soon developed a love for the smithy which he was formally allowed to join at the age of fifteen. He progressed rapidly and became

---

[504] T. Philipot, *Villare Cantianum*, 1659, 72. In: Raymond A. Anselment (see fn 503).

[505] C. E. Challis, 'Bowes, Sir Martin (1496/7-1566)', *Oxford Dictionary of National Biography*, Oxford University Press, 2004; online edn, Jan 2008 [http://www.oxforddnb.com/view/article/3055, accessed 22 November 2016].

an expert smith, best known for his forging of light iron-work and making trivets out of solid pieces of iron. By the time he was eighteen, in 1789, his fame as one of the most dexterous hands in the trade had spread to London. He was taken on by Joseph Bramah who had taken out a patent for a lock in 1784 but could not develop the machines to manufacture the very precise parts it required. Maudslay did so and production commenced. It was not long before he married Sarah Tindale, Bramah's housekeeper. Because Bramah would not increase his wages beyond 30/- per week, Maudslay left him in 1798 to set up his own workshop in Wells Street, off Oxford Street. It was soon successful and he moved to larger premises in Margaret Street, Marylebone. His best-known invention was the slide rest, the influence of which upon machinery was likened by his pupil Nasmyth to the influence of the steam engine on manufacturing and commerce. He also obtained a reward of £1,000 offered by the Government for a three-threaded screw required at the Royal Observatory. Maudslay soon became acquainted with Brunel, for whom he built 44 machines Brunel had been commissioned to construct at Portsmouth Dockyard for the bulk production of ships' blocks, essential items in rigging. Their parts were interchangeable, making him and Brunel early exponents of mass production. The patents he took out included, in 1805, one for a table engine, so called because it became popular in applications that only required a small amount of power. He moved his factory for a third time in 1810 to premises in Westminster Bridge Road. The firm, by now trading as Maudslay, Sons and Field, developed a strong business in marine engines, replacing overhead beams with levers alongside the engines which made them more suitable for marine use.

Maudslay's contribution to engineering was not so much the machines his firm made as the machine tools he used to develop them. These – lathes, planes, slotting machines and drills – were of the highest quality and used equally high-quality materials, thus making mass duplication of output achievable. His micrometers were accurate to within one ten-thousandth of an inch. He had introduced scientific accuracy to the world of machine manufacturing and many were the workmen he trained who achieved fame and distinction as engineers in their own right. He died from a cold on 14 February 1831 and, by his direction, was buried in Woolwich where a cast-iron tomb made to his own specification was erected over his remains.

The 'Sons' in the firm's name were his eldest and third sons, Thomas Henry (1792-1864) and Joseph (1801-1861) respectively. Thomas had considerable commercial ability and gave evidence about steam navigation before a select committee of the House of Commons in 1831. He, too, was buried at Woolwich. Joseph had served an apprenticeship as a shipbuilder before joining his father's business. He patented an improved oscillating steam engine in 1827 that did away with a beam or a slide rest by allowing the cylinder to rock on trunnions with each stroke. In 1841-2, the firm made the engine for *Rattler*, the first screw-propelled steamship built for the Admiralty.[506]

Moira Road

This road is named after the person born in Dublin as Francis Rawdon (7 December 1754 to 28 November 1826). He was the eldest son of Sir John Rawdon. Sir John became Earl of Moira in 1762. Francis was styled Lord Rawdon from then until 1783 when he became Baron Rawdon of Rawdon in the British peerage. In 1790 he added Hastings to his surname by Royal Licence when he inherited most of the estates of his maternal uncle, Francis Hastings, 10th Earl of Huntingdon. He succeeded as 2nd Earl of Moira upon his father's death in 1793.

His Army career began in August 1771 when he was commissioned ensign in the 15th Foot. He was promoted to lieutenant, 5th Foot in 1773 and saw service in America where he was commended for fearlessness. He left America in 1781 after contracting a severe illness. The ship he was on was captured by a French cruiser. Following his release in an exchange of prisoners, he began a long involvement in Irish politics two years before he took his seat in the House of Lords as Baron Rawdon.

At the time of his succession as Earl of Moira he had an income estimated at £18,000 a year, £3,000 of which he had inherited from his maternal uncle. He saw further military service in France, having been promoted to major general on 12 October 1793, and continued to pursue Irish matters from his seat in the House of Lords. In September 1803 he was appointed commander-in-chief in Scotland and promoted

---

[506] R. Angus Buchanan, 'Maudslay, Henry (1771-1831)', *Oxford Dictionary of National Biography*, Oxford University Press, 2004; online edn, Oct 2007 [http://www.oxforddnb.com/view/article/18357, accessed 22 November 2016].

to general the following month. He was close to the Prince of Wales who, on 8 February 1806, approved his becoming Master-General of the Ordnance with a Cabinet seat and Privy Councillorship in order to stop his being made Irish Viceroy. Four days later, the Constableship and Lord Lieutenancy of the Tower of London were added. He resigned from the Ordnance Office in March 1807 and took his seat in the Lords as Baron Hastings from 19 January 1809 following the death of his mother in April 1808, which caused him to inherit the English baronies vested in the Hastings family. He went to India as Governor-General from April 1813 to March 1822 and died aboard HMS *Revenge* off Naples. He was buried in Malta.[507]

Phineas Pett Road

Phineas Pett (1 November 1570 to 1647) was the eldest son of Peter Pett, Master Shipwright at Deptford. He left Emmanuel College, Cambridge, in 1589 after his father's death and before graduating to become apprenticed to Richard Chapman, another Master Shipwright of Deptford. Unfortunately, Chapman died after three years and for economic reasons Pett joined the privateer *Gallion Constance*, bound for the Mediterranean, as a carpenter's mate. The twenty-month cruise was not a financial success so, come 1594, Pett was again out of work. He took up employment as an ordinary workman with his brother (also Peter), one of Elizabeth's master shipwrights, on the *Defiance* in a Woolwich dock where it was being sheathed (the term for the boarding of the hull) for the voyage of Sir Francis Drake and Sir John Hawkins. In 1595 he was engaged on a new ship, the *Triumph*, which was also to be included in the voyage that was to be Drake's last. He was out of regular work for several years but spent his time studying mathematics, model-making and other educational work under the tutelage of Matthew Baker, another master shipbuilder. In 1601, his brother made him assistant Master Shipwright at Chatham where he so pleased the Earl of Nottingham, the Lord High Admiral, that he obtained Royal Letters Patent, giving him the 'next presentation' to the

---

[507] Roland Thorne, 'Hastings, Francis Rawdon, first Marquess of Hastings and second Earl of Moira (1754-1826)', *Oxford Dictionary of National Biography*, Oxford University Press, 2004; online edn, Jan 2008 [http://www.oxforddnb.com/view/article/12568, accessed 22 November 2016].

Office of Master Shipwright which happened on the death of another of his brothers, Joseph, in 1605. In the meantime, in 1599-1600 and with Nottingham's patronage, he became the Purveyor of Timber in Norfolk and Suffolk and, in June 1600, Keeper of the Stores at Chatham. He used both for his own financial ends, as was the norm at a time when naval administration was at its most dishonest. His dubious practices were to cause his near downfall in the years that followed, when the levels of corruption forced King James I to set up a commission of inquiry in 1608. One of its leaders was Nottingham.

Pett settled in Woolwich on 15 April 1606 and, in 1607, made a model of a great ship which so impressed Nottingham that he presented it to King James. His Majesty was mightily pleased and a magnificent vessel, the *Prince Royal*, was ordered to be built, based on the model. The keel was laid in October 1608, the date coinciding with the 1608 commission of inquiry. Pett's past dealings caught up with him and he fell victim to allegations, not all necessarily completely true, brought by other shipwrights and adversaries. Corruption charges followed which ended in a hearing before the Royal Court in Woolwich. The King heard both sides and dismissed the case, letting Pett off with nothing more than a lecture; to have done otherwise would have implicated many of the Navy's principal officers and possibly even Nottingham himself.

Pett continued to build ships according to the mores of the day and became the first Master of the Shipwrights' Company after their new charter of incorporation was granted in 1612.[508] In the same year he fitted out the *Resolution* and the *Discovery* at Woolwich for an Arctic expedition. Between March and December 1615 he built the Destiny in the Galley Dock at Woolwich for Sir Walter Raleigh. He is believed to have died in Chatham in 1647, where the parish register records the burial of 'Phineas Pett, Esquire and captain, on 21st August 1647'.

Prince Rupert Road

Prince Rupert (18 December 1619 to 29 November 1682) was the third son of the King of Bohemia and Princess Elizabeth, eldest daughter of James VI of Scotland and James I of Great Britain. He was educated

---

[508] Roy McCaughey, 'Pett, Phineas (1570-1647)', *Oxford Dictionary of National Biography*, Oxford University Press, 2004; online edn, Jan 2008 [http://www.oxforddnb.com/view/article/22060, accessed 23 November 2016].

THE EVOLUTION OF THE ESTATE

for the Army and fought for Charles I, his uncle on his mother's side, during the rebellion. On 24 January 1644, during the First English Civil War (1642-1647),[509] Charles elevated Rupert to the peerage, entitling him the Earl of Holderness and Duke of Cumberland.

As a military commander, the Prince was considered brave but rash; some consider his hasty and unguarded tactics contributed to his uncle's (Charles I's) downfall. He went to France with a pass by Parliament in August 1646 and continued to live there and in The Netherlands, operating as a privateer off Western European shores as well as in the West Indies. He was invited to return after the Restoration (1660) and appointed along with the Duke of Albemarle to command the fleet In 1666.

Prince Rupert lived mostly at Windsor Castle, of which he was Governor, spending a great deal of his time in chemical and philosophical experiments as well as the practice of the mechanical arts. He was a skilled painter and, if not its inventor, the first to use the process of mezzotint in England in 1658. He designed locks for firearms and invented 'pinchbeck', an alloy of iron and zinc that became known as Prince's metal. He communicated his gunpowder improvements to the Royal Society, of which he and his royal cousins had been made honorary founder members in 1664. He also acquainted them with an engine he had contrived for raising water and an early machine gun that discharged several bullets with, according to Vincent, 'the utmost speed, facility and safety'.

The Price was appointed by his cousin, Charles II, by Royal Warrant dated 13 June 1667 to construct batteries at Woolwich (see page 178) and may have lived for the duration of the work in Tower House, a 14th-century structure built on the Warren. He died at his house in Spring Gardens, Whitehall, a few days after catching a chest infection at the theatre and was buried in the Henry VII Chapel in Westminster Abbey.[510]

---

[509] en.wikipedia.org/wiki/Timeline_of_the_English_Civil_War, accessed 5 May 2017.

[510] Ian Roy, 'Rupert, prince and count palatine of the Rhine and Duke of Cumberland (1619-1682)', *Oxford Dictionary of National Biography*, Oxford University Press, 2004; online edn, May 2011 [http://www.oxforddnb.com/view/article/24281, accessed 23 November 2016].

Rochester Way

Boughton Road, Gilbourne Way and the northern section of Admiral Seymour Road that ran from the end of Gilbourne Way to the eastern boundary of the Estate were absorbed into Rochester Way. It also took in the very northern end of Moira Road, between its last houses and the junction with Granby Road.

The time taken to build the road belies any idea that delays in the completion of infrastructure projects are a modern phenomenon. The authorities knew, when they approved the plans for the Estate in 1915, that a Shooters Hill bypass road would become necessary. Thus the houses either side of Boughton Road and Gilbourne Way were set back to ensure that compulsory purchase for their demolition would not be required at a future date. Various aspects of the road's construction are recorded in the minute books of Metropolitan Borough of Woolwich from November 1924 to September 1932.

For the road as a whole, phase I was to be the easterly section from the Welling end of Dover Road[511] to Well Hall Road.[512] In due course, the completion of phase II to the west would link it from Well Hall Road to Woodville Road near Kidbrooke Green.[513] Woodville Road would then reconnect it to Shooters Hill Road in the west.

On 23 October 1924, the Chief Engineer at the Ministry of Transport wrote to Woolwich Council stating that the Minister was anxious for work to 'begin at an early date'.[514] The road as a whole was to run through the boroughs of Bexley, Woolwich and Greenwich. The Woolwich section was a distance of 1.64 miles,[515] from the western end of Briset Road (near where the Lower Kidbrook drained into the River Quaggy) to the eastern boundary of Oxleaze Woods on Welling Way. The Minister supported the idea that each council should construct that part of the

---

[511] National Library of Scotland, Ordnance Survey sheet Kent II. SW & SE (includes: Bexley; Borough of Greenwich; Borough of Woolwich; Erith.) revised 1931, published: ca. 1935.

[512] National Library of Scotland, Ordnance Survey sheet London Sheet P (includes: Borough of Greenwich; Borough of Woolwich), revised 1938, published: ca. 1946.

[513] WBC 1929-1930, p. 428, Works Committee, minute no. 12, 14 April 1930.

[514] MBW 1924-1925, p. 78, Works Committee, minute no. 16, 17 November 1924.

[515] MBW 1931-1932, p. 216, Works Committee, minute no. 12, 18 January 1932.

road in its area. This, for the Progress Estate, involved the widening of Boughton Road, Gilbourne Way and the northern section of Admiral Seymour Road to a total width of 70 feet, which was to include a 40-foot-wide carriageway.[516] Less major works were required in Deansfield Road, the carriageway immediately to the east of these three.[517] A complication was that the hutments – wooden bungalows H.M. Office of Works had erected (and owned) along Deansfield Road east of Glenesk Road in 1915/16 as additional housing for munitions workers at the Royal Arsenal, Woolwich[518] – remained occupied. The initial arrangement, made between the LCC and the Office of Works, was that they could be demolished as they became vacant. The first two to be removed were nos. 134 and 144 and the materials were sold for £20.[519] If the expectation was that people would soon move out, the reality proved otherwise. By October 1927, two years later, Woolwich Council's Housing Committee was involved, minuting that the Office of Works had finally agreed to grant Woolwich Borough Council vacant possession (and thus demolition rights) upon receipt of £34 per hutment from the Council. Some of the tenants declined to be rehoused on a council housing estate in Eltham, thereby creating a need for the Office of Works to offer them alternative hutments. The Committee had 'fully considered the whole matter from a financial point of view and ... having regard to the urgent necessity for the completion of the Arterial Road' recommended the payment of £34 per hutment to the Office of Works 'and variations to earlier Resolutions where so required to implement this'.[520]

The process of obtaining rights to various parcels of land necessary for the road to be built had been underway since May 1926 at the latest. On the 18th, Progress Estates Ltd. minuted receipt of a letter

---

[516] MBW 1924-1925, p. 180, Works Committee, minute no. 26, 19 January 1925.

[517] A proposal by Woolwich Borough Council to compulsorily purchase thirteen houses in Deansfield Way and thereby increase its width to 65 feet did not proceed when a petition against was signed by 84 residents. Instead, automatic traffic signals were installed at the junction of the road and Westmount Road 'which it is hoped will prevent further accidents'. MBW 1931-1932, p. 352, Works Committee, minute no. 14, 6 April 1932 and p. 479, Works Committee, minute no. 18, 8 June 1932.

[518] Kennett (1985), pp. 2-3.

[519] MBW 1924-1925, p. 587, Works Committee, minute no. 4, 21 September 1925.

[520] MBW 1926-1927, p. 666, Housing Committee, minute no. 12, 13 October 1927.

from the Treasury Solicitor 'requiring the Company to convey to the LCC the strip of land agreed to be sold for an Arterial Road'.[521]

The project was finally considered shovel-ready when, on 4 December 1928, the Chief Engineer of the LCC wrote to Woolwich Council 'stating that he had instructions to proceed with the completion of the Shooter's Hill By-Pass, and asking that arrangements may be made by this Council to start on the work so far as it is in this Borough'. Woolwich Council was fed up with the time it was taking for the Office of Works to transfer land that had been occupied by the hutments and decided, after a phone call to the LCC, to commence work on Monday, 10 December[522] in two sections, one of which was Deansfield Road. On the Tuesday, the Office of Works telephoned Woolwich Council, informing them that they were trespassing on their land and must withdraw the twenty men who had started work that day. The Council did not comply with the request and, at the insistence of the Office of Works, representatives of the parties concerned held at a conference at the Treasury Solicitor's offices. All was resolved, work continued[523] and a week later the number of workmen had increased to sixty-four.

Correspondence between the LCC and Woolwich Borough Council about the naming of the bypass lasted, in fits and starts, from February 1928 until April 1932. The LCC wrote to the Council on 24 February 1928 saying they had approved the name 'Kidbrooke Way' for phase II (the western section from Well Hall Road to Kidbrooke).[524] The Council then wrote to the LCC on 4 December 1929 requesting that the section between Well Hall Road and Grangehill Road be named Progress Way.[525] However, probably unbeknown to them, the LCC had already written to them on 29 November stating they had approved the name Rochester Way.[526] Nevertheless, the LCC replied on 31 January 1930 pointing out that 'in its opinion, it is undesirable, especially from a traffic point of view that the Shooters Hill By-Pass should bear

---

[521] PEL, 18 May 1926, minute no. 1.

[522] MBW 1927-1928, p. 141, Works Committee, minute no. 8, 17 December 1928.

[523] Kennett (1985), p. 31.

[524] MBW 1927-1928, p. 270, Works Committee, minute no. 4, 19 March 1928.

[525] MBW 1929-1930, p. 88, Works Committee, minute no. 15, 4 December 1929.

[526] MBW 1929-1930, p. 138, Works Committee, minute no. 9, 16 December 1929.

sectional names'. They now suggested that the entire length from Dover Road to Kidbrooke should be named Kidbrooke Way. For its part, the Council resolved to raise no objection although it noted that the LCC would have to obtain the concurrence of Bexley Council in respect to the length in their area. It did not anticipate that Bexley Council would raise any objection thereto because the greater length of the road would be in the county of London's area.

The LCC may have run into problems with Bexley Council and certainly discovered that the renumbering of houses along the entire length of phases I and II was problematic. They put the problem back to their committee, asking them to reconsider their proposal for the whole road to be called Kidbrooke Way. This resulted in their writing again to Woolwich Borough Council on 28 March 1930. Whilst adhering to the principle that one name should be applied to the whole of the bypass, they had decided that no action should be taken as regards the portion to the west of Well Hall Road known as Kidbrooke Way until the bypass was extended to link Well Hall Road to Woodville Road. The western section including Kidbrooke Way and Woodville Road could then be incorporated with the section east of Well Hall Road, for which they now suggested the name Welling Way. They further suggested that the numbering east of Well Hall Road should commence at 501 and 502 so as to render it practicable to include the western section without disturbing the numbers now to be applied. On 14 April 1930, the Borough Council resolved that they disapproved of the name 'Welling Way' and saw no reason to depart from its previous decision approving of the name 'Kidbrooke Way'.[527]

The LCC replied on 11 July 1930 saying they had again reconsidered the naming of the new thoroughfare, pointing out that Bexley Council had approved of the adoption of the name 'Welling Way'. They remained of the opinion that 'Kidbrooke' would be inappropriate. The longer portion of the road would be in Eltham and when it was built over and numbered, the numbers would commence at the Kidbrooke end and run in the reverse direction to the implication of the name – towards Welling and not towards Kidbrooke. The Council were not convinced, and wrote back to the LCC accordingly.[528]

---

[527] MBW 1929-1930, p. 428, Works Committee, minute no. 129, 14 April 1930.

[528] MBW 1929-1930, p. 600, Works Committee, minute no. 15, 14 July 1930.

The LCC must have continued the debate internally or with Bexley and/or Greenwich Councils because nothing further is minuted by Woolwich Borough Council until 6 April 1932 when they discussed a letter the LCC had written to them on 25 February. It enclosed a plan showing proposals to rename the Shooters Hill By-Pass as Rochester Way, and to renumber it accordingly, with effect from 1 July 1932.[529] The Borough Council resolved not to object to the LCC's proposals. However, it was not until January 1933 that they finally resolved to take over responsibility for the maintenance of that portion of the new road in their Borough. The carriageway that had formed Deansfield Road was breaking up under the rapidly increasing traffic flows and they attempted to persuade the LCC to strengthen and rebuild it before they took it over. They had also tried to persuade the LCC to make them a general percentage contribution to the 1.64 miles of the road that passed through their borough because it was an arterial road. They were unsuccessful on both counts, the LCC arguing that the new road had taken pressure off other roads in its vicinity for which Woolwich had 100% responsibility for maintenance. Furthermore, the new road had added to the attractions of the area, thereby paving the way for Woolwich to increase the rateable value of local properties.[530]

Ross Way

Sir Hew Dalrymple Ross (5 July 1779 to 10 December 1868) entered the Royal Military Academy at Woolwich on 9 October 1793. He saw service with the Royal Horse Artillery in Ireland from 1798 to 1803, by which time he had been made up to captain lieutenant. On 12 September 1803 he was appointed adjutant to the 5th Battalion of Royal Artillery at Woolwich. He saw service in the Duke of Wellington's army during the Peninsular War, rising from captain of the 'A' troop, Royal Horse Artillery in November 1808 to brevet lieutenant colonel in June 1813. This was followed by service at Waterloo and, on 2 January 1815, he was made KCB for his services in these two theatres as well as being deservedly decorated with many campaign medals, including the Waterloo Medal when it was distributed later. He married Elizabeth

---

[529] MBW 1931-1932, p. 351, Works Committee, minute no. 7, 6 April 1932.

[530] MBW 1932-1933, p. 117, Works Committee, minute no. 34, 4 January 1933.

Margaret Graham in 1816. Their son John Ross (1829-1905) saw much service in India and Canada and became a general, GCB and Deputy Lieutenant of Cumberland.[531] By 1852 Sir Hew had risen to Colonel Commandant of the Royal Horse Artillery. He was Deputy Adjutant-General of the Royal Artillery, a headquarters post, from 1840 until 1854, during which time he was instrumental in the appointment of an officer at Woolwich whose role was to instruct young officers of the Royal Artillery when they first joined the service. This led to the formation of the Department of Artillery Studies. On his initiative, classes were also established at Woolwich to instruct officers in the various departments of the Royal Arsenal. A gun-practice range was set up on the Woolwich marshes, and a small station for artillery was formed at Shoeburyness for experimental practice which later developed into a school of gunnery. The duty of preparing the artillery force for Crimea fell to him.

He was Lieutenant-General of the Ordnance from 29 April 1854 until Palmerston, shortly after becoming Prime Minister in February 1855, ended its separate role on 16 June of the same year. Its civil duties were transferred to the War Office and command of the artillery and engineers to the Horse Guards. He received the GCB on 19 July 1855. He was promoted to field marshal on 1 January 1868, the first person to be promoted to the rank from the Royal Artillery. The achievement was celebrated at a public dinner on 9 March 1868 that was organised by the officers of the Royal Artillery and Royal Engineers and presided over by the colonel of the two corps, the Duke of Cambridge. His final appointment was as Lieutenant Governor of Chelsea Hospital, London, on 3 August 1868. He died at his London home, was buried in Woolwich churchyard, and is commemorated on a brass plaque in the Garrison Church, Woolwich.[532]

---

[531] H. M. Vibart, 'Ross, Sir John (1829-1905)', rev. James Lunt, *Oxford Dictionary of National Biography*, Oxford University Press, 2004; online edn, Sept 2011 [http://www.oxforddnb.com/view/article/35836, accessed 24 November 2016].

[532] R. H. Vetch, 'Ross, Sir Hew Dalrymple (1779-1868)', rev. John Sweetman, *Oxford Dictionary of National Biography*, Oxford University Press, 2004 [http://www.oxforddnb.com/view/article/24119, accessed 24 November 2016].

Sandby Green

Paul Sandby was baptised in 1731 and lived until 8 November 1809. He and his elder brother Thomas were probably apprenticed to the Nottingham land surveyor Thomas Peat who, in 1742, was engaged as military draughtsman in the Ordnance Office of the Tower of London. In March 1747, Paul submitted specimens of his work to the Board of Ordnance. Eight are in the British Museum and one in the Victoria and Albert Museum, London. Probably as a result of this, he was appointed draughtsman to a military survey of Scotland established in September 1747. Its purpose was to map the Highlands as part of the campaign to restore peace following the 1745 rising. The maps on which he was employed (he was largely responsible for their colouring) were of a very high standard. Sandby remained with the survey for five years, during which time he completed many landscape and figure studies. The latter, in particular, are considered to be very mature works for someone of in his late-teens and early twenties and many are to be found in public collections. He was appointed Chief Drawing Master at the Royal Military Academy, Woolwich, in August 1768 at a salary of £150 per annum. When there, he lived in lodgings at Old Charlton in Kent. He retained the post until his retirement in January 1796 when he was succeeded by his son, Thomas Paul (died 1832).[533]

Sandby was a prodigious landscape and portrait painter, a popular artist whose output ranged from fancy etchings to drawings of country houses and magazine illustrations. He is said to have amassed a large fortune through his work.

Shrapnel Road

Henry Shrapnel (3 June 1761 to 13 March 1842) is most famous for inventing the shell that bears his name. He was commissioned into the Army on 9 July 1779 and served in Newfoundland from 1780 to 1784, becoming first lieutenant on 3 December 1781. He started to develop his shell, at his own expense, in 1875 after returning to England. It was to be a hollow, spherical case filled with small round shot and a powder

---

[533] Luke Herrmann, 'Sandby, Paul (*bap.* 1731, *d.* 1809)', *Oxford Dictionary of National Biography*, Oxford University Press, 2004; online edn, May 2006 [http://www.oxforddnb.com/view/article/24613, accessed 24 November 2016].

charge, capable of being fired from the artillery's existing guns. The charge was ignited by a fuse, whose length could vary. He proposed his shell to the Board of Ordnance in 1799 and it was eventually approved in 1803.

By now regimental lieutenant colonel, Shrapnel was made first Assistant Inspector of Artillery at Woolwich on 10 February 1804 which gave him wide responsibility for ordnance research and development as well as for shells. Shells made to his initial design were first used in 1804. The reports were favourable and (notwithstanding criticism by Wellington, rapidly revoked) considered instrumental in both field and naval victories thereafter. The shells were cast and perfected by Gunner John Henderson, RA, who afterwards was appointed Master Founder at the Royal Arsenal at £2 per day of attendance, a post he held until his death on 16 October 1826. The shells continued to be manufactured based on Shrapnel's original principles until the end of the First World War. Parliament granted him a pension of £1,200 a year in 1814 in recognition of his discovery only after he had reminded the Board of Ordnance, in 1813, that he had spent several thousands of pounds of his own money in developing the shell over a period of 28 years.

Shrapnel was made major general on 12 August 1819 and retired from active service on 29 July 1825. He continued to experiment with the machinery of war and was made Colonel Commandant of the Royal Artillery on 6 March 1827 and its Lieutenant General on 10 January 1837. He died at his residence in Southampton and is buried in the family vault at Holy Trinity Church in Bradford on Avon, Wiltshire.[534]

Well Hall Road

Well Hall Road is a very antiquarian route. John Rocque's map of London, surveyed between 1737 and 1744,[535] clearly shows it traversing between fields from Eltham to Shooters Hill. The area around a junction where

---

[534] John Sweetman, 'Shrapnel, Henry (1761-1842)', *Oxford Dictionary of National Biography*, Oxford University Press, 2004; online edn, Sept 2010 [http://www.oxforddnb.com/view/article/25473, accessed 24 November 2016] and 'Henry Shrapnel', www.findagrave.com/cgi-bin/fg.cgi?page=gr&GRid=21024132, accessed 29 April 2017.

[535] John Rocque, *An Exact Survey of the Cities of London, Westminster, ye Borough of Southwark, and the Country near Ten Miles round*, 1746. British Library Online Gallery, www.bl.uk/onlinegallery/onlineex/crace/a/007zzz000000019u00018000.html, accessed 27 June 2016.

a lane (now Kidbrooke Lane) turns off towards the unpopulated area then named Keed Brook is called Wale Hall. Its countrified appearance can be seen in the upper illustration on page 144. The creation of Well Hall Road as we know it today has been described in the chapter *Cecil Henry Polhill and the Site for the Estate*.

The buildings between the southern end of the Estate in Well Hall Road and Eltham High Street were originally known by names given to them by their owners. Mr. E. Wilson, a dental surgeon, lived in one of them and wrote to Woolwich Council in December 1924, asking for his house to be numbered. Although the Council had previously discussed the issue with the London County Council, the matter had been held over 'pending the building of houses south of the railway bridge'. His letter thus prompted them to take up again 'the question of renumbering Well Hall Road, to include the new houses erected, or in the course of erection, on the south side of the railway bridge'.[536]

The LCC submitted a plan that the Council discussed on 16 February 1925. It showed a renumbering on the east side from Eltham High Street through to Eltham Common, somewhat beyond the northern limit of the Estate, and on the west side from the churchyard adjacent to St. John the Baptist church to Kidbrooke Lane. The Borough Engineer thought the LCC had made insufficient allowance for the number of building sites yet to be developed on the west side of the road so, subject to this concern, the meeting resolved to approve the scheme.[537] Five months later, the LCC wrote to the Council suggesting the renumbering should be limited to the east side of the road. The Council agreed and the exercise was apparently completed in early 1926,[538] thus increasing the numbers of all the Estate's even-numbered houses along Well Hall Road by 80.

Consequent upon the construction of Rochester Way, the LCC needed to obtain vacant possession of land forming part of the front gardens of the odd-numbered houses around what is now the roundabout at the junction of Well Hall Road with Rochester Way. The board of Progress Estates Ltd. resolved to accede to their request insofar as it related to their tenanted houses, subject to some probably non-

---

[536] MBW, 1924-1925, p. 128, Works Committee, minute no. 9, 15 December 1924.

[537] MBW, 1924-1925, p. 238, Works Committee, minute no. 9, 16 February 1925.

[538] MBW, 1925-1926, p. 191, Works Committee, minute no. 9, 21 January 1926.

consequential conditions recommended by their surveyors, Messrs. Eley and Allen of Woolwich, in a letter dated 27 August 1930. They subsequently received a letter from the Cheltenham & Gloucester Building Society relating to compensation payable by the LCC to Mr. Byard and Mrs. L. Kelly of nos. 109 and 115 Well Hall Road, respectively, for the acquisition of land in front of the homes they owned on long leases, asking the Company (as freeholders) if there was any objection to this. There was not, and the Secretary was asked to make a recommendation 'to deal with all cases of this nature'.[539]

The roundabout was first referred to as such in a Woolwich Council minute in October 1931.[540] Prior to this it had been described as Well Hall Road Circus.[541]

Whinyates Road

Edward Charles Whinyates (6 May 1782 to 25 December 1865) entered the Royal Military Academy in Woolwich as a cadet on 16 May 1796. He had a brilliant battlefield career and was especially noted for his attack on Copenhagen with the siege batteries in 1807. On 24 July 1812, at Ribera, he made such good use of two guns that the French Commander Lallemand sent him a message saying that if it had not been for his bravery, the English cavalry would have been beaten. Come 17 November, his unit was attached to a cavalry unit under General Long at the retreat from Burgos. Afterwards, Long wrote of the artillery troop that he had never witnessed 'more exemplary conduct in quarters, nor more distinguished zeal and gallantry in the field'. On 24 January 1813 Whinyates was promoted to captain and, in 1814, commanded the 2nd Rocket Troop at Waterloo. In one day's fighting he had three horses shot under him and was struck on the leg and severely wounded in the left arm. He was awarded the Waterloo Medal and, afterwards, the Peninsular Silver Medal with clasps for Busaco and Albuera. He commanded a troop of horse artillery from 1823 and became regimental lieutenant colonel on 22 July 1830. Knighted in 1823, he was made a CB in 1831. He commanded the Horse Artillery at Woolwich from

[539] PEL, 27 August 1930 (minute no.1) and 5 May 1931 (minute no. 4).

[540] MBW, 1931-1932, p. 44, Works Committee, minute no. 8, 19 October 1931.

[541] MBW, 1930-1931, p. 344, Works Committee, minute no. 16, 20 October 1930.

November 1834 to May 1840 and was made up to regimental colonel on 23 November 1841. He was made Director General of Artillery at Woolwich on 1 April 1852 and Commandant at Woolwich Garrison from 19 August of the same year, becoming Major General on 20 June 1854. He became a KCB on 18 May 1860. He had become colonel commandant of a battalion on 1 April 1855 and was transferred to the Horse Artillery on 22 July 1864. He was said to be 'an officer whose ability, zeal, and services have hardly been surpassed in the regiment'.

The Whinyates were something of a military dynasty. Sir Edward was the third son of Major Thomas Whinyates (1755-1806) and his wife Catherine. His marriage to Elizabeth at the age of 45 did not produce any children, but four of his five brothers served with distinction in the Army or the Navy. Two died unmarried and one died married but without issue. The fourth and youngest, Frederick, and his wife Sarah, had six children, four of whom became Army officers.[542]

---

[542] E. M. Lloyd, 'Whinyates, Sir Edward Charles (1782-1865)', rev. H. C. G. Matthew, *Oxford Dictionary of National Biography*, Oxford University Press, 2004; online edn, May 2006 [http://www.oxforddnb.com/view/article/29208, accessed 27 November 2016].

1915-1924:
The Estate's Early Years

The Estate in 1915 was far starker than it is today. All the rendering was left unpainted and there was little vegetation; although many have emphasised that no trees were felled during its construction, there were only about 80 growing on the land before the builders moved in and many of these were elms growing close together in rows, as seen in the lower illustration on page 144.

By June 1915 H.M. Office of Works had decided, in consultation with the Chief Superintendent of Ordnance Factories, that the Estate's dwellings were to be let to men employed at the Royal Arsenal's factories who were lodging in Woolwich apart from their families,[543] which explains the various reports that exist of people moving to it from elsewhere in the country. Men were attracted to the munitions business by the wages it offered.

H.M. Office of Works was not in the business of estate management and probably began to seek a suitable subcontractor in June 1915. Although the Metropolitan Borough of Woolwich had offered to collect the rents for a fee of 3½%,[544] the Office needed a more comprehensive service than this. Accordingly, they contracted with the London County Council who already managed other cottage estates in London. The deal with the LCC was agreed, possibly as early as mid-July 1915[545] – a couple of months after Mr. and Mrs. Aylward had moved into their Well Hall Road house on 22 May. Its main terms were:

1. That the Estate be managed on the lines of the LCC cottage estates.
2. That the houses only be let to people recommended by the Royal Arsenal, Woolwich.
3. That the Council undertake cleansing and minor repairs, to be charged to the Office of Works.
4. Any major repairs were to be referred to the Office of Works.
5. All stationery was to be supplied by the Office of Works.

[543] MBW 1914-1915, p. 597, Committee of the Whole Council, minute no. 2, 30 June 1915.

[544] MBW 1914-1915, p. 753, General Purposes Committee, minute no. 3, 28 September 1915.

[545] MBW 1914-1915, p. 674, General Purposes Committee, minute no. 4, 28 September 1915.

6. That the LCC would take commission at rate of 4½% of the gross rentals.
7. That all rates, taxes and water charges be paid by the Office of Works.[546]

The LCC transferred Mr. E. J. Turner from their Norbury Estate to be Superintendent of the Estate at a rate of pay of £2/10/- per week plus a 10/- allowance and removal expenses of £34. His home and office were at 1 Downman Road, since split into four flats. They provided him with a clerical assistant whose wages were £2 per week and a youth at £1 per week.[547]

The LCC had begun to acquire land on which to develop its own estates in 1900, consequent upon powers granted to local authorities under the Housing of the Working Classes Act, 1890. The first, the Totterdown Fields Estate, Tooting (1903-1911 – 38½ acres) was followed by Norbury (16½ acres completed between 1901 and 1912) and White Hart Lane, Tottenham (963 homes built on 40 acres, 1912-1915). Land for the fourth, the Old Oak Estate, Acton was purchased in 1905 but the estate was built largely after 1919.

The first two had a density of about 227 people to the acre so the Totterdown and Norbury estates housed some 12,500 people. White Hart Lane might have housed about 5,000 people. Add a few much smaller, pre-1900 estates and the LCC was probably housing, at most, 20,000 people.[548] On this basis, the addition of the Estate's 6,490 residents increased the population of their estates by 30-35%. Its weekly rent roll was some £720, so the LCC's commission amounted to about £1,700 p.a. Under normal LCC procedures, tenants were required to visit the Estate office on Mondays to pay their rent weekly in advance. It was only open during normal working hours, which did not fit at all conveniently with shift patterns at the Royal Arsenal factories. During the first two years of the war, men were employed on

---

[546] LCC (Housing of Working Classes Committee) 14 July 1915, p. 111. In: Hills, pp. 16-17.

[547] Hills, p. 17.

[548] Tarn, pp. 137-142 and 'The White Hart Lane Estate, Tottenham: Houses, the very best of their kind', *Municipal Dreams in Housing, London*, municipaldreams.wordpress.com/2013/07/16/the-white-hart-lane-estate-tottenham-houses-the-very-best-of-their-kind, accessed 1 November 2016.

a shift system on 27 days out of 28 and those on overtime sometimes worked a 96-hour week. Women worked for 13 or 13½ days out of 14 and frequently on seven consecutive night shifts, normally of twelve hours' duration.[549] The newly-formed Well Hall Garden City Tenants' Association successfully argued that rent should be collected from their homes and, in October 1915, the LCC employed an additional rent collector and purchased a bicycle for £8/0/8d. to assist their staff in carrying out their duties.[550]

It was stated at the beginning of the chapter *His Majesty's Office goes to work* that the Estate's 1,298 homes were designed to house 6,490 people – an average of exactly five per home. Probably most of the Estate's adults would have been of an age to have started their families.

It is possible to estimate the number living on the Estate who were liable for conscription. Munitions work was a certified occupation under the Military Service Act, 1916 so we can assume for the purposes of such a calculation that none of the fathers would have been called up.[551] Ignoring the fact that a few householders had one or more of their parents living with them, or that they had taken in lodgers, the Estate was intended to house 3,894 children, an average of three per house. For the purposes of this estimate, men are assumed to have fathered their first child at the age of either 25 or 30 and to have sired two more at three-yearly intervals. Thus, for example, the children of a man of 45 would be either 20, 17 and 14 years old, or 15, 12 and 9. Although boys aged eighteen and over were not liable for conscription under the Act until mid-1916, the calculation assumes all the boys aged eighteen or over volunteered from the time they arrived on the Estate (that is, six to twelve months before conscription began). The final two presumptions are that the age of fathers was evenly spread and that none of their children had moved away from the family home.

The estimated number of boys of conscription age would have increased as the lowest ages of fathers decreased; their children would have been older, so a higher proportion of the total would have been of conscription age. No data has been found indicating the age range

---

[549] Hogg, p. 975.

[550] Hills, p. 18.

[551] Philip Snowden, MP, *The Military Service Act Fully and Clearly Explained*, National Labour Press, 1916, pp. 4-5.

of people working at the Royal Arsenal, so this is, perforce, a matter of conjecture. Given the assumptions made, the estimated number of men who saw active service during the First World War would have been:

ESTIMATED NUMBER OF MALE RESIDENTS
AGED 18 AND OVER

Age of fathers	Estimated no. male children over 18	Age of fathers	Estimated no. male children over 18
25-40	nil	30-40	nil
25-45	100	30-45	133
25-50	399	30-50	499
25-55	665	30-55	798
25-60	855	30-60	997

The age range of men living on the Estate is unlikely to have been weighted towards the lower end, given the decision by H.M. Office of Works to let its houses to Royal Arsenal workers lodging in Woolwich away from their family homes. One might speculatively conclude that some 400-500 boys and men living on the Estate saw active service. The estimate serves to put the impact of the war on families into stark relief. If the fatalities mirrored the proportion for the British Army as a whole, one in ten would have died during the conflict.[552]

The Royal Arsenal factories were shut down 66 times during the First World War on account of air-raid warnings. Although 37 of these were caused by aeroplane attacks and 29 by Zeppelin airships, the factories only received six direct hits. Five were incendiaries and one a high-explosive bomb that fell on the main machine shop. Of the incendiaries, three fell in front of the hospital, one through the roof and upper floor of a machine shop adjacent to the hospital and the fifth in the street outside. Altogether nine men were injured, one of whom subsequently died from his wounds.[553] One might therefore consider it to have been exceptionally bad luck that four people were killed outright when by a bomb dropped from a Zeppelin L31 destroyed what was then 210 Well

---

[552] Proportion of deaths derived from 'Some British Army statistics of the Great War', *The Long, Long Trail: The British Army in the Great War of 1914-1918*, www.1914-1918.net/faq.htm, accessed 14 November 2016.

[553] Hogg, pp. 959-960.

Hall Road in the early hours of 25 August 1916.[554] A police sergeant had seen the airship whilst crossing the Estate at about 2:00 a.m. and had heard two or three explosions. All that was left standing when he arrived at the house was the staircase and a small portion of the front wall. He found the body of a 38-year-old munitions worker, Frederick Allen, lying on the staircase. A native of Bolton in Lancashire, he had been working on munitions since the war broke out.

The Coroner's inquest was held three days later on Monday, 28 August. The sergeant said he believed Frederick Allen had been going down the stairs when the explosion occurred. The body of their 11-year-old daughter Gladys was found in the centre of the debris along with that of his 36-year-old wife Annie. Their lodger Annie Tunnell, a married woman aged 29 and the wife of a corporal in the Life Guards, on active service in France, had rented two unfurnished rooms three months earlier. She was employed in the stores department of a local war hospital. Her body was found at about 5:00 a.m., covered in masonry. It seemed as though the bomb had exploded, either as it hit the roof or, after falling through it, as it made contact with a bedroom floor. Her bed had fallen through to the ground floor and falling masonry from the roof and walls had killed her. A caged bird was found alive in the rubble, another indicator that the blast had not occurred at ground-floor level.[555]

The glass in all the adjacent houses was shattered, the roofs were extensively damaged and the tiles for a considerable distance around appeared to have been peppered with shots from a machine gun. Two or three houses in Congreve Road – behind the one destroyed – were declared insecure and the owner of one of them had been startled by the appearance of the leg of a bedstead through his window after a loud report. Other bombs dropped in the same raid fell in the garden of a house in Lovelace Green. Lumps of clay were blown in all directions, one huge piece lodging itself between the chimney stack and the roof of a house.[556]

The destroyed house was rebuilt and is now 290 Well Hall Road; even-numbered houses in the road had their numbers increased by 80 in 1926.

[554] Bernard Ashley, *Shadow of the Zeppelin*, Orchard Books, London, 2014, pp. 161, 290, 312.

[555] 'Inquest on Seven Victims: Four cases in another district', *The Pioneer*, Friday 1 Sep. 1916.

[556] 'Incidents of the Raid', *The Pioneer*, Friday 1 September 1916.

1925-1938:
The Early Co-op Years

Much of the information in this chapter has been gleaned from the minutes of meetings of the Directors of Progress Estates Limited. These are contained in two books, 29 May 1925 to 12 April 1957, and 2 September 1957 to 2 October 1974, held in the National Co-operative Archive, Manchester.

H.M. Office of Works took back the administration of the Estate from the London County Council in 1920[557] and, by the autumn of 1923, had begun negotiations that would result in its sale to Progress Estates Ltd. ('PEL'), a subsidiary of the Royal Arsenal Co-operative Society ('RACS'),[558] for £375,000.[559] Sixty-four houses spread across the Estate were excluded from the sale because the Office had either sold their freeholds to their occupiers since 1920 (fifty-nine) or were in the process of doing so at the date of transfer (five).[560] RACS had resolved to purchase the Estate by a Resolution of its members in December 1924[561] and the transfer documents were signed off by Mr. R. R. Wale JP and Mr. J. T. Sheppard during the meeting of the Directors of PEL held on 8 June 1925. William Baker Neville was appointed Company Secretary and the directors resolved to appoint William Tait as their clerk on the Estate at 'the usual wage rate' of £3/16/- per week.[562] He worked from what had been the LCC's estate office at 1 Downman Road. On 25 June, Mr. Wale was appointed Chairman of the Board and Mr. H.W. Winn, an employee in the RACS General Office, was appointed Manager of the Estate for six months on probation at a salary of £300 per annum.[563] He evidently survived his probationary period,

---

[557] Beaufoy (1950), p. 261.

[558] Documents and correspondence relating to the transfer of 272 Well Hall Road, National Archives, Kew, document no. TS59/52.

[559] Kennett (Progress Estate).

[560] Beaufoy (1950), p. 261, PEL, 24 February 1926, minute no. 1 and reports included in PEL minute books for years ending January 1932 and 1933.

[561] Plaque erected by the Royal Arsenal Co-operative Society to mark the purchase of the estate and opening of the Progress Hall, Admiral Seymour Road, November 1935.

[562] PEL, 8 June 1925, minutes nos. 1, 2 and 4.

[563] PEL, 25 June 1925, minutes nos. 2, 8 and 9.

because his name reappears in the minutes of meetings in July and November 1926. The 25 June meeting also confirmed the appointment of eight rent collectors who would be employed from RACS offices for one day per week.

PEL was no more than the structure through which RACS chose to own the Estate. The seven directors of the company were all the committee members of the Royal Arsenal Co-operative Society. These were the aforementioned Messrs. Wale and Sheppard, together with S. Curtis, J. Farrell, F. Lockyer, Mrs. E. Real and H. Sykes. Of the initially authorised 100 £1 ordinary shares, 95 were allotted to RACS, one to William Baker Neville, the Company Secretary and one to William Bethell, the Manager of RACS. The purchase of the Estate was financed by a loan of £380,000 from RACS to PEL and, simultaneously, PEL created a legal charge over the Estate in favour of RACS by way of security. £4,500 of the excess over the £375,000 purchase price was to settle professional fees in connection with the purchase of the Estate.[564] RACS's financial interest was strengthened following advice from their solicitors associated with income tax on profits. PEL held an Extraordinary General Meeting on 17 December 1926, at which (a) the ordinary shares were reclassified as preferred ordinary shares carrying a fixed dividend of 5% and (b) a further 50,000 new ordinary shares were created. These were issued to RACS and entitled them to all PEL's profits in excess of the preferred dividends and, in the event of a winding-up, to all the company's surplus assets after repayment of the capital paid-up on the preferred ordinary shares.[565]

PEL continued to sell houses on long leases from the outset, five such transfers being reported to the aforementioned 8 June 1925 directors' meeting. Judging by the subjects discussed at their meetings, there seems little doubt that the directors were the hands-on managers of the Estate, dealing with such day-to-day matters as the action to be taken over rent arrears, requests from tenants to move from one sized house to another and agreeing to the redecoration of houses prior to their being offered for sale.

By 30 June, the Board had resolved the staffing of the Progress Estates Works Department. Mr. Magon was to be appointed Foreman

[564] PEL, 23 June 1925, minute no. 1.

[565] PEL, 17 December 1926 EGM and 8 January 1927.

Painter at £4 per week and to have twelve painters working for him. A carpenter, plumber and labourer were to be engaged at trade union rates and a greensman was to be engaged at £3 per hour.[566]

On 1 September 1925, it was reported at a board meeting that 326 Well Hall Road had been sold for £725 at a ground rent of £5/10/-.[567] This is the first indication of the size of ground rents on the Estate. There was a clause in the leases preventing leaseholders from reselling their houses within three years. A subsequent minute notes that tenants had been given a discount to their home's open market value and, on the minuted occasion, a sale within three years was permitted on the proviso that the tenant paid PEL a sum equal to this discount on completion.[568] The owner of a house in Congreve Road offered her house back to PEL, having spent £195 on improvements. They agreed to repurchase it for the original selling price, plus £195.[569]

PEL were not averse to buying properties in. The earliest recorded instance was in the autumn of 1925 when they had been asked to purchase the freehold of 44 Admiral Seymour Road and agreed to do so for £510, subject to vacant possession.[570]

As a general rule, improvements to tenanted houses were paid for by PEL subject to tenants agreeing to an increase in their rent. The earliest minuted example is on 1 December 1925, when the board agreed with the Estate Manager's estimate for replacing "register" grates with "kitcheners". The cost would be £8/10/- in Class III houses and £11 in Class II. (Presumably Class I houses and the flats had different systems.) Only eight days later, he reported to the board that 58 open grates had been fixed and 115 further applications were waiting to be processed.[571]

On 17 December 1925 the London County Council's Architect's Department wrote to PEL about a scheme for the development of land lying between the Estate on the east side of Well Hall Road and 'the open space known as Castlewood'. They wanted a communication

---

[566] PEL, 30 June 1925, minute no. 1.

[567] PEL, 1 September 1925, minute no. 1.

[568] PEL, 11 August 1950, unnumbered minute.

[569] PEL, 21 May 1962, minute no. 1.

[570] PEL, 6 October 1925, minute no. 4.

[571] PEL, 1 December 1925, minute no. 10, and 9 December 1925, minute no. 2.

road between the two. The Board resolved that the Council be asked if they would make a pathway if the Company surrendered the land. The footpath from Granby Road, opposite the Cornwallis Walk junction, through to Grangehill Road was finally constructed in 1936 when the Borough Council agreed to pay PEL £100 compensation for the loss of the strip of land as well as their legal costs and surveyor's charges.[572]

The Board noted, at its meeting on 18 May 1926, receipt of documents from the Solicitor to the Treasury requiring the Company to convey to the LCC the strip of land it had previously agreed to transfer in connection with the construction of what became Rochester Way.[573] Also noted was receipt of a letter dated 5 May from the Town Clerk to the Metropolitan Borough of Woolwich. It gave notice that the Council proposed to develop the land immediately adjoining the Company's Estate on the west side and required that certain roads be made up to give access to new roads on the Council's estate, 'in accordance with covenants made by the Government with the Vendor at the time of purchase'. Although the Secretary was asked to report on the matter,[574] there are no subsequent minutes detailing his findings.

The Estate may have obtained its first resident dentist when, in June 1926, Mr. F. R. Christian offered to purchase 416 Well Hall Road, subject to him being permitted to carry on the business of a dentist. It was resolved that the Secretary negotiate the sale.[575] This building houses a dental practice to this day.

On 27 October 1926, Mr. D.L. Berry of 20 Congreve Road wrote to the Board asking for permission to have a telephone installed at his residence. It was resolved that permission be granted subject to power being reserved to the Company to withdraw its consent at any time.[576]

It appears as though rectification work was required to the foundations of some houses. On 1 November 1926 Mr Winn, the Estate Manager, advised the Board that underpinning had been completed and all defects made good at 29/31 Arsenal Road, the total cost of the job being

---

[572] PEL, 5 January 1926, minute no. 11, and unnumbered minute dated 11 August 1936.

[573] PEL, 18 May 1926, minute no. 1.

[574] PEL, 18 May 1926, minute no. 2.

[575] PEL, 1 June 1926, minute no. 5.

[576] PEL, 2 November 1926, minute no. 6.

£43/16/5d.[577] Settlement was also reported on 18 September 1929 at 29 Arsenal Road (for the second time) and at 44 Moira Road, the repairs being agreed at estimated costs of £95 and £18, respectively.[578]

Telephone kiosks arrived on the Estate in the second half of 1927. The London Telephone Service asked for permission to erect the first on 'the green at the side of the entrance to the Estate'. Subject to its position being clarified, permission was granted, and was also given for a kiosk 'in the vicinity of Dickson Road'.[579]

By 1928, there had been several incidences of pedestrians and a number of perambulators falling over the edge of the raised pathway in Ross Way because of a lack of any protection along its 160-yard length. Woolwich Borough Council therefore adopted a recommendation that the Borough Engineer be instructed to erect an oak post and rail fence along its edge, at an estimated cost of £170.[580]

A fence was erected around the green in Sandby Green in 1929. It was four feet in height and made from round, wrought iron bars of ⅝-inch diameter. The cheapest estimate received was approximately £60. The Board resolved that the work be put in hand at the figure mentioned, but that an effort be made to buy the material direct instead of through agents if better terms could thereby be arranged.[581]

On 18 May 1934, the Board resolved that the Secretary obtain a sketch plan for the erection of a hall and premises on the vacant site in Admiral Seymour Road, the main meeting room to be capable of seating 250 persons, and for there also to be included two classrooms with kitchen, etc. It was not a unanimous decision; Directors Mr. Comerton and Mr. Dashwood requested that their names be recorded as voting against the resolution. Plans submitted by PEL's architect, Mr. S.W. Ackroyd, were agreed on 7 September 1934 at an estimated cost of £5,587. He was asked to submit them to the LCC and the local authority, Woolwich Council, for approval and to prepare specifications for tenders. By March 1935, eight tenders had been received at prices ranging from £5,163 to

---

[577] PEL, 2 November 1926, minute no. 9.

[578] PEL, 1 October 1929, minute no. 49.

[579] PEL, 14 June 1927 (minute no. 4), 20 September 1927 (minute no. 3) and 3 January 1928 (minute no. 3).

[580] MBW, 1928-1929, p. 47, Works Committee, minute no. 26, 22 October 1928.

[581] PEL, 4 July 1929, minute no. 8.

£6,760. It was resolved to grant the contract to Douglas Halse & Co in the sum of £5,364, the second-lowest tender. Separately, a quotation was accepted from the RACS Engineer for heating by a low-pressure hot water system, powered by a thermostatically controlled gas boiler (£180). This excluded the classrooms which were to be heated by gas radiators. The lowest quotation for the electrical installation (£223/2/9d) was submitted by Messrs T Clarke & Co Ltd and accepted. The furniture included steel-framed chairs at 11/- each and a piano. The architect was requested to submit suggestions for a commemorative tablet to be unveiled by the Chairman, Mr. J.T. Sheppard, when the premises were officially opened on 4 November 1935. It remains in place to this day. Hire charges for the hall for up to three hours ranged from 12/6d to £2 for non-profit organisations, depending upon the nature of the event. Hire of the piano was an additional 10/-. Functions run for private profit were charged an additional 50%. The classrooms were 3/6d per meeting for the smaller one and 6/6d for the larger. The premises were available Monday to Saturday and were to be evacuated by 11:00 p.m.[582]

Covers were provided for domestic water storage tanks so as to comply with the provisions of the Public Health (London) Act. Messrs Croggan & Co provided galvanised covers with a one-inch-deep rim to fit 30-gallon tanks at a cost of 1/8d each – slightly over £100 for the whole Estate.[583]

The first evidence of private motorised transport impacting on the Estate's appearance under PEL's ownership came in February 1928 when Mr. P.H. Bushnell of 230 Well Hall Road asked PEL if the gateway leading to his house could be altered to enable him to wheel his motorcycle combination through it. The directors turned his request down and offered him a transfer to a property with a suitably sized gate if one became available. By the autumn of 1935 there was a demand for garages because the board asked their architect, Mr. Ackroyd, to draw up plans to erect five lock-ups on the vacant land between 40 and 42 Whinyates Road. This was land opposite the southern end of the communal gardens shown on the site layout plan on page 152. Work began in July or August 1936.[584] It was presumably the slow but

[582] PEL, various minutes between 18 May 1934 and 1 November 1935.

[583] PEL, 3 September 1935, minute no. 9 and 1 October 1935, minute no. 11.

[584] PEL, 12 November 1935, minute no. 7 and 14 July 1936, minute no. 8.

inevitable increase in vehicular traffic that caused PEL, in 1963, to transfer to Woolwich Borough Council sufficient land at the corners of the road in Sandby Green for each to be rounded off to a 25-foot radius.[585] In the same year, the company decided to allow all tenants, upon application and acceptance of its standards, to park their cars in the front gardens of their houses.[586] Towards the end of 1971, PEL increased the rent on each of the four garage plots it owned adjacent to 68 Whinyates Road from £1 to £16 per annum.[587]

Signs that lessees wanted to change the appearance of their homes began as early as March 1936 when PEL gave permission to Mr. L. Robinson to erect a wood and brick porch at 5 Sandby Green, and to Mr. J.W. Hughes of 21 Granby Road for the erection of a timber and asbestos garage.[588] Mr. H.P. Golding of 2 Arsenal Road was also given permission to erect a garage in June 1939. Its method of construction is not recorded, although it was to cost £58/17/- and the lessee's ground rent was to be increased by 10/- per annum.[589]

The raised section of Ross Way takes in even-numbered houses nos. 34-84, and the absence of front fences caused the occupants of nos. 40 to 76 to complain of a lack of privacy. Their case is fairly obvious from this illustration.

Ross Way.

[585] PEL, 24 May 1963, minute no. 1.
[586] PEL, 8 November 1963, minute no. 1.
[587] PEL, 19 November 1971, minute no. 2.
[588] PEL, 10 March 1936, minute no. 7.
[589] PEL, 13 June 1939, minute no. 7.

The matter was resolved in 1938 when PEL surrendered to the Council a four-foot strip of land inside the fence the latter had built along the edge of the section ten years earlier. Save for a section where the front walls of the houses abut this four-foot line (outside nos. 64-68), front fences were erected along the boundary of the strip furthermost from the road at an estimated cost (to PEL) of £103 over and above the value of the land.[590]

The first mention of the Progress Estate Residents Association is on 23 August 1938 when their application to pay 'specially reduced fees' for hiring the Progress Hall was turned down.[591] On 7 November of the same year, Mrs. E.M. Hider submitted a resolution on behalf of PERA 'regarding houses being sold to purchasers for speculative letting, which was noted'.[592]

---

[590] PEL, 5 October 1937 (minute no. 10), 11 January 1938 (minute no. 8B) and 24 May 1938 (minute no. 6).

[591] PEL, 23 August 1938, minute no. 7.

[592] PEL, 13 December 1938, minute no. 9.

1939-1944:
Second World War Aerial Attacks

There are four sources of information for the damage wrought to the Estate during the Second World War. They are the Metropolitan Borough of Woolwich's bomb damage maps, the Incident Logs complied by the Air Raid Precautions service, the Record of Flying Bomb Incidents, probably also created by the ARP and the minutes of meetings of the Directors of Progress Estates Ltd. The first three are to be found in the Greenwich Heritage Centre.

The governments of Britain and France guaranteed Polish independence on 31 March 1939.[593] Twelve days later, the London Fire Brigade wrote to Progress Estates Ltd. asking for the use of a portion of the company's premises as a fire alarm station in the event of hostilities breaking out. Their request was granted.[594] Although Britain declared itself at war with Germany when Germany invaded Poland on 1 September 1939, the civilian population was not drawn into the conflict *en masse* until the Blitz began on 7 September 1940.[595]

The government and the civil service continued to plan for war during the summer of 1939 and, on 8 June, the Ministry of Health issued circular no. 1811, *Return as to War Damage to property*: 'It will be the duty of the local authority in the event of war to furnish returns giving particulars of properties in their area which have been damaged by enemy action ... The return is required in connection with claims for compensation for war damage and in considering questions of emergency repairs to housing accommodation and other essential buildings'. For London, it was decided that the Architect's Department of the London County Council, a large department with about 1,200 staff, should be the body to whom the 28 metropolitan boroughs[596] made their returns. Following an air raid, district rescue officers and their teams inspected the affected streets to categorise the damaged

---

[593] Lee, p. 480.

[594] PEL, 18 April 1939, minute no. 6.

[595] Gardiner, pp. 97-114.

[596] en.wikipedia.org/wiki/Metropolitan_boroughs_of_the_County_of_London, accessed 4 December 2016.

buildings, relaying their conclusions to borough councils on the forms *Incident Report and Record of War Damage* that were provided by the Architect's Department. Damage was described on the forms in one of five categories, in accordance with the Ministry of Health's circular:

a) Totally destroyed
b) Requiring demolition
c) Capable of repair but uninhabitable
d) Capable of repair but inhabitable
e) Slightly damaged

The high volume of minor blast damage in the London region caused the addition of a sixth category – blast damage, minor in nature. This was for damage in excess of mere broken windows and missing roof tiles or slates which was not to be reported.

It was the job of each Metropolitan Borough's District Surveyor to present the information returned on the incident forms on large-scale plans (1:1056, or 88 feet to the inch) by colour-coding effected properties. The coding, whose descriptions were slightly renamed from the Ministry of Health's circular, was:

a) Black – total destruction
b) Purple – damaged beyond repair
c) Dark red – seriously damaged; doubtful if repairable
d) Light red – seriously damaged, but repairable at cost
e) Orange – general blast damage; not structural
f) Yellow – blast damage; minor in nature

Upon receipt of these maps from District Surveyors, the Superintending Architect of the LCC's War Damage Survey Section transferred the information to smaller scale maps (1:2500) which were stamped 'LCC Architect's Plan Room' followed by a reference number in the format [letter and number]/[two-digit number] whose precise meaning is a matter of conjecture. Although not relevant to the Estate, the Architect's Department added a seventh colour code: green, for clearance areas. In London, it marked heavily damaged domestic property, often cheek by jowl with the docks or industry along the Thames. The buildings had been noted as being of poor-quality construction before the war, and the code was to indicate that the areas ought to be redeveloped, rather than repaired, once hostilities ceased.[597]

The Air Raid Precautions Act,1937 had made local authorities responsible, from 1 January 1938, for 'the protection of persons and property from injury and damage in the event of hostile attacks from the air'.[598] Air Raid Precautions personnel were the authors of the World War Two Civil Defence Incident Logs for the Metropolitan Borough of Woolwich. The logs reflect their chief concern: dealing with people and property close to the epicentres of attacks. The ARP very probably also created the Borough's Record of Flying Bomb Incidents, June 16th to August 31st, 1944.[599] Every incident and flying bomb attack is dated, which helps to interpret the bomb damage maps whose coding is undated.

Woolwich was one of the boroughs that chose to keep mapped information for its own purposes. It used 1:2500 sheets, rather than a 1:1056 scale that would have matched the sheets it sent to the LCC's Architect's Department. The Estate covers parts of London Ordnance Survey sheets X.7, X.10 and X.11.[600] Whilst adopting the LCC's colour-coding, the representation of damage caused to any one property in second and subsequent air raids differs. The policy of the Architect's Department was to change the colour by overpainting if a greater degree of damage was sustained in successive raids.[601] Woolwich's approach was to colour the outline of the house when it was first damaged and to add a coloured dot within its curtilage for second and subsequent attacks. The difference is most evident in the extreme western portion of the Estate that will be referred to in this chapter as the Whinyates Road area. This comprises the whole of Whinyates Road, the portion of Phineas Pett Road between Whinyates Road and Kakehill Lane, Dickson Road between Cobbett Road and Whinyates Road, Sandby Green and Cobbett Road itself. Only 32 of its 160 houses escaped recordable damage. 62 have one

---

[597] Saunders; Ward; maps of the LCC's Architect's Department, London Metropolitan Archives, viewed 1 December 2016.

[598] Gardiner, pp. 97-114.

[599] Both records are stored in the Greenwich Heritage Centre.

[600] Ordnance Survey;, London sheet X.11 and Kent sheets II.14 & VIII.2 (Parts of), rev. 1914, pub. 1916; London sheet X.10, rev. 1914, pub. 1935; London sheet X.7 and Kent Sheet II.14 (Part of), rev.1914, pub. 1916.

[601] Ward, p. 6.

coloured dot inside the boundaries of their gardens, 21 two dots and 2, three. Thus, for example, all the houses in the block in Dickson Road that straddle the footpath to Sandy Green are coloured yellow (blast damage; minor in nature). All also have two orange dots inside their boundaries (general blast damage, not structural) and two have dark red ones (seriously damaged; doubtful if repairable). That these dots represent damage from second or subsequent attacks is borne out by the documentary records for two separate incidents. The first was at 39 and 41 Lovelace Green. The Incident Logs state that at 3:40 a.m. on 31 March 1944 a bomb fell at the junction of Lovelace Green and Martin Bowes Road. It failed to explode on impact but did so at 10:35 a.m., badly damaging these two houses. The outlines representing 39 and 41 Lovelace Green are coded yellow (blast damage; minor in nature), as are about 24 others in their immediate vicinity. These two, however, are the only houses in the area with light red dots (seriously damaged, but repairable at cost). The second relates to even nos. 40-44 Dickson Road. Again, the outlines of all the houses are coloured yellow (blast damage; minor in nature). Orange dots (general blast damage; not structural) have been added at nos. 40 and 42 and purple ones (damaged beyond repair) appear in front of all three. Further documentary confirmation for this highest level of damage is a set of architect's drawings dated September 1947 entitled 'Proposed rebuilding war damaged houses at nos. 40 42 44 Dickson Road, Eltham, SE9'.[602]

The number of damaged houses recorded on the Borough's bomb damage maps exceeds that recorded on the maps produced by the Architect's Department. A clue as to why this might be is the instruction issued by the latter in its circular of 12 July 1944, which said that category E damage (general blast damage; not structural) no longer needed to be reported.[603] Presumably the same applied to category F (blast damage; minor in nature). V1 flying bomb (doodlebug) attacks began on 13 June 1944. By the time they ended the following October, when the last launching site was overrun by Allied forces, 9,521 had been launched towards south-east England, peaking at over 100 per

---

[602] Fred[k] H. Jones, FIAA&S, FFAS, M. Inst. RA, Registered Architect & Surveyor, 247 Bexley Road, Eltham, SE9, drawing no. 5099, Sept. 1947; photocopies kindly supplied by David Hallam, partner, David Evans & Co., 2015.

[603] Ward, p. 19.

day.[604] Their destructive power was such that the Department may have been overwhelmed by the sheer number of reports within a month of the start of this phase of the war; on average, each V1 landing in the London area damaged 400 houses.[605] Extensive damage in the Whinyates Road area occurred as a result of a V1 attack on 10 July 1944.

Progress Estates Ltd. had acquired 1,299 houses and flats from H.M. Office of Works (the original 1,298 plus the manager's house) less 64 the government had sold or agreed to sell prior to the transfer of ownership. PEL subsequently repurchased 20 of this sixty-four so, by 6 January 1940, owned the freeholds of 1,255 houses and flats. Of these, 376 had been sold on 99-year leases[606] for considerations totalling £223,367/10/- and ground rents of £1,653/12/6d per annum. These numbers remained unchanged throughout the war.[607] The tenanted properties thus numbered 879, and it is only these whose war damage would have been reported at board meetings because long-leaseholders would have been responsible for their own repairs. It is quite likely that the minutes include houses damaged to a lower level than the minimum reported by Woolwich's District Surveyor to the LCC's War Damage Survey Section, because the company would have been liable to undertake all repairs to its tenanted properties.

The Estate was first affected by the war the day after the Blitz began when 3 Brome Road was struck by an incendiary bomb at 9:49 p.m. on 8 September 1940.[608] PEL's directors' list of vacant houses as at 8 October included eight that had been damaged in air raids and a further two that had been appropriated by the local Council Billeting Officer. These were this Brome Road house along with 7, 85 and 99 Congreve Road, 14 Prince Rupert Road and even numbers 318-322 Well Hall Road.[609] As a demonstration of the differing reporting criteria – and maybe also understandable differences of opinion between one observer and another during and immediately after the chaos of a raid

---

[604] en.wikipedia.org/wiki/V-1_flying_bomb, accessed 2 January 2017.

[605] Gardiner, p. 285.

[606] Beaufoy (1950), p. 261.

[607] PEL, reports included in minute books for years ending January 1940-45.

[608] Incident Logs complied by the Air Raid Precautions service, Greenwich Heritage Centre.

[609] Incident Logs complied by the Air Raid Precaution service, Greenwich Heritage Centre.

– Woolwich's bomb damage maps do not record any damage to houses in Brome Road, Congreve Road or Prince Rupert Road. In Well Hall Road, 318 is marked as seriously damaged, but repairable at cost, 320 seriously damaged; doubtful if repairable and 322 blast damage; minor in nature. Woolwich's maps also record damage at even numbers 308-316. Classifications for 308 and 310 were seriously damaged; doubtful if repairable and 312-316 damaged beyond repair. 324 was recorded as having sustained blast damage; minor in nature. The Incident Logs note that 308-310 had their walls cracked and windows damaged, and 318-322 suffered broken chimney stacks and roof damage. There were two non-fatal casualties in the group as a whole. The Incident Logs also reported a further nine raids on 11 September 1940 between 00:02 and 08:05 a.m. – the most concentrated the Estate endured – followed by single incidents on the 15th, 16th and 19th. Five of these thirteen reports were for the investigation of actual or suspected unexploded bombs, five did not damage houses (although a high-explosive bomb that fell at the junction of Admiral Seymour and Moira Roads caused casualties), but three did. An empty property, 63 Arsenal Road, was hit by an incendiary bomb that caused considerable damage to its roof and a bedroom, police securing the premises and neighbours undertaking to notify the owners. A high-explosive bomb detonated outside 3 Congreve Road, causing damage to this house as well as no. 9. Another broke a gas main and caused three casualties at 34 Granby Road.

Two further raids caused damage to the Estate during October 1940. A high-explosive bomb that fell on 59 Prince Rupert Road on the 17th injured four people, one of whom was taken to the local Brook Hospital for treatment. Six houses were affected in the early afternoon of the 20th; oil bombs, high-explosive bomb cases filled with an inflammable oil mixture designed to spread burning oil,[610] fell on even numbers 8-10 Lovelace Green (the first having its front windows broken) 282-284 Well Hall Road (rear of houses badly damaged) and 38-40 Phineas Pett Road (fire in the back garden burnt out without causing damage). The Luftwaffe ceased dropping oil bombs in January 1941 because they often failed to detonate.[611]

[610] Steve Hunnisett, *Metropolitan Borough of Woolwich – World War Two Civil Defence Incident Logs*, Greenwich Heritage Centre.

[611] en.wikipedia.org/wiki/Incendiary_device#Development_and_use_in_World_War_II, accessed 29 November 2016.

A high-explosive bomb raid on 5 November 1940 blew in part of 23 Dickson Road at 4:45 a.m. No further raids are reported in the Incident Logs until 19 April 1941, when another high-explosive attack resulted in two fatal casualties at 52 Lovelace Green.

The report of Mr. Tait, PEL's Estate Manager, to the directors on 21 March 1941 advised them of further damage by enemy action to an unspecified number of properties on the night of Wednesday, 19 March 1941 and commended two fire watchers, Messrs. Fenwick and Alcorn, for tackling fire bombs which fell on the roof of the Estate Office at 1 Downman Road. The directors resolved 'that a suitable letter be sent to the men concerned'.[612]

The next incident was at 9:15 p.m. on 17 January 1943 when a raid comprising an estimated 70 incendiary bombs, nearly all of which fell to the west of the Estate, damaged 26-32 Whinyates Road beyond repair and caused three fatal casualties.[613] Mr. Tait confirmed the loss of three of the houses, the destruction of the five garages that PEL had erected in Whinyates Road between nos. 40 and 42 and 'two other [houses] so badly damaged as to necessitate demolition'.[614] These would have been nos. 22-24 Whinyates Road, classified on the Woolwich bomb damage maps as seriously damaged; doubtful if repairable.

The Estate suffered further damage in the 'Baby Blitz' which began on 21 January 1944[615] and ended the following May.[616] St. Barnabas church, at the junction of Rochester Way and Cobbett Road, was hit by an incendiary bomb in the early hours of 2 March 1944 and the uncontrollable fire that resulted left it gutted and roofless.[617] At 1:15 a.m. on the same night, the Incident Logs reported phosphorous incendiary bombs causing fires at 156, 196 and 226 Well Hall Road, although they were brought under control – presumably meaning the houses were not gutted. At 3:40 a.m. on 31 March a bomb fell at the

---

[612] PEL, 24 March 1941, minute no. 1.

[613] Incident Logs.

[614] PEL, 22 January 1943, minute no. 1.

[615] Blake, pp. 134-139.

[616] en.wikipedia.org/wiki/Operation_Steinbock, accessed 5 December 2016.

[617] Blake, p. 138.

THE EVOLUTION OF THE ESTATE

junction of Lovelace Green and Martin Bowes Road. As discussed on page 221 in the context of the methods used by Woolwich to code its maps, it failed to explode on impact but did so at 10:35 a.m., badly damaging 39 and 41 Lovelace Green.

The single-most damaging raid of the war occurred at 10:39 a.m. on 10 July 1944 when a V1 (doodlebug) flying bomb landed in Whinyates Road.[618] V1 attacks were recorded on the Woolwich maps by 1½-inch diameter black circles. One, whose centre is in the back garden of no. 32, was erased because it had been drawn in error. A second replaced it, centred nine houses down the road on no. 50. The correction is corroborated by the Record of Flying Bomb Incidents which describes the bomb as having landed in 'Whinyates Road – opposite the green at junction with Dickson Road'. This is a near-perfect description of the position of no. 50. The Incident Log records 'extensive damage to properties' and eight casualties, some of whom were hospitalised. A very high proportion of the damage recorded on the Woolwich bomb damage maps in the Whinyates Road area might have been caused by this incident; all are within a 300-yard radius from the point where the V1 landed. Carrying a ton of explosive apiece, they had a devastating effect in urban areas. Roofs could be ripped off, doors blown out and window frames wrenched from their casements half a mile (800 m) away.[619]

PEL's directors began to minute less and less after 24 March 1941 (other work caused by the war gradually took precedence?) and there is no immediate report of the 10 July 1944 V1 attack. However, on 25 April 1947, the Secretary reported 'the receipt of a licence to rebuild the seven demolished houses nos. 28-40 Whinyates Road, and that a licence to deal similarly with the other five houses in [the] road was expected in the near future'.[620] Nos. 28-40 had been hit during the 1943 incendiary raid. The Woolwich bomb damage maps show 32 and 40 as totally destroyed and 26-30 together with 34-38 as damaged beyond repair.

The following table summarises the Estate's bomb damage.

[618] *Record of Flying Bomb Incidents, 16th June to 31st August 1944*, Greenwich Heritage Centre.

[619] Waller, p. 24.

[620] PEL, 25 April 1914, minute no. 1.

WWII BOMB DAMAGE

Category of damage	Woolwich map totals	Whinyates Road area	Elsewhere on the estate
Total destruction	8	5	3
Damaged beyond repair	18	10	8
Seriously damaged; doubtful if repairable	45	32	13
Seriously damaged, but repairable at cost	8	8	-
General blast damage; not structural	76	57	19
Blast damage; minor in nature	117	16	101
TOTALS	272	128	144

Where a house was hit more than once, it is included for the worst category of damage. Most of the incidents occurred in one of three areas. By far the worst concentration was in the Whinyates Road area, where 80% of its 160 houses were hit.

Second were the 38 properties on the eastern (odd-numbered) side of Granby Road from its junction with Well Hall Road to slightly south of Cornwallis Walk that suffered minor blast damage, possibly as a result of a raid which destroyed or damaged beyond repair nine houses on the outside of the bend in Castlewood Drive immediately south-west of the underground reservoir on the edge of the Castle Wood area of Oxleaze Woods and rendered all 21 between them and the Drive's junction with Westmount Road seriously damaged; doubtful if repairable.

The third concentration concerns an area centred upon nos. 48, 50, 52 and 51 in the unusually-numbered Lovelace Green and even numbers 70-74 Arsenal Road. They are behind one another and all were seriously damaged though repairable at cost. Perhaps a single bomb fell in the gardens between them. Almost every house on either side of Arsenal Road between its intersections with Cornwallis Walk and Prince Rupert Road suffered minor blast damage, as did about twenty on either side of the Lovelace Green houses. Altogether, these and the abovementioned Granby Road group account for about 120 of the 144 houses described in the table as being elsewhere on the Estate.

The damage assessments recorded on the Woolwich bomb damage maps may well have resulted from fairly superficial inspections. This may account for the small numbers assessed as being 'Seriously damaged; repairable at cost'. A number of homes classified as 'Seriously damaged; doubtful if repairable' may, upon later (and more qualified?) inspection, have been found to be repairable.

War damage was an excluded risk from insurance policies and the government had made it clear that compensation for bomb damage would be paid 'at the end of the war and not before'. Repairs during wartime were not just a financial issue. Materials had to be sourced and adequately-qualified labour was in short supply. Houses were made weatherproof by stretching tarpaulins over broken roofs and whatever was available was used to board up broken windows.[621] Thus, in October 1940, PEL authorised Mr. Tait to obtain equitable rents for partially damaged houses that remained partly habitable.[622]

---

[621] Gardiner, p. 131.

[622] PEL, 8 October 1940, minutes nos. 5 and 7.

1945-1947:
Post-War Rebuilding

The principles for the terms upon which the country would compensate people for losses caused by enemy action (either directly or consequentially) were contained in the War Damage Act, 1941. The Act created the War Damage Commission whose members were to be appointed by the Treasury. Under section 1, it had complete freedom of choice in the selection and numbers of its members save that Members of Parliament could not serve on it. Under section 3, compensation would take one of two forms. The first was payment for the cost of works. If war damage was to be made good by reinstating property to 'the form in which it existed immediately before the occurrence of the damage' the amount of the payment was to be 'equal to the proper cost of the works executed for the making good thereof', including necessary professional fees. The Estate has this section to thank for its damaged houses being rebuilt to their original specification even when, as in Whinyates Road, house after house was badly damaged so would in all probability have otherwise been rebuilt to a less costly specification. Today, it is all but impossible to tell the repaired or rebuilt homes from those that escaped serious damage. The section included an override that repairs could not result in a more valuable property than had existed immediately prior to the loss occurring.

The second form of compensation was a value payment, under which the owner was to be paid compensation equal to the fall in the value of the property caused by the damage in lieu of the damaged house being repaired. At the time the Act was passed, the pre-damage value was to be the open market value as of 1 March 1939 and the damaged value a professional estimate of the sum the property would be expected to fetch immediately after the damage occurred.

Section 4 provided for value payments rather than payments for the cost of works to be made in the case of totally-destroyed houses where the cost of rebuilding was expected to exceed their 1 March 1939 values. Here, the value payment was to be the difference between the 1 March 1939 value and the value of the land upon which the house had stood.

Owners could opt for a hybrid payment. For example, they might elect for payment for the cost of repairs to make a house wind- and weather-proof, but elect for a value payment in lieu of reconstructing a conservatory that might be destroyed for a second time before hostilities ceased.

Section 8 gave the Treasury powers to determine the timing of payments by the War Damage Commission. Save for certain payments on account, value payments were to be made at 'such time or times as may be specified in regulations made by the Treasury' and would in the meantime accrue interest at 2½% per annum. Insofar as compensation for damage to houses was concerned, the chief cause of payments on account had to do with mortgaged homes that were totally destroyed or so seriously damaged as to be uninhabitable. The owners could claim a grant of £800. As there was no legal liability for lenders to finance repairs, the intention was that the grant would be used wholly or partially to pay off the mortgage. The Building Societies Association had readily agreed with the government that they would grant such mortgagees new loans on alternative houses.[623] It turned out that no other value payments were made before November 1947, albeit the amount was enhanced as March 1939 values were by then considered to be inappropriate.

A month before the War Damage Act received Royal Assent on 26 March 1941, the Ministry of Home Security, which had been established in 1939 principally to direct the Civil Defence,[624] published its estimates for repairs. It was expected to cost £750 to rebuild a totally-destroyed house, £100 to repair one that was seriously damaged and £30 to pay for minor damage.[625]

Aerial bombing fell into three phases. The Blitz lasted from 8 September 1940 until May 1941 and the Baby Blitz from January to May 1944. V1 attacks, followed by V2s, lasted from 13 June 1944 to 27 March 1945. As to the first, the Ministry of Home Security stated that, by 15 February 1941, 93,865 homes in England and Wales had been destroyed or damaged beyond repair, 298,915 were seriously damaged but repairable and a further 1,094,190 were damaged to a lesser extent. Out of the overall total, 36% were in London. Although the Baby Blitz

---

[623] Waller, p. 126.

[624] en.wikipedia.org/wiki/Ministry_of_Home_Security, accessed 29 December 2016.

[625] Gardiner, p. 284.

caused much less damage,[626] the V1 and V2 attacks were devastating for South-East London. Two-thirds of the housing in Peckham was estimated to have been destroyed or damaged.[627] In total, 1,104,000 homes were destroyed by V1s alone.[628]

On 4 October 1945, five months after the war ended in Europe,[629] Woolwich Borough Council's Works and Housing Committees held a Special Joint Meeting to consider war damage repairs, the licensing of building work and housing.[630] Probably due to the proximity of the docks in the Thames basin, the Council had realised when war broke out that bombing was likely to be very serious so had divided the borough into areas. Each had been allocated a member of the Borough Engineer's staff, to which local builders were assigned. During the Blitz, the large number of houses damaged and the frequency of incidents meant their work was restricted to carrying out first-aid repairs to make houses wind- and weather-proof. As and when time permitted, second-stage repairs were carried out to make damaged houses reasonably comfortable by using temporary materials to repair ceilings and internal joinery. By the time the Blitz ended nearly 45,000 houses had been first-aided and the builders' work forces had averaged 1,500 men. In all, 1,163 homes had been destroyed or demolished, 1,049 seriously damaged and 30,668 slightly damaged. By the end of the Baby Blitz in May 1944 a further 37 houses had been demolished and approximately 11,500 received first-aid repairs. By this time the labour force had reduced to about 800 men although private work, up to the value of £100, was being fairly extensively undertaken. Come June 1944, repairs were fast drawing to a close and would have been completed by the following winter had the V1 flying bomb attacks not started. These resulted in the demolition of a further 418 houses and the need for nearly 43,000 first-aid repairs. The workforce had been increased to over 2,700 by bringing in provincial firms and providing billeting and feeding accommodation for their employees in eight large

---

[626] en.wikipedia.org/wiki/Operation_Steinbock, accessed 29 December 2016.

[627] Waller, p. 33.

[628] Waller, p. 128.

[629] en.wikipedia.org/wiki/Victory_in_Europe_Day, accessed 15 December 2016.

[630] MBW, 1944-1945, pp. 259-265, 4 October 1945.

houses the Council had requisitioned along with other depots and a school. The V2 rocket attacks resulted in the demolition of another 137 houses and 25,000 first-aid repairs.

The Borough had begun the war with about 38,000 houses. Very few escaped, and most were damaged on several occasions. In all, 124,500 had been first-aided (the equivalent of repairing every house more than three times). Second-stage repairs had been made to 29,274 houses, many on more than one occasion. Seriously damaged houses partly rebuilt or made habitable totalled 1,106.

The Council was now faced with the 'colossal' task of completing repairs to all these houses, to which end the government had allocated it a workforce of about 4,000. They were assisted by 7 surveyors, 44 Clerks of Works and their Assistants and 37 timekeepers. In addition, 41 Clerical Assistants and the staffs of three firms of quantity surveyors were engaged in dealing with correspondence and contractors' accounts.

The workforce of 4,000 was permitted to operate in one or more of seven ways:

1. Repair to war-damaged properties.
2. The erection of temporary bungalows.
3. The erection of permanent council houses.
4. Repair of war-damaged houses privately by building licence.
5. Rebuilding of demolished war-damaged houses.
6. Completion of houses under construction by private enterprise at the beginning of the war.
7. The erection of new houses by private enterprise.

The first two were the Borough's absolute priority and were absorbing the entire allocation of labour. Although the Government had intimated that local authorities should proceed with (3) and (4) and formulate a plan for completing (5) within two years, this would only be possible in the south-east boroughs that had borne the brunt of the V1 and V2 attacks with a greatly increased allocation of labour. This had not been forthcoming despite the Council's strong representations to the Government.

A shortage of plasterers and plastering materials meant that in many houses there was a prolonged gap between new plasterboard ceilings being erected and their being skimmed. Similarly, the initial decoration of walls was often limited to a single coat of distemper and, of joinery, a coat of primer together with, if it was external, a single coat of undercoat. A shortage of tradesmen made it impossible to create properly-balanced gangs, resulting in much work being undertaken by unqualified labourers to a standard that should not have been acceptable in peacetime.

In October 1943 the Government, faced with shortages of materials and labour on the one hand and massive amounts of repair work required simply to make premises habitable on the other, decided to require private owners to obtain a licence from the Ministry of Works if they wanted to carry out work in excess of £100 in value, the cost of repairing a seriously damaged house as estimated by the Ministry of Home Security in February 1941. The Ministry of Works referred all applications to Borough Councils who were asked to provide them with Certificates of Essentiality confirming the category into which the application fell:

1. The repair of war damage to houses.
2. Work necessitated by a statutory notice issued by the local authority.
3. Essential works of repair or maintenance to avoid danger to health or grave deterioration of the structure.
4. Repair and adaptation for the conversion of premises to bring into use more housing accommodation.
5. Necessary works for the completion of partly built houses to relieve the urgent housing need.

Upon receipt of the Certificate, the Ministry of Works would issue a building licence to the applicant that allowed the materials to be purchased and the work to proceed.

The rules were tightened from 3 October 1944 to control works of £10 or more. Now, local authorities were responsible for issuing licences for works costing between £10 and £100. For larger amounts they were required to forward the application together with a Certificate of Essentiality to the Ministry who would then issue the building licence to the applicant.

A final procedural change was made with effect from 1 August 1945. Because local authorities had a better idea than central government of housing needs in their own areas, they were made responsible for issuing building licences regardless of the value of the work.

By 25 September 1945, under all three variations of the licensing scheme, Woolwich Borough Council had received 1,586 applications for private work of which all bar 60 had been processed. They had issued 182 Certificates of Essentiality to the Ministry of Works and 618 building licences directly to applicants. They had disapproved 45% of the applications that had been made – 606 applications for licences under £100 and 120 for sums in excess of this. Whilst this appeared to be a high rejection rate, they had to be mindful of the fact that if an applicant's work was to be carried out by a firm that was under contract to carry out war damage repairs for the Council, the granting of a licence gave the firm the right to withdraw men from war damage repair work to undertake the licenced work. The Council's policy was to ensure all war-damaged houses were repaired as a matter of urgency. The granting of licences in these circumstances would therefore only result in the giving of priority to applicants at the expense of others. Also, many applications were to rebuild demolished houses. So far, no licences had been granted for such work, although applicants had been reminded that much preliminary work was required, and they had been advised to instruct an architect to draw up detailed plans and specifications and to seek the necessary consents under the Building Acts. Although the meeting recommended that the Council began to issue licences for the rebuilding of houses where a cost of works payment would be granted by the War Damage Commission, the repair of war damage and the construction of temporary and permanent houses should continue to be given the highest priority.

The Ministry of Health (which had been given responsibility for first-aid repairs to houses)[631] issued its circular no. 219/45 to local authorities in London in December 1945 stating that, upon request, they should release provincial building firms contracted to undertake war damage repairs in the metropolis in order to undertake housing work in their own localities. The Ministry would inform individual local authorities when they considered provincial labour who did not request to return home should have their contracts discontinued. Local authorities were also told to review their contracts with all builders

[631] Waller, p. 131.

with a view to ending cost-plus arrangements in favour of the usual peacetime fixed-price arrangements.[632] Woolwich Council terminated cost-plus contracts for war damage repairs on 8 October 1946 except for works to roofing and casements; the Ministry agreed these could continue on this basis.[633]

The Ministry continued to nudge local authorities to return to usual peacetime, private sector contracting methods. In July 1946, Woolwich Council received a communication from them stating, amongst other things, that it seemed unreasonable to refuse building licences to applicants where their chosen contractors were not engaged on Local Authority work because granting them would in effect be adding to the war damage repair force in the district. The Council concurred, provided the Borough Engineer was satisfied that materials would not be unduly diverted from work being carried out by building firms engaged by the Council on repair work (slates, plaster and plasterboard still being in short supply).[634] In October 1946 the issuing of building licences for the rebuilding of demolished houses and the construction of new homes reverted to the Borough Engineer, having been controlled by the Building Licences Sub-Committee formed a year earlier.[635]

By the autumn of 1946, Progress Estates Ltd. had apparently decided they would set up a contracting business and tender for work offered by Woolwich Borough Council. At their meeting on 4 December of that year it was reported that contracts with Woolwich Borough Council for war damage work to 596 properties had been secured at a contract price of £20,573/0/5d. Tenders in respect of 130 houses in Admiral Seymour Road, Phineas Pett Road and Lovelace Green had been unsuccessful, and in respect of 34 houses in Maudslay Road the Company had not been invited to tender. The Estate Manager stated that the profit margin on these contracts was quite reasonable, and that he was now hiring labour of the right type and in sufficient quantities to cover present requirements.[636] This minute confirms two interesting matters. Firstly,

---

[632] MBW 1945-1946, p. 83, Works Committee, minute no. 9, 17 December 1945.

[633] MBW 1945-1946, p. 382, Works Committee, minute no. 27, 23 September 1946.

[634] MBW 1945-1946, p. 327, Works Committee, minute no. 26, 15 July 1946.

[635] MBW 1946-1947, p. 26, Works Committee, minute no. 24, 18 November 1946.

[636] PEL, 4 December 1946, minute no. 3.

the value of the contract to work on the 596 properties amounts to an average of £34/10/4d. per house. This is one-third of the estimated cost of restoring a seriously-damaged house, implying that some of the damage must have been fairly superficial. Secondly, there are some 175 flats and houses in Admiral Seymour Road, Phineas Pett Road and Lovelace Green, so the implication is that 74% were in need of repair. Maudslay Road has 54 houses, so 63% of these had been damaged (assuming the 34 houses mentioned were all the damaged houses in the road). These far exceed the numbers shown on Woolwich's war damage maps discussed earlier, thus providing confirmation that huge numbers of houses suffered damaged below the minimum reportable level.

In an effort to keep work moving apace, the Ministry of Health informed local authorities in March 1947 that they should cease including the cutting out and making good of plaster cracks in ceilings and walls in their contracts for the repair of war damage unless the condition of the wall or ceiling was dangerous or the work was necessary to make a house wind and weather-tight. In cases where schedules had been prepared but tenders not yet invited, they were to be adjusted. If, after excluding the work, the amount remaining to be carried out in any particular house was small, the local authority should consider deleting that house from its present programme. Woolwich Council objected on the grounds that its war damage repair work was at an advanced stage, but without success. Nationally, the Ministry wanted the grave shortage of labour working on new housing reduced by the labour this would release. Furthermore, the present house-to-house survey and scheduling of occupied houses was to be discontinued. The Council estimated this would leave 3,888 houses unrepaired.[637] Possibly not coincidentally, Progress Estates Ltd. was granted a building licence to rebuild the seven demolished houses nos. 28 to 40 Whinyates Road the following month and expected a second to rebuild the other five houses in Whinyates Road shortly thereafter. The directors agreed to advertise for a works foreman to take charge and that he be paid £450 per annum.[638] The purchase of a light builder's lorry for £184/10/6d, 'required mainly for private work', was approved a year later, in April 1948.

---

[637] MBW 1946-1947, p. 219, Works Committee, minute no. 21, 17 March 1947.

[638] PEL, 25 April 1947, minute no. 1.

1948-1966:
Modernisation and Renewal

The increasing demand for electricity had caused PEL to grant Woolwich Borough Council permission to construct a substation at the rear of 27 Arsenal Road on 9 May 1947. The Council would pay a rent of £5 per annum and the tenant's rent was reduced accordingly.[639] Despite the availability of electric light, 51 of PEL's tenanted properties (some houses, some flats) still had gas lighting in early 1959, although 35 had agreed to change over to electricity for which they would pay an additional rent of between 10d. and 1/7d. per week. The change would cost PEL an estimated £1,489/9/11d. The staircases in at least some of the flats were lit by gas until early 1970.[640]

On 17 October 1949 PEL considered an application received from the Woolwich Labour Party to rent the land between even nos. 172 and 182 Well Hall Road in order to erect a prefabricated divisional office.[641] Initially turned down, the Directors resolved after 'further consideration' on 17 November 1949 to enter the tenancy agreement requested at a ground rent of £10 per annum.[642] As is evident from the plan included in the conveyance of the land (see illustration on page 141) the site, at its southern boundary, ends in a triangle so there was a point beyond which houses could not be built. When the east side of Well Hall Road was renumbered in 1926 (see the chapter *The Estate's road names*) the LCC presumably made provision for potential new housing plots on the land the Labour Party leased, allocating them even nos. 174-180. The land is now the site of the Eltham Medical Practice, whose address is 180 Well Hall Road, and its car park. Eltham Funeralcare (the Co-operative Society's undertaker's business) is number 172; there are no buildings nod. 174-176. It is worth mentioning that no. 182, the southernmost Estate house, shows every sign of having been rebuilt at some time although it is not marked on Woolwich's maps as having been bomb-damaged during the Second World War. The brickwork surrounding the front door is unique in the block. There is a blank

[639] PEL, 9 May 1947, minute no. 1.

[640] PEL, 13 February 1970, minute no. 1(b).

[641] PEL, 17 October 1949, minute no. 1.

[642] PEL, 17 November 1947, minute no. 1.

plaque with a brick surround above the door at first-floor level that one might assume was intended to carry the date of rebuilding, but does not. Finally, there are no first-floor windows on the right-hand side of the property, thereby giving the facia an asymmetry unusual for the Estate as a whole. Perhaps the house was seriously damaged for reasons unconnected with the war and subsequently rebuilt at a currently-unknown date.

Coal bunkers were offered to all PEL's tenants in May 1950. They would cost approximately £12/5/- each and the rent for tenants electing to have one installed would be increased to reflect this price.[643]

There were occasional structural problems to be resolved. On 25 September 1950 the Directors resolved, upon receipt of an architect's report, to deepen and widen the foundations of 6 Dickson Road below the front wall at an estimated cost of £250.[644]

By the mid-1950s the Estate's fencing, now some 40 years old, was in need of renewal. In April 1954, PEL's Architect & Works Manager recommended the wooden structures be replaced with brick walls and the Directors resolved that specimens be erected for their inspection before a final decision was made.[645] The following month, presumably after the Directors had inspected the specimen walls, they resolved to erect concrete walls in side roads, at a cost of £11,750, and brick walls in Well Hall Road, at a cost of £848/14/6d, subject to the Architect & Works Manager confirming whether the Royal Arsenal Co-operative Society's Works Department could carry out the work at this price.[646] (The Directors had decided in March 1954, following repeated losses, that PEL's contracting business should not take on any new work.)[647] However, nothing happened immediately and the original resolution to erect concrete walls in side roads was rescinded on 25 March 1955 in favour of a decision to build them with 4½-inch bricks instead at an increased cost of £12,250.[648]

[643] PEL, 24 May 1950, unnumbered minute.

[644] PEL, 25 September 1950, minute no. 1.

[645] PEL, 2 April 1954, minute no. 3

[646] PEL, 14 May 1954, minute no. 1.

[647] PEL, 3 March 1954, unnumbered minute.

[648] PEL, 25 March 1955, minute no. 1.

Fortunately that was not the end of the matter. The Estate Manager reported to the Directors just five days later that oak fencing and gates had become available. All the Estate's fencing could be replaced at a cost of £8,783/6/6d.[649] PEL's Directors' report for the year to 7 January 1956 stated that, although some of the Estate's fencing had been replaced by walls, 'in respect of the remainder we have decided to keep to the traditional oak fence'. The walls that were almost certainly built for the directors' inspection are those fronting 392-398 Well Hall Road, 471-475 and 496-500 Rochester Way (these being immediately to the east of the Well Hall Road/Rochester Way roundabout) and that fronting 182-186 Well Hall Road, the Estate's southernmost block of houses. The wall outside 1 Shrapnel Road appears to be of similar design and vintage; the common denominator is that all are castellated. Possibly others were built but have since been demolished. It may, therefore, be safely concluded that, with two possible exceptions, many of the Estate's brick walls date from 1955.

The first possible exception is the brick wall fronting 111-123 Well Hall Road. The LCC compulsorily acquired part of the front gardens of some of the houses in this part of the road when the Well Hall Road/Rochester Way roundabout was built.[650] Judging from the change in the angle of the road, 101-115 appear to have been the houses concerned.[651] The original fence would have been demolished not long after the LCC's acquisition, apparently in the second half of 1931,[652] so this length of brick wall could have been built at that time. It is not in the castellated style of others. Although these two sets of numbers have only three overlapping houses – nos. 111-115 – it could be that constructing a brick wall to no. 123, the house whose plot forms the corner with Dickson Road, was more aesthetically acceptable than retaining the wooden fence between nos. 117 and 123. Nos. 101-109, who lost nearly all their front gardens, have wooden fences constructed in the style of the Estate as a whole.

[649] PEL, 30 March 1955, minute no. 1.

[650] PEL, 27 August 1930, minute no. 1, and 5 May 1931, minute no. 4.

[651] Ordnance Survey, TQ4275, Includes: London (Charlton; Eltham), surveyed 1949, pub. 1951 and TQ4275NW, Includes: London (Charlton; Eltham), surveyed 1949, pub. circa 1950. Maps.nls.uk/view/103033791, accessed 27 January 2017.

[652] MBW 1931-1932, p. 44, Works Committee, minute no. 8, 19 October 1931.

The second exception is the wall fronting 34-40 Whinyates Road. Although of a not dissimilar style, it is lower and probably dates from the rebuilding of these houses after the Second World War.

Oak fencing appears to have a life of 40-50 years. That enclosing the communal gardens on the east side of Well Hall Road is believed to have been replaced by The Hyde Group in the late-1990s, and they renewed the west side fence in 2015. Considerable numbers of individual houses have been granted planning permission to renew their original fences with matching structures since the Estate became a conservation area in 1971. Individual brick walls may well have been constructed before Greenwich Council's Article 4 Direction required homeowners to, *inter alia*, apply for planning permission to renew their front fences.

PEL decided, probably in 1953, to build a pair of semi-detached houses on the land in Whinyates Road between nos. 40 and 42. This had been the site of garages that had been destroyed in the V1 attack on 10 July 1944. Their Directors report for the year ending on 2 January 1954 stated 'the work of building two houses on the site of 40A and 40B Whinyates Road is making good progress. A deposit had been received for 40A and 40B is still for sale'.

The largest single change made to the original design of the Estate's homes was the gradual creation of internal bathrooms and WCs for those that had been built with baths in their sculleries (plumbed with cold but not hot running water) and/or had WCs that, although within the building line, were accessed externally. This comprised virtually all the Class III houses and a very small number of the Class IIs together with all 212 flats which had baths in their sculleries (an estimated 28 also lacking internally-accessible WCs).[653] Thus two-thirds of the homes on the Estate needed modernising (see table on page 158). By January 1959 PEL had sold off 483 houses on long leases, a steady process that had continued throughout its ownership of the Estate save for the years of the Second World War.[654] Presumably at least some of these had been modernised by their leaseholders over the years. Tenanted homes had not been improved, so in February 1961 PEL wrote to their occupants advising them that consideration was being given to the possibility

---

[653] Numbers based on H.M. Office of Works site plans and detailed drawings, Greenwich Heritage Centre.

[654] PEL, based on extracts from their annual accounts.

of providing bathrooms, indoor toilets and hot water subject to an increase in rent based on a percentage of the cost involved. This would bring their facilities up to the standard to which Class I and virtually all Class II houses had been built in 1915. By 3 March, 151 had requested further details, 103 had said they were not interested, and some had not replied.[655]

Nowadays there are probably, very few homes that remain as originally constructed. Although this modernisation has not altered the appearance of the Estate's street scene, it has brought about a substantial reduction in the number of three-bedroomed houses. Each block of houses has a sewer running behind it which is joined to the main sewer by pipes running between the blocks at their downhill ends. New facilities therefore had to be provided at the backs of houses. As most people elected to install bathrooms upstairs (the remainder having had single-storey extensions built at the back) there has been a general loss of second bedrooms; the third (smallest) was built over the front living room. The modernisation of tenanted properties took a very long time. Hyde Housing Association, who bought out RACS's interest in the Estate, wrote to all their tenants in 1990. They said these facilities were absent in most of the properties when they acquired them in September 1980.[656]

---

[655] BV, February 1961 and PEL, 3 March 1961, minute no. 1(b).

[656] BV; undated circular from Hyde Housing Association apparently issued in early 1990.

1967-2015:
The Growth of Freehold Home Ownership

H.M. Office of Works had sold the freeholds of 64 houses prior to Progress Estates Ltd's purchase in 1925. Of these, 20 had been subsequently repurchased by the company,[657] and so by the mid-1960s it controlled 1,255 homes (including the building that had previously been the Estate Manager's office) in one of two ways. Around 500 had been sold on 99-year leases[658] and the remainder were tenanted.[659] Because the leases contained conditions governing lessees' actions, the aesthetic control of the Estate was in the hands of the company.

This status quo was changed by the Leasehold Reform Act, 1967. Coming into force on 1 January 1968,[660] it gave the tenant of a leasehold house who occupied it as his residence 'a right to acquire on fair terms the freehold ... of the house ... where (a) [he has] a long tenancy at a low rent and the rateable value of his house [in Greater London] is not more than £400 and (b) he has been a tenant occupying it as his residence for the last five years ...'.[661] It was popular legislation. By January 1974, 304 of the Estate's leaseholders – nearly a quarter of its householders – had purchased their freeholds.[662] The potential problem was that the Estate's architectural values were being compromised as individual owners began to change the appearance of their homes.

The Civic Amenities Act, 1967 arrived on the statute book whilst the Leasehold Reform legislation was going through Parliament and attempted to give local authorities the ability to counter this forthcoming risk. It received Royal Assent on 27 July and required 'every local authority' to determine from time to time 'which parts of their area are areas of special architectural or historic interest the character

---

[657] PEL, based on extracts from their annual accounts.

[658] Beaufoy (1950), p. 261.

[659] PEL's annual accounts for the year to 3 January 1959 state that 483 homes were leased. This is the last year whose records are held in the National Co-operative Archive; an average of seven had been leased each year since 1952.

[660] The Leasehold Reform Act, 1967 Commencement Order 1967.

[661] s.1, Leasehold Reform Act, 1967.

[662] PEL, based on extracts from their annual accounts.

or appearance of which it is desirable to preserve or enhance'.[663] The Progress Estate, the environs of Eltham Palace and the Charlton Village Area were to be the first conservation areas created at the behest of the London Borough of Greenwich (as it then was) once the Greenwich Conservation Area itself had been formed and became so designated on 4 March 1971.[664]

The Royal Arsenal Co-operative Society Ltd. (RACS) decided to run down its tenancy operation in 1972. At a meeting for the Estate's residents held in the Town Hall, Woolwich on 19 July Mr. S.H. Kennard, a RACS director, stated that its subsidiary Progress Estates Ltd. (PEL) would sell all tenants their homes for a 20% discount to their market value. Houses would be sold freehold and flats on 999-year leases at peppercorn rents. Interested tenants were asked to contact Martin Couchman Properties Limited, Blackfen, Messrs H.J. Furlong & Sons, Eltham High Street or Messrs Bernard H. Skinner & Co., Well Hall Road for a valuation without charge and assistance with their mortgage requirements. Mr. Kennard also announced that PEL would sell properties on the Estate as they became vacant.[665]

Although the Estate had been declared a Conservation Area, the problem the Council faced was that the status did not allow it to control alterations individual owners chose to make to the external appearance of their properties. As a general rule, people are permitted to carry out works to their houses that are classified as Permitted Developments under Orders issued by virtue of the Town and Country Planning Acts. The way in which Councils can restrict these is, after public consultation and the agreement of the Secretary of State for the Environment, to issue Orders requiring homeowners to obtain grants of planning permission before carrying out works specified in the Orders. These Orders are called Article 4 Directions. Accordingly, on 4 December 1973 the London Borough of Greenwich issued an Order under which owners were required to apply for planning permission for the erection or construction of garages, porches, building extensions

---

[663] s. 1(1), Civic Amenities Act, 1967.

[664] London Borough of Greenwich, Minutes of Proceedings, Planning and Development Committee, p. 194, 15 October 1970, minute 3(b) and pp. 435-436, 4 March 1971, minute 7.

[665] BV, 19 July 1972.

and additions, front and/or side entrance doors, gates, fences, walls or other means of enclosure or for the change of roofing materials if the works were to be visible from the public highway. The erection of satellite dishes constitutes works to walls or roofs as the case may be. Many of the changes to, in particular, doors and windows that would not receive planning permission today were made before the Direction came into force. Separately, a Notice was issued following confirmation by the Secretary of State on 8 February 1974 that houses on the Estate could not be demolished without planning permission.[666]

On 2 October 1974, PEL's assets were transferred to RACS in consideration for the latter issuing paid-up shares in the Society equal to the nominal value of each PEL preferred ordinary share.[667] 95 out of 97 of these were owned by RACS itself.[668] Despite the plurality implied by the company's name, there is no evidence from PEL's minute books that it owned any houses other than those on the Progress Estate. It ceased to operate as a company separate from RACS on 4 November 1974.[669]

RACS continued to remind its tenants that they could purchase their homes at a 20% discount to their market value. In April 1976 they also offered tenants, 'in certain special cases', 10% of the surveyor's valuation if they preferred to give RACS vacant possession instead. A further letter in July 1977 extended the 20% discount to close relatives who wished to purchase tenants' homes. By September 1978 the 10% offer to vacating tenants had been replaced by an undertaking to 'consider making an ex-gratia payment' which continued into 1980. In the meantime, come 1st March 1979, the 20% discount made been changed to 'an allowance of up to 25%'.[670]

On 25 September 1980 RACS wrote to its remaining tenants advising them that they now owned 'less than one half of the Estate'. Most of the greens had been acquired by the London Borough of Greenwich who had thus become responsible for their maintenance,

[666] BV, undated circular from Greenwich Council.

[667] PEL, 2 October 1974, minute no. 1.

[668] PEL share register counterfoils.

[669] Memorandum from A. J. Nobbs, Financial Controller, RACS to RACS Office Managers, 6 November 1974, National Co-operative Archive, Manchester.

[670] BV.

and the Progress Hall was being 'leased to the local authority for the benefit of residents on the Estate'. They had therefore decided to sell their remaining tenanted houses to the Hyde and South Bank Housing Association Limited[671] which resulted in almost 500 tenants having a new landlord.[672]

Only a few homes (together with the Progress Hall) have been added since the Estate was built in 1915. The Estate Manager's house and office at 1 Downman Road were eventually converted into four flats and, much later (in 2011),[673] planning permission was granted to build the semi-detached houses 3A and 3B Downman Road on land that was originally the site of the Estate's workshops. 40A and 40B Whinyates Road were built by Progress Estates Ltd. in 1954 (see the chapter *1948-1966: Modernisation and renewal*). 25 Cobbett Road was built in 2005[674] on what had been part of the land belonging to no. 23 and no. 26 was built on land attaching to no. 24. 53 Whinyates Road, the last house on the east side at the southern end of the road, is also not a 1915 house. There are two other houses which appear to be later additions. The first is 290 Well Hall Road, rebuilt after the original was destroyed in the 1916 Zeppelin raid (see the chapter *1915-1924: the Estate's early years*). The second, the brick-faced 37 Prince Rupert Road, looks as though it is a rebuild but it is not. It is in the same colour-wash as all the brick chimneys in H.M. Office of Works drawing no. 111 and thus is, in the words of one of the Estate's architects, George Edward Phillips, is an example of how the Estate should look 'as if it had grown and not merely been dropped there'.[675]

---

[671] BV, 25 September 1980.

[672] BV; undated circular from Hyde Housing Association apparently issued in early 1990.

[673] Royal Borough of Greenwich, planning application no. 10/3339/F.

[674] Royal Borough of Greenwich, planning application no. 04/3003/F.

[675] Beaufoy (1950), p. 260.

Afterword

The principal objective of this book has been to describe the Estate's place in the history of architecture and town planning. The industrial age required large numbers of people to live close to the factories in which they worked. Commerce was quick to exploit the production methods that became available. Agricultural life was not the bucolic dream painted on the tops of chocolate boxes. For many it involved poor, damp housing, and economic insecurity. The lure of the new industrialised towns was magnetic, yet the rate at which they grew created the great social problems that have been described. To paraphrase Newton's third law, every action causes a reaction. For housing, there was a threefold reaction. First were the themes pursued by John Ruskin which led to what became known as the Arts and Crafts movement. Second was the determination of people such the Quaker Cadburys and Rowntrees who believed they had a moral duty to show that it was economically possible to provide decent housing for the working classes. Their influence led thirdly to the creation of communities, rather than merely areas of housing, as epitomised in the schemes designed by Barry Parker and Raymond Unwin. The more politically-inclined Unwin went on to create Town Planning. These three themes were at work over about three-quarters of a century, during which time the parallel activities of political agitators and their parliamentary supporters were, at the rate practical politics would permit, placing legislation on the statute book that caused their endeavours to endure.

The impact of leading thinkers and practitioners on those who followed them has been evident. Anyone who achieved anything was influenced, through social intercourse if not actual pupillage, by a predecessor. Such is the course of human history. It is wrong to say there is no such thing as original thought, but it is rare. Change is generally developmental.

The Estate is not unique because there are others that display similar characteristics. However, it seems to represent a particular pinnacle of architectural achievement. Parker and Unwin (either in partnership or individually) contributed to the design of at least ten of the eighteen garden suburbs constructed between 1906 and 1915 and their former pupils were often these developments' architects. *Nothing Gained by Overcrowding!*, Unwin's 1912 pamphlet that attempted to give his style of site-layout economic parity with by-law housing schemes, hugely influenced the design of housing estates. Once the decision had been taken to build the Estate as a Government Housing Scheme, Herbert Samuel, President of the Local Government Board, possibly encouraged by Unwin who was by then Town Planning Inspector at the Board, was determined it should be a showcase estate. He countered the Treasury's complaints about cost overruns because the housing of employees at the Royal Arsenal was a matter of national urgency.

So why did Baines and his team decide to plan an estate whose houses, with their changing rooflines and projecting gables, would be so much more difficult to build than a set of more uniform designs? A more standardised approach would almost certainly have had the backing of the housing fraternity who were moving towards simplified designs. Unwin himself had long argued for the avoidance of 'useless features' and the next munitions housing estate, built at Gretna by the Department of Explosives Supply under Unwin's direction commencing June 1915 whilst on secondment from the Local Government Board, was a far plainer affair.[676] The answer may be to do with Baines's background. His career had not brought him into close proximity with those concerned about the design of houses. His architectural mentor, Charles Ashbee, was deeply involved with and influenced by the Arts and Crafts movement *per se*. The illustration on page 123 hints at his approach to housing design. Here is a row of four houses, constructed as one scheme, that look as though they were built as three separate projects. The team of architects Baines assembled within H.M. Office of Works to design the Estate had all had housing experience before they joined the Office so would have learned of Unwin's thinking during their training.

Perhaps, therefore, a convergence of these four elements – a lack of budgetary pressure; political direction to build a showcase estate; Ashbee's influence on Baines; and Unwin's influence on the training of architectural students around the end of the 19th and the beginning of the 20th centuries – caused the Estate to be built in the way it was.

---

[676] Pepper and Swenarton, p. 370.

APPENDICES

Appendix A:
Conversion of Pre-Decimal to Decimal Currency

Prior to 15 February 1971, £1 was divided into 20 shillings and a shilling into 12 pennies. Pennies were denoted by the letter 'd', Roman for denarius. Until 1969, a penny was divided into two halfpennies (pronounced 'hape-knees'). Before 1960, a halfpenny could be divided into 2 farthings. The pre-1960 divisions of a penny were thus 1 farthing (written as ¼d), a halfpenny (½d) and 3 farthings (¾d).

There were various ways of annotating pre-decimal currency. This book adopts the style of £x/y/zd for pounds, shillings and pence. If the shillings or pence are nil, the amount is written as £x/-/zd or £x/y/- respectively. Whole pounds are written as £x, whole shillings y/-, shillings and pence y/zd, and pence zd.

The following table shows the decimal equivalents of pre-decimal amounts up to £1. For example, 4/5d is (to the nearest single decimal place) equal to 22.1p.

Pence Shillings	0d	1d	2d	3d	4d	5d	6d	7d	8d	9d	10d	11d
0/-	0.0	0.4	0.8	1.3	1.7	2.1	2.5	2.9	3.3	3.8	4.2	4.6
1/-	5.0	5.4	5.8	6.3	6.7	7.1	7.5	7.9	8.3	8.8	9.2	9.6
2/-	10.0	10.4	10.8	11.3	11.7	12.1	12.5	12.9	13.3	13.8	14.2	14.6
3/-	15.0	15.4	15.8	16.3	16.7	17.1	17.5	17.9	18.3	18.8	19.2	19.6
4/-	20.0	20.4	20.8	21.3	21.7	22.1	22.5	22.9	23.3	23.8	24.2	24.6
5/-	25.0	25.4	25.8	26.3	26.7	27.1	27.5	27.9	28.3	28.8	29.2	29.6
6/-	30.0	30.4	30.8	31.3	31.7	32.1	32.5	32.9	33.3	33.8	34.2	34.6
7/-	35.0	35.4	35.8	36.3	36.7	37.1	37.5	37.9	38.3	38.8	39.2	39.6
8/-	40.0	40.4	40.8	41.3	41.7	42.1	42.5	42.9	43.3	43.8	44.2	44.6
9/-	45.0	45.4	45.8	46.3	46.7	47.1	47.5	47.9	48.3	48.8	49.2	49.6
10/-	50.0	50.4	50.8	51.3	51.7	52.1	52.5	52.9	53.3	53.8	54.2	54.6
11/-	55.0	55.4	55.8	56.3	56.7	57.1	57.5	57.9	58.3	58.8	59.2	59.6
12/-	60.0	60.4	60.8	61.3	61.7	62.1	62.5	62.9	63.3	63.8	64.2	64.6
13/-	65.0	65.4	65.8	66.3	66.7	67.1	67.5	67.9	68.3	68.8	69.2	69.6
14/-	70.0	70.4	70.8	71.3	71.7	72.1	72.5	72.9	73.3	73.8	74.2	74.6
15/-	75.0	75.4	75.8	76.3	76.7	77.1	77.5	77.9	78.3	78.8	79.2	79.6
16/-	80.0	80.4	80.8	81.3	81.7	82.1	82.5	82.9	83.3	83.8	84.2	84.6
17/-	85.0	85.4	85.8	86.3	86.7	87.1	87.5	87.9	88.3	88.8	89.2	89.6
18/-	90.0	90.4	90.8	91.3	91.7	92.1	92.5	92.9	93.3	93.8	94.2	94.6
19/-	95.0	95.4	95.8	96.3	96.7	97.1	97.5	97.9	98.3	98.8	99.2	99.6

Appendix B:
Metric Equivalents of Imperial Weights and Measures

Distance

The smallest unit of imperial measurement is the inch (in). There are 12 inches to the foot (ft) and 3 ft to the yard (yd). Metric equivalents of these distances are:

1in	2.54cm
1ft	30.48cm
1yd	91.44cm

A mile (ml) is 1,760 yards which is the same distance as 1,609 metres.

Area

The basic area of imperial measurement is the acre, being 4,840 square yards. Although no longer in common usage, one-quarter of an acre is a rood and a rood is subdivided into 40 perches. There are 640 acres to the square mile. The metric equivalents of imperial areas – 1 hectare (ha) being 10,000 square metres (m^2) – are:

1 sq ft	$0.093m^2$	1 rood	$1,012.50m^2$
1 sq yd	$0.836m^2$	1 acre	0.405ha
1 perch	$25.30m^2$	1 sq ml	259.2 ha

Weight

An imperial ton is divided into 20 hundredweights (cwt). A cwt comprises 4 quarters (qt), and a quarter 2 stones (st). A stone is made up of 14 pounds (lb), each of which is divided into 16 ounces (oz). The metric equivalents of these (1 kilogram being 1000 grammes) are:

1 oz	28.35g	1 qt	12.79kg
1 lb	453.59g	1 cwt	50.80kg
1 st	6.35kg	1 ton	1,016.054kg

APPENDICES

Appendix C:
Inflation 1850-2017[677]

This table shows the estimated year-to-year change in consumer prices for 1850-1948 and the change in the Retail Price Index (all items) for 1949 onwards. The number is negative for the years when there was deflation. To obtain an estimate of the 2017 equivalent of money in an earlier year, multiply the original value by the number in the Multiplier column. Remember that not everything has risen by these averages. For example, average wages have increased by more.

Year	Inflation	Multiplier	Year	Inflation	Multiplier	Year	Inflation	Multiplier	Year	Inflation	Multiplier
1850	-6.40%	116	1892	0.40%	117	1934	0.00%	65.7	1976	16.50%	7.71
1851	-3.00%	124	1893	-0.70%	117	1935	0.70%	65.7	1977	15.80%	6.62
1852	0.00%	128	1894	-2.00%	118	1936	0.70%	65.3	1978	8.30%	5.72
1853	9.30%	128	1895	-1.00%	120	1937	3.40%	64.8	1979	13.40%	5.28
1854	15.10%	117	1896	-0.30%	121	1938	1.60%	62.7	1980	18.00%	4.66
1855	3.30%	102	1897	1.50%	122	1939	2.80%	61.7	1981	11.90%	3.95
1856	0.00%	98.5	1898	0.30%	120	1940	16.80%	60.0	1982	8.60%	3.53
1857	-5.60%	98.5	1899	0.70%	120	1941	10.80%	51.4	1983	4.60%	3.25
1858	-8.40%	104	1900	5.10%	119	1942	7.10%	46.4	1984	5.00%	3.10
1859	-1.80%	114	1901	0.50%	113	1943	3.40%	43.3	1985	6.10%	2.96
1860	3.70%	116	1902	0.00%	112	1944	2.70%	41.9	1986	3.40%	2.79
1861	2.70%	112	1903	0.40%	112	1945	2.80%	40.8	1987	4.20%	2.69
1862	-2.60%	109	1904	-0.20%	112	1946	3.10%	39.7	1988	4.90%	2.59
1863	-3.60%	112	1905	0.40%	112	1947	7.00%	38.5	1989	7.80%	2.46
1864	-0.90%	116	1906	0.00%	112	1948	7.70%	36.0	1990	9.50%	2.29
1865	0.90%	117	1907	1.20%	112	1949	2.80%	33.4	1991	5.90%	2.09
1866	6.50%	116	1908	0.50%	110	1950	3.10%	32.5	1992	3.70%	1.97
1867	6.10%	109	1909	0.50%	110	1951	9.10%	31.5	1993	1.60%	1.90
1868	-1.70%	103	1910	0.90%	109	1952	9.20%	28.9	1994	2.40%	1.87
1869	-5.00%	104	1911	0.10%	108	1953	3.10%	26.4	1995	3.50%	1.83
1870	0.00%	110	1912	3.00%	108	1954	1.80%	25.6	1996	2.40%	1.77
1871	1.40%	110	1913	-0.40%	105	1955	4.50%	25.2	1997	3.10%	1.72
1872	4.70%	108	1914	-0.30%	105	1956	4.90%	24.1	1998	3.40%	1.67
1873	3.10%	104	1915	12.50%	106	1957	3.70%	23.0	1999	1.50%	1.62
1874	-3.30%	100	1916	18.10%	94.0	1958	3.00%	22.2	2000	3.00%	1.59
1875	-1.90%	104	1917	25.20%	79.6	1959	0.60%	21.5	2001	1.80%	1.55
1876	-0.30%	106	1918	22.00%	63.6	1960	1.00%	21.4	2002	1.70%	1.52
1877	-0.70%	106	1919	10.10%	52.1	1961	3.40%	21.2	2003	2.90%	1.49
1878	-2.20%	107	1920	15.40%	47.4	1962	4.30%	20.5	2004	3.00%	1.45
1879	-4.40%	109	1921	-8.60%	41.0	1963	2.00%	19.6	2005	2.80%	1.41
1880	3.00%	114	1922	-14.00%	44.9	1964	3.30%	19.2	2006	3.20%	1.37
1881	-1.10%	111	1923	-6.00%	52.2	1965	4.80%	18.6	2007	4.30%	1.33
1882	1.00%	112	1924	-0.70%	55.5	1966	3.90%	17.8	2008	4.00%	1.27
1883	-0.50%	111	1925	0.30%	55.9	1967	2.50%	17.1	2009	-0.50%	1.23
1884	-2.70%	112	1926	-0.80%	55.8	1968	4.70%	16.7	2010	4.60%	1.23
1885	-3.00%	115	1927	-2.40%	56.2	1969	5.40%	15.9	2011	5.20%	1.18
1886	-1.60%	118	1928	-0.30%	57.6	1970	6.40%	15.1	2012	3.20%	1.12
1887	-0.50%	120	1929	-0.90%	57.8	1971	9.40%	14.2	2013	3.00%	1.08
1888	0.70%	121	1930	-2.80%	58.3	1972	7.10%	13.0	2014	2.40%	1.05
1889	1.40%	120	1931	-4.30%	60.0	1973	9.20%	12.1	2015	1.00%	1.03
1890	0.20%	118	1932	-2.60%	62.7	1974	16.00%	11.1	2016	1.80%	1.02
1891	0.70%	118	1933	-2.10%	64.3	1975	24.20%	9.58	2017		1.00

[677] http://inflation.stephenmorley.org, accessed 7 February 2017.

Bibliography

Archive material

BV   Bill Venn's papers (see Acknowledgements)
BVT   Bournville Village Trust Archive, Library of Birmingham
JRVT   Joseph Rowntree Village Trust Archive, Borthwick Institute for Archives, University of York
MBW   Metropolitan Borough of Woolwich, Minutes of Proceedings, Greenwich Heritage Centre
PEL   Progress Estates Ltd., Minutes of meetings of the Directors, 29 May 1925 to 12 April 1957 and 2 September 1957 to 2 October 1974, National Co-operative Archive, Manchester

Books and articles

The web addresses for books accessed online is in parentheses after the publication's details.

Ashbee, Charles Robert, *An Endeavour Towards the Teaching of John Ruskin and William Morris*, Edward Arnold, London, 1901, Nabu Public Domain reprint, USA, 2015

Ashbee, Felicity, *Janet Ashbee*, Syracuse University Press, New York, 2002

Baines, Frank, 'A government housing scheme', *Municipal Journal*, vol. xxvi (28 September 1917)

Baines, Frank, 'Planning, Design, and Construction of Small Houses', *The Architects' and Builders' Journal*, 1 May 1918

Baines, Frank, *History of John Mowlem & Co*, undated typescript bound in two volumes, principally based on the diaries of John Mowlem (1788-1868) and concluding in the mid-1880s. London Metropolitan Archive, file no. ACC/2809/58

Barnett, Dame Henrietta, DBE, *The Story of the Growth of Hampstead Garden Suburb 1907-1928*, Hampstead Garden Suburb Archive Trust reprint, 2006

Beaufoy, S. L. G., 'Well Hall Estate, Eltham', *Town Planning Review*, October 1950

Beaufoy, S. L. G., 'Well Hall Estate', *Town Planning Review*, July 1952

BIBLIOGRAPHY

Benson, John, *The Working Class in Britain 1850-1939*, I.B. Tauris, London, 2003

Blake, L., *Red Alert, the Story of South East London at War, 1939-1945*, 1992

Burnett, John, *A Social History of Housing*, 1815-1985, Routledge, London and New York, 1986

Cadbury, Deborah, *Chocolate Wars*, Harper Press, London, 2010

Cobb, Henry S. and Saunders, Ann, eds: *Handlist of the Hampstead Garden Suburb Archive*, Hampstead Garden Suburb Archive Trust and London Metropolitan Archives, 2001

Cooper, Peter, *Building Relationships: The History of Bovis 1885-2000*, Cassell, 2000

Crawford, Alan, *C. R. Ashbee: Architect, Designer and Romantic Socialist*, Yale University Press, New Haven and London, 2005

Fraser, Derek, *The Evolution of the British Welfare State*, Macmillan Press, London, 1984

Gardiner, Juliet, *The Blitz: The British Under Attack*, Harper Press, London, 2011

Gauldie, Enid, *Cruel Habitations, A History of Working-Class Housing 1780-1918*, George Allen & Unwin, London, 1974

Gibbs, John, Brasier, Clive and Webber, Joan, 'An attempt to stop the spread of Dutch Elm Disease', *Dutch Elm Disease in Britain*, The Forestry Commission Research Information Note 252, September 1994

Gilbert, Bentley B., *The Evolution of National Insurance in Great Britain*, Michael Joseph, London, 1966

Government Housing Scheme at Well Hall, Eltham, Kent, *The Architects' and Builders' Journal*, Wednesday 27th December, 1916, vol. XLIV no. 1147 (Supplement)

Halsey, A.H., ed., *British Social Trends Since 1900*, Macmillan, London, 1988

Harrison, Michael, *Bournville: Model Village to Garden Suburb*, Phillimore, Chichester, 1999

Harvey, W. Alexander, *The Model Village and its Cottages: Bournville*, B. T. Batsford, London, 1906, undated reprint by HardPress Publishing, Miami

Hillier, Richard, *Clay That Burns*, London Brick Company Limited, 1982

Hills, Alan B., *The Progress Estate*, unpublished thesis prepared for the University of London diploma in history, scheme C: Local History, 1976, the Greenwich Heritage Centre, ref: G711

Hogg, Brig. O.F.G., *The Royal Arsenal, its Background, Origin and Subsequent History vol. II*, Oxford University Press, London, 1963

Hopkins, Eric, *A Social History of the English Working Classes 1815-1945*, Edward Arnold, 1979

Howard, Ebenezer, *Garden Cities of To-morrow*, S. Sonnenschein & Co., Ltd., London, 1902, undated reprint by Dodo Press

Jackson, Frank, *Sir Raymond Unwin: Architect, Planner and Visionary*, A. Zwemmer Ltd., London, 1985

Jones, D.T., *The Well Hall Estate, Eltham, London SE9: How successful were the solutions to the functional, social, and aesthetic problems faced by the designers of the Well Hall Estate?*, unpublished project for the Open University's course 'Architecture & Design 1809/1939', the Greenwich Heritage Centre, ref A305/Project

Kennett, John, *Eltham Hutments*, Eltham Books, London, 1985

Kennett, John, *Trams in Eltham*, The Eltham Society, 2007

Kennett, John, 'Progress Estate', *Ideal Homes: A History of South-East London Suburbs*, www.ideal-homes.org.uk/case-studies/progress-estate, accessed 22nd September 2016

Lee, Christopher, *This Sceptred Isle, Twentieth Century*, BBC Worldwide, London and Penguin Books, London, 1999

Lees, Lynn Hollen and Lees, Andrew, eds., *The Rise of Urban Britain*, Garland Publishing, 1985

Macfadyen, Dugald, *Ebenezer Howard and the Town Planning movement*, Manchester University Press, 1933 (cashewnut.me.uk/WGCbooks/web-WGC-books-1933-1.php#IV)

Miele, Chris, *William Morris on Architecture*, Sheffield Academic Press, 1996

Miller, Mervyn, *Letchworth, the First Garden City*, Phillimore, Chichester, 2002

Miller, Mervyn, *English Garden Cities: an introduction*, English Heritage, Swindon, 2010

Morris, William, Ed: David Leopold, *News From Nowhere*, Oxford University Press, 2003

Parker, Barry and Unwin, Raymond, *The Art of Building a Home*, Longmans, Green & Co, London, New York & Bombay, 1901

(archive.org/details/artofbuildinghom00park)

Pepper, Simon and Swenarton, Mark, 'Home Front: Garden Suburbs for Munition Workers', *The Architectural Review*, 1978, vol. CLXIII, no. 976

Port, M. H., *Imperial London: Civil Government Building in London 1850-1915*, Yale University Press, New Haven & London, 1995

Powell, C. G., *The British Building Industry Since 1800*, E. & F. N. Spon, 1996

Rackham, Oliver, *The History of the Countryside*, J. M. Dent & Sons Ltd., 1986

Rackham, Oliver, *Trees and Woodlands in the British Landscape*, 2nd edition, J. M. Dent & Sons Ltd., 1990

Ramsey, Dave, *Greenwich Industrial History* (greenwichindustrialhistory.blogspot.co.uk/2011/02/woolwichs-19th-century-chp-council.html)

Richardson, Margaret, *Architects of the Arts and Crafts Movement*, Trefoil Books 1983

Robeck, Cecil M., Jnr., *Azusa Street Mission and Revival: the Birth of the Global Pentecostal Movement*, Thomas Nelson Inc., Nashville, Tennessee

Rowntree, B. Seebohm, *Poverty and Progress: a second social survey of York*, Longmans, Green and Co., London, 1941

Saunders, Ann [ed.], *The London County Council Bomb Damage Maps*, 1939-1945, London Topographical Society, publication no. 164

Swenarton, Mark, *Homes fit for Heroes*, Heinemann Educational Books, London, 1981

Swenarton, Mark, *Artisans and Architects: The Ruskinian Tradition in Architectural Thought*, Macmillan Press, 1989

Tarn, John Nelson, *Five Per Cent Philanthropy*, Cambridge University Press, London, 1973

Thirsk, Joan, ed. *The Agrarian History of England and Wales*, Vol. VII (Part II), 1850-1914, Cambridge University Press, 2000

Thompson, W., *Handbook to the Housing and Town Planning Act 1909*, National Reform Council, London, 1910, p. 7 (archive.org/stream/handbooktohousin00thom#page/6/mode/2up)

Thurley, Simon, *Men From the Ministry*, English Heritage, Yale University Press, New Haven and London, 2013

Unwin, Raymond, 'The Planning of the Residential Districts of Towns',

Transactions of the VIIth International Congress of Architects, London, 1906, the Royal Institute of British Architects, 1908

Unwin, Raymond, *Town Planning in Practice*, T. Fisher Unwin, London, 1909

Unwin, Raymond, *Nothing Gained by Overcrowding!*, P. S. King & Son, London, for the Garden Cities & Town Planning Association, 1912 re-published by the Town and Country Planning Association, 2012

Usher, John M., 'Cecil Henry Polhill: The Patron of the Pentecostals' *Pneuma*, vol. 34, issue 1, 2012

Waddilove, L. E., *One Man's Vision; the Story of the Joseph Rowntree Village Trust*, George Allen & Unwin Limited, London, 1954. L. E. Waddilove's authorship of the book is acknowledged on p. xiii and also confirmed in a letter written by Richard Fraser of Louis de Soissons, Peacock, Hodges, Robertson and Fraser (architects) on 11th August 1969 (Joseph Rowntree Village Trust Archive, Borthwick Institute for Archives, University of York, ref: NE 21/14(e)

Waller, Maureen, *London 1945*, John Murray, London, 2004

Ward, Laurence, *The London County Council Bomb Damage Maps, 1939-1945*, Thames & Hudson, London, 2015

White, Gus, *The Bexleyheath Railway at Eltham 1895-1995*, The Eltham Society, 1996

White, Ken, *The Quaggy River and its Catchment Area*, private publication, 1999, copy held in the Lewisham Local History & Archive Centre, Lewisham Library

Wingham, Gaynor, *A Hundred Years of a London Street*, private publication, 2002

Index

Page numbers relating to tables and illustrations or footnotes are, respectively, in **bold** type and *italics* if there is no other reference to their subjects on the same page. If a theme runs from one page to another, the page numbers are hyphenated.

Acts of Parliament: Air Raid Precautions Act, 1937, 220; Ancient Monuments Consolidation and Amendment Act, 1913, 126; Ancient Monuments Protection Act, 1882, 126; Artisans' and Labourers' Dwellings Improvement Act, 1875, 35, 45; Artisans' Dwellings Act, 1875, 98; Cheap Trains Act, 1883, 36; Civic Amenities Act, 1967, 241; Defence of the Realm Act, 1914, 15; Hampstead Garden Suburb Act, 1906, 103-104, 107, 110; Housing Act, 1890, 40; Housing Act, 1914, 140, 170, 173; Housing of the Working Classes Act, 1890, 80, 107, 111, 116; Housing of the Working Classes Acts, 1890-1909, 108-109; Housing, Town Planning, &C. Act, 1909, 103, 107, 109, 115-116, 118, 119, 130; Leasehold Reform Act, 1967, 241; Leeds Improvement Act, 1842, 35; Local Government Act, 1858, 38; Local Government Board Act, 1871, 38; Lodging Houses Act, 1851, 34, 44; London Building Act, 1774, 34; London Building Acts, 149, 150; Metropolis Management and Building Acts Amendment Act, 1878, 39; Metropolitan Buildings Act, 1844, 29, 37; Military Service Act, 1916, 207; Public Health Act, 1848, 34; Public Health Act, 1875, 38; Public Health Acts Amendment Act, 1890, 40; Redistribution of Seats Act, 1885, 48, 107; Reform Act, 1867, 107; Representation of the People Act, 1884, 48; Representation of the People Act, 1918, *108*; Sanitary Law Amendment Act, 1874, 38; War Damage Act, 1941, 228

Adams, Thomas, Secretary, Garden City Association, 90; Manager, Letchworth Garden City, 114; Town Planning Assistant, Local Government Board, 119

Admiralty, 16

Adult School Movement, Birmingham, 62

Air raids: bomb damage maps, 218, 220, 223, 224, 225, 227; flying bomb incidents, 218, 220, 225; Incident Logs, 218, 220-221, 223, 224, 225; V1 flying bombs, 221-222, 230, 239. See also WWII bomb damage

Albemarle, Duke of, 193

Albert, Price Consort, 44

Allen, Annie, 209

Allen, Frederick, 209

Allen, Gladys, 209

Ancient Monuments Board, 126

Architectural Association, 59

Armitage and Rigby cotton mills, 73

Armitage, G. Faulkner, architect, 73, 93

Arsenal Football Club, 178-179

Arts and Crafts Movement, 53, 57, 62, 89, 90, 245-246

Ashbee, Charles Robert, 77, 99, 122-123, 127, 246

Ashley, Lord, 33, 34, 44

Asquith, Herbert, Prime Minister, 1908-1915, 16

Aylward, Mr. and Mrs. Sidney, first Estate residents, 157, 205

Baines, Frank, Principal Architect, H.M. Office of Works, *19*, 24, 77, 99, 122, 123, 124, 126-129, 147, 148, 150, 151, 156, 157, 158-159, 161, 170, 174, 246; belief in better working-class housing, 160; knighthoods,125,129; pressure within Whitehall, 172-173; wartime responsibilities, 128-129; work ethic, 128
Baker, Matthew, Master Shipbuilder,191
Barnett, Canon Samuel, 46, 74, 97-101, 106, 111, 122
Barnett, Henrietta, 46, 96-102, 106, 111, 122
Barron, Emily Frances, 133, 135
Barron, Sir Henry Winston, 1st Bt., 133, 135
Battelsden Park estate, Bedfordshire, 134-5
Bennett, Robert, Parker & Unwin assistant architect, 88
Bexley, Borough of, 194, 197-198
Bexleyheath railway line, 138
Bidlake and Lovatt, 56
Bidlake, William Henry, architect, **54**, 59-60, 62, 122
Billing, John, architect, 56
Birmingham Architectural Association, 59
Birmingham Guild of Handicraft, 59
Birmingham School of Art, **54**, 59,62
Birmingham University, town planning faculty, 114
Birmingham West Suburban Railway, 61
Bodley and Garner, architects, 122
Bodley, George Frederick, architect, **54**, 55-56, 59, 122
Boer War, 111; Mafeking, relief of, 49
Bohemia, King of, 192
Booth, Charles, 46-47, 79, 98, 111; maps, **47**

Boughton, Sir Edward, 179
Bournville, 61-63, **67**, 113; Bourn, River, 61; Bournbrook, 61-62; building materials, cost of, 63; Laburnum Road, 62; Village Trust, 64, 65, 71, 80
Bowden, James Albert, architect, H.M. Office of Works, 148, 160, 164
Bowerman, Charles, Independent Labour M.P., 108
Bowes, Martin, 179, 188
Bowman, W.T., H.M. Office of Works, 169, 172
Bramah, Joseph, lockmaker, 189
Brassey, Lord (Thomas), 100
Brentham Garden Suburb, *109*
British Museum, 200
Brome, General Joseph, 179
Brook Hospital, 223
Brown, James, solicitor's clerk, Letchworth, 87
Brunel, Isambard Kingdom, 189
Bunney, Michael Frank Wharton, architect, 106
Burns, John, Liberal M.P.,108, President of the Local Government Board, 108-109, 115, President of the Board of Trade,118

Cadbury, George, 61-66, 79, 82, 87, 114, 245
Cadbury, Richard, 61, 245
Caernarfon Castle, Investiture of the Prince of Wales, 1911, 125
Cambridge Seven, 136
Cambridge, King's College, 122; University, 136
Carpenter Edward, 75-76, 122
Castlewood Estate, 212, 226
Cellars, as homes, 26-27
Cenotaph, Whitehall, 102, 147
Chadwick, Edwin, Secretary to the Board of the Poor Law Commissioners, 28

256

INDEX

Chapman, Richard, Master Shipwright, 191
Charity Organisation Society, 46, 74, 98
Charles, King, I, 193
Charles, King, II, 193
Charlton & Kidbrooke, parish boundary, 142
Cheltenham & Gloucester Building Society, 203
Clemenceau, Georges, Prime Minister of France, 98
Cobbett, William, 180
Commonwealth War Graves Commission, 102, 147
Condition of the people, 48, 49, 111
Congregational Church, 68, 73
Congreve rocket, 181
Congreve, Lt. Gen. Sir William, 181
Congreve, Sir (hon: Colonel) William, 2nd Bt., 181
Corbett, Cameron, housebuilder, 149
Cornwallis, Charles, 5th Baron, 181
Cornwallis, Charles, Viscount Brome and Earl, 181-182
Cornwallis, Elizabeth, 181
Cornwallis, Frederick, Archbishop of Canterbury, 183
Cornwallis, James, Dean of Canterbury, 183
Cornwallis, William, 182
Covent Garden Theatre, 133
Crickmer, Courtenay Melville, architect, 106
Crook, Harry Steward, construction worker killed on the Progress Estate, 174
Crooks, Will, Labour M.P., 22, 147
Cross, Sir Richard, Home Secretary, 98

Darwin, Charles, 26, 74
Davies, Dr. Sidney, Medical Office of Health, Woolwich, 21

Delhi, Secretariat Buildings, 102
Dickens, Charles, 51
Dickson, Gen. Sir Collingwood, 184
Dickson, Maj. Gen. Sir Alexander, GCB, 183
Disraeli, Benjamin, Conservative Prime Minister, 68
Ditges, Henrietta Monica Margaretta, 96
Downman, Gen. Sir Thomas, 184
Downman, Lt. Gen. Sir C. Downman, 184
Drake, Sir Francis, 191
Dulwich Picture Gallery, 97
Dutch elm disease, 145

Earle, Sir Lionel, Permanent Secretary, H.M. Office of Works, 126, 128
Earswick, 79. See also New Earswick
East End Dwellings Company, 98
East India Company, 134
Eaton Cricket Club, 136
Edis, R.W., architect, 59
Edward, Prince of Wales and King, VI, 177
Elizabeth, Princess, mother of Prince Rupert, 192
Elizabeth, Princess and Queen, I, 178
Eltham High Street, 202
Eltham railway station, 137
Eltham, parish boundary, 142

Fabian Society, 46, *48*
Fire Brigade, London, 218
First Garden City Co. Ltd., 88
Five per cent philanthropy, 45
Form of By-laws, control of buildings and inhabitation, 38-39
Foster, Sir Walter, Liberal M.P., 108
Franklin, Sir John, 185
Fry's, 79

Garden Cities and Town Planning Association, 118

257

Garden Cities Association, 69, 82, 87, 88, 119
Garden City Conference, 1901, 82, 87
Garden City Movement, 68, 103
Garden City Pioneer Company, the, 87
Garden City, plan for, 69-71
Garden suburbs, 95, 120, 245; early influences, 60
Garner, Thomas, architect, 59
Garrison Church, Woolwich, 199
Gladstone, William Ewart, Liberal Prime Minister, 68
Gothic, architecture and revival, 51-53, 55, 56, 57
Government Housing Scheme at Well Hall, 7, 137, 139, 149, 246
Graham, Elizabeth Margaret, 199
Granby, Marquess of – see Manners, John, Marquess of Granby
Greenwich Council/Metropolitan Borough/Royal Borough of, 8, 142, 194, 198, 242, 243
Guild and School of Handicraft, 99, 123
Gurney & Sons, 68

H.M. Office of Works, 124, 126, 140, 246; agreement to road widths without prejudice, 150; attempts to economise, 152, 172; destruction of records during Second World War, 148; detailed drawings, 7, 12, 148, 151, 169, 244; hutments, ownership of, 195-196; Monuments, projects, 127; public exhibition for Progress Estate housing, 156; published plans, **152-153**; site layout plans, 7, 12, 142-143, 145, 146, 148, 151, 152, 155, 156; staffing, 127
H.M. Treasury, 172, 246
Haddon sisters, 96
Hampstead Garden Suburb, 46, 74, 86, 100, 109, 113, 150; land for, 100;

Hampstead Garden Suburb Trust, 101
Hansard, 68
Hardie, Keir, Independent Labour M.P., 68, 77
Harvey, W. Alexander, architect, **54**, 62-63, 65, 68, 122
Hawkins, Sir John, 191
Health of Towns, Committee on the, 29
Henderson, John, Master Founder, Royal Arsenal, 201
Henry, King, VIII, 177, 179
High Victorian architecture, 55
Hill, James, aural surgeon and philosopher, 96
Hill, Octavia, 96-98, 100, 111
Hinton, James, 96
Homes fit for Heroes, 39, 130
Housing, back-to-back, 28-29, 31, 35, 87, 109; drainage of, 30; by-law, 40-42, 87, 116; garden suburbs, 106; growth of suburbs, 87; jerry-building, 37-38, 39; of munitions workers, 106; opposition to municipal provision, 97, 100; sanitary conditions, 29, 34, 39, 40; weekly rents for, 23, 35; rural shortage, 107
Howard, Ebenezer, 68, 75, 82, 87, 101, 139
Howbury Hall, Renhold, 133, 135-136
Howell, Frances, 133, 134
Hutments, 195
Hyde Group, 8, 239, 240, 244

Independent Labour Party, see Labour Party

James, John, surveyor and carpenter, 134
James, King I, 192
Jardim America Garden Suburb, São Paulo, Brazil, 94
Joseph Rowntree Trusts, 80

INDEX

Labour Church, 77
Labour Party, *48*, 51, 68, 77, 108, 111, 236
Land prices, 87
Latimer, Lord, 177
Leslie, N., Ltd., 162, 172
Lesnes Abbey, confiscation of estates of, 179
Letchworth Garden City, 86-87, **103**, 106, 116, 130; Bird's Hill, 92-93; building regulations for, 90; Cheap Cottages Exhibition, 90-92
Lethaby and Ricardo, architects, 90
Lever, William, 64
Lloyd George, David, Liberal M.P., Minister of Munitions, 16; Prime Minister, 39
Local Government Board, 38, 40, 80, 107, 108, 109, 110, 119, 126, 140, 246
London County Council, Building Acts Committee, 150; estate management, 205-207, 210; naming of roads, 152, 156, 176, 196-198; Superintending Architect, 149, 150; Architect's Department, 218, 219, 220-221, 222
Long, Walter, M.P., 109
Lovelace family, 187
Lower Kidbrook River, 143
Lucas, (Thomas) Geoffry, architect, 106
Lutyens, Edwin, 73, 101-102, 148
Lyttelton, Alfred, Liberal politician and sportsman, 101-102

Macassar Oil Company, 96
Mackarness, Dr. Frederick, Liberal M.P., 108
Mackinnon, William Alexander, Conservative M.P., 29
Macnamara, Dr. Thomas, Liberal M.P., 108
Manners, John, Marquess of Granby, 182, 186

Marmsworth, Cecil, Chairman, Garden Cities and Town Planning Association, 118
Maudslay, Henry, 188
Maudslay, Joseph, 190
Maudslay, Sons and Field Ltd., 189
Maudslay, Thomas Henry, 190
Mawson, Thomas Hayton, landscape architect and town planner, America, 114
Metropolitan Association for Improving the Dwellings of the Industrious Classes, 44
Metropolitan Improvements Commission, *30*
Military service, est. nos. of Estate residents on, WWI, 207-208
Ministry of Health, *83*
Ministry of Munitions, 16, 160, 172
Missenden, Eustace, Traffic Superintendent, S.E. Railways, 161
Model Dwellings Companies, 44-45
Model Lodging Houses, 45
Moira, 2nd Earl of, 190
Mole, Charles, architect, H.M. Office of Works, 155, 170
Morris, William, **54**, 55, 57-59, 73, 74, 76, 93-94, 101, 122
Morris, Marshall, Faulkner & Co., 55-56
Mowlem, John & Co. Ltd., 156-157, 162, 170-171, 172

Napoleonic Wars, 183, 185
National Gallery, 97
National Trust, 97
Nell Gwyn's Cottages, 143
Nelson, Lord Horatio, 183
New Earswick, 80-85, 103, 109, 116
Norbury Estate, 206
Nottingham, Earl of, Lord High Admiral, 191, 192

Oder of the Bath, 176
Old Oak Estate, Acton, 206
Oxford and University of Oxford, 56; Magdalen College Choir School, 74; Slade School, 74; St. John's College, 99; University of, 57, 73; Wadham College, 98
Oxleaze Woods, 194

Page, Sir Gregory, 1st Bt., 134
Page, Sir Gregory, 2nd Bt., 134, 139
Page, Sir Gregory, 3rd Bt., 134
Page-Turner Barron, Sir Henry, 2nd Bt., 135, 136, 139
Page-Turner, Anna Leigh Guy, 133, 135, 139
Page-Turner, Sir Gregory Osborne, 4th Bt., 135, 139
Page-Turner, Sir Gregory, 3rd Bt., 134, 139
Paget, Sir William, 177
Paine, Tom, author, 180
Parker & Unwin partnership, 72, 77-78, 82-83, 86, 88, 89, 91-92, 101, 106, 112, 118, 120
Parker, Barry, architect, 72, 74, 76, 77, 89, 93-94, 245
Parker, Dr. Joseph, Congregational preacher, 68
Parker, Ethel, 77
Parker, Frances, 72
Parker, Gerald, architect, H.M. Office of Works, 148, 160
Parker, Robert, 72
Parr, Katherine, 177
Peabody Trust, 45
Peabody, George, 45
Peat, Thomas, surveyor, 200
Peers, Charles, Inspector of Ancient Monuments, H.M. Office of Works, 126
Pentecostal missionary movement, 136
People's Palace School, 99, 124

Pepler, George, Town Planner, Local Government Board, 119
Pett, Joseph, 192
Pett, Peter, 191
Pett, Phineas, 191
Pevsner, Sir Nikolaus, 106
Phillips, George Edward, architect, H.M. Office of Works, 148, 151, 160, 244
Pitcher, A.J., architect, H.M. Office of Works, 148, 151, 160
Plumstead churchyard, 180, 183
Polhill, Cecil Henry, 12, 134, 135, 136, 137, 138, 139
Polhill, Cecil Henry, trustees of, 137, 138, 139
Polhill, Frances Margaretta, 133
Polhill, Frederick, 133
Polhill, Frederick Charles, 133
Polhill, Nathaniel, 133
Polhill-Turner, Arthur, 134
Polhill-Turner, Cecil Henry, see Polhill, Cecil Henry
Polhill-Turner, Emily, 135
Polhill-Turner, Frederick Charles, 133, 135
Polhill-Turner, Frederick Edward Fiennes, 134, 135
Poor Law, Board, 38; Commissioners, 29; operation of, 44, 45, 49
Population, England and Wales, 1851, 25
Population, growth rates, 25, **26**, **36**
Porcupine, Peter, *nom de plume*, William Cobbett, 180
Port Sunlight, 64, 109
Porto, Portugal, 94
Poverty line, 47-48
Progress Estate: accommodation, classes of, 157; additions to buildings, 216; Article 4 Direction, 239, 242; building costs, control of, 163; building materials, 163-165, 169;

coal bunkers, 237; Conservation Area, 242; construction cost per house, 173; contractors' employees, average weekly earnings of, 170-171; contractors' employees, transport for, 171; freehold and leasehold homes, creation of, 210-211, 212, 222, 239, 241, 242, 243; garden city lines, to be built on, 152; names, previous, 7; number of dwellings, 140; parlours, 158-159; boundaries, shape of, 140, 167; west of Estate, development, 213; electricity and gas providers, 173-174; fencing and walls, 166-168, 214, 237-238, 239; houses and flats, design of, 7, 23, 24; labour disputes, 172; Letchworth Garden City, influence of, 93; motorised transport, parking, 215-216, 224; narrow-gauge railway to transport materials, 161; objectives, 175; original tenants, 205; popularity of, 175; rents, 159; speculative letting, 217; street lighting, 174; telephones, 213-214; tendering not pursued, 160-161; trees growing on the, 144-145, 146, 205; underpinning of houses, 213-214, 237; Unwin's influence, 107; upgrading of tenanted homes, 212, 239; volume of building materials, 161; Woolwich Borough Council, involvement with roads and sewers, 150, 166

Progress Estate Residents Association, 217

Progress Estates Ltd., 210-217, 250, Works Department and contracting, 211, 235, 237; domestic gas lighting, 236; electricity and electric light, 236

Progress Hall, 214-215, 244

Progress Residents Association, 7

Public Works Loan Commissioners, 80, 82

Quaggy, River, 143, 194
Quakers, influence of, 61, 79, 93

Railways, growth of commuting, 35, 87
Raleigh, Sir Walter, 192
Ravensbourne, river, 143
Rawdon, Francis, Lord Rawdon/Baron Rawdon/Baron Rawdon-Hastings, see Moira, 2nd Earl of
Rawdon, Sir John, Earl of Moira, 190
Red House, The, Bexleyheath, 58, 60
Reid, Anne, 180
Republicanism, American and French, 180
Roads, construction standards for, 30; widths, 39, 149, 150, 165
Roads on the Estate: Admiral Seymour Road, 10, 143, 145, 151, 154, 166, 167, 176, 177-178, 194-195, 212, 214, 223; Arsenal Road, 145, 154, 178, 213-214, 216, 223, 226; Boughton Road, 145, 154, 165, 179, 194-195; Brome Road, 179-180, 222; Cobbett Road, 176, 180, 220, 224, 244; Congreve Road, 151, 181, 209, 212, 213, 222, 223; Cornwallis Walk, 145, 154, 167, 181-183, 213, 226; Dickson Road, 142, 143, 144, 155, 183-184, 214, 220-221, 224, 225, 237; Downman Road, 143, 184-185, 224, 244; Franklin Passage, 142, 154, 185; Gilbourne Way, 154, 166, 186, 194-195; Granby Road, 145, 146, 154, 167, 168, 186, 194, 213, 216, 223, 226, 227; Kakehill Lane, 142, 220; Lovelace Green, 187-188, 209, 221, 223, 224, 225, 226, 227; Martin Bowes Road, 176, 188, 221, 225; Maudslay Road, 188-190; Moira Road, 146, 158, **159**, 190-191, 194, 214, 223; Phineas Pett Road, 142, 154, 176, 191-192, 220, 223; Prince Rupert Road, 151, 176, 192, 222,

223, 226, 244; Rochester Way, 143, 145, 146, *150*, 151, 154, 166, 179, 186, 194-198, 202, 213, 224, 238; Ross Way, *44*, 144, 154, 155, 166, 176, 198-199, 214, 216-217; Sandby Green, 144, 200, 214, 216, 220-221; Shrapnel Road, 200-201, 238; Well Hall Road, 138, 139, 142, 143, 144, 146, 151, 154, 157, 166, 167, 173, 175, 176, 194, 201-203, 208-209, 212, 213, 215, 222, 223, 224, 226, 236, 238, 244 ; re-numbering, 202; Whinyates Road, 143, 154, 166, 168, 203-204, 215, 220, 224, 225, **226**, 228, 239, 244

Roads, other: Appleton Road, 168; Briset Road, 143, 194; Craigton Road, 167; Deansfield Road, 195, 196, 198; Dover Road, 194; Glenesk Road, 195; Grangehill Road, 167, 196, 213; Kidbrooke Lane, 202; Shooter's Hill, 137; Welling Way, 194; Westmont Road, 226; Woodville Road, 194

Robinson, Charles Mumford, Professor, Civic Design, University of Illinois, 113

Rocque, John, map of London, 143, 201

Ross, Capt. Sir James, 185

Ross, John, 199

Ross, Sir Hew Dalrymple, 198

Rossetti, Dante Gabriel, 58

Rosyth, development of naval base, housing of employees, 130

Rowland, Alexander William, 96

Rowland, Henrietta, see Barnett, Henrietta

Rowntree, B. Seebohm, 41, 79, 80, 83, 85, 245

Rowntree, Joseph, 79-82, 83, 85, 103, 245

Rowntree, Julia, 79

Royal Academy Architecture School, 59

Royal Arsenal Co-operative Society, 210-211

Royal Borough of Greenwich, see Greenwich Council

Royal College of Art, 73

Royal Courts of Justice, London, 55

Royal Institute of British Architects, 51, 73, 75, 76, 94, 102, 112, 114, *148*; International Congress, 1906, 120

Royal Military Repository, Woolwich, 181

Royal Statistical Society, 47

Runciman, Walter, President of the Board of Agriculture, 118, 131

Rupert, Prince, Earl of Holderness and Duke of Cumberland, 178, 192

Ruskin, John, 51-53, 55, 57, 60, 61, 69, 73, 74-75, 76, 97, 101, 122, 123, 245

Salisbury Cathedral, 51

Salisbury, Marquess of, 68

Salt, Titus, 64

Saltaire, 64

Samuel, Herbert, President of the Local Government Board, 119, 140, 147, 246

Sandby, Paul, 200

Sandby, Paul Thomas, 200

Sandby, Thomas, 200

Scott, Samuel, 55

Scott, Sir George Gilbert, architect, 53, **54**, 55, 59

Seebohm, Antoinette, 79, 82

Self-help, 46

Settlement Work, 98

Seymour, Edward, 177

Seymour, Jane, 177

Seymour, Margery, 177

Seymour, Mary, 178

Seymour, Sir John, 177

Seymour, Thomas, 177

INDEX

Shaftesbury, 7th Earl of, social reformer, 33
Shaw, George Bernard, *46, 48*
Shaw, Richard Norman, architect, 57
Sheffield Socialist League, 75, 77
Sheffield Socialist Society, 122
Shooter's Hill Bypass, 194; naming of, 196-198; see also Roads on the Estate, Rochester Way
Shrapnel, Henry, 200
Simmonds, T.C., Atelier of, 72-73
Simon, Sir John, Secretary of State for the Home Department, 16
Smiles, Samuel, 46
Social altruism, 96
Socialist League, 75
Society for Improving the Condition of the Labouring Classes, 44
Society for the Protection of Ancient Buildings, 58
South Kensington Schools, 73, 93
Southwood Smith, Dr. Thomas, pioneer of sanitary reform, 97
Southwood Smith, Caroline, 96-97
St. Augustine, Canterbury, dissolution of, 179
St. Barnabas Church, Eltham, 224
St. Georges, Hanover Square, 33
St. Giles, 47
St. John the Baptist church, Eltham, 137, 202
St. Jude's, Whitechapel, 98
St. Mary's Bryanston Square, Marylebone, 98
Standen House, Sussex, 60
Stanier, Robert Spenser, historian of Magdelen College, Oxford, 74
Staveley Coal and Iron Company, 74, 77
Street, George Edmund, architect, **54**, 55, 56, 57
Survey of the Memorials of Greater London, 1894, 124

Tanner, Sir Henry, Principal Architect and Surveyor, H.M. Office of Works, 127
Theatre Royal, Drury Lane, 133
Third National Conference and American City Planning, 1911, 114
Tindale, Sarah, 189
Totterdown Fields Estate, Tooting, 206
Town and Country Planning Association, 69
Town planning, 95, 101, 103, 107, 108, 112, 114-116; economics of, 116-118
Town Planning Exhibition and Conference, 1910, 112-113, 116
Town Planning Institute, 119
Toynbee Hall, 99, 122, 123; Settlement work, 98-99
Tram service, Woolwich to Eltham, 137, 138, 140, 143, 162
Tunnell, Annie, 209
Tyler, Henry Bedford, architect, 66

Unwin, Raymond, architect and town planner, 72-73, 74-75, 77, 82-83, 89, 100-102, 101, 105, 106, 107, 112-114, 116-120, 122, 130, 140, 148, 150, 245-246; socialist beliefs, 95
Unwin, Edward, 73
Unwin, William, 72

Victoria and Albert Museum, 200
Victoria, Queen, 44
Vivian, Henry, Liberal M. P., 103, 107

Wages, agricultural, 91
Wale Hall, 202
Walpole, Horace, 182
Walpole, Sir Robert, 181
Waltham Abbey gunpowder factory, 181
War Office, 16, 172, 174, 199

Warren, Herbert, solicitor, The Garden City Pioneer Company, 87
Webb, Beatrice, 46
Webb, Philip Speakman, architect, **54**, 56-57, 58, 60
Webb, Sidney, *46*, 48, 49
Well Hall Estate, 7
Well Hall Garden City Tenants Association, 207
Well Hall railway station, 137, 138, 161, 164, 171
Well Hall Road Circus/Roundabout, 203, 238
Wellington, Duke of, 183, 198, 201
Whinyates, Edward Charles, 203
Whinyates, Elizabeth, 204
Whinyates, Frederick and Sarah, 204
Whinyates, Maj. Thomas and Catherine, 204
White Hart Lane Estate, Tottenham, 206
Whitman, Walt, American intellectual, 75
Woolwich Dockyard, beginnings, 178
Woolwich Green, 178
Woolwich Housing Scheme, 7
Woolwich Ropeyard, 178
Woolwich, housing shortage, 21-23, 147, 149
Woolwich, Metropolitan Borough of, 142, 194-198, 205, 250
Worcester and Birmingham Canal, 61
Workforce, structure of, **27**
Wren, Sir Christopher, 102
Wricklemarsh estate, Blackheath, 134, 139
WWII bomb damage: compensation for repairs, 218, 227, 228-229; duties of local authorities, 218; Blitz, 218, 222, 224, 229; post-war repairs, 230-235; temporary repairs and re-building, 227, 230, 235, 239; War Damage Commission, 228, 229. See also Air raids
Wythenshawe, Manchester, 94

Zeppelin airship raids, 208-209, 244